Ideas That Shaped Buildings

Ideas That Shaped Buildings

Fil Hearn

The MIT Press

Cambridge, Massachusetts

London, England

This book was set in Sabon by Graphic Composition, Inc. and
was printed and bound in the United States of America.

Library of Congress Cataloging-in-Publication Data

Hearn, M. F. (Millard Fillmore), 1938–
    Ideas that shaped buildings / Fil Hearn.
        p. cm.
    Includes bibliographical references and index.
    ISBN 0-262-58227-9 (pbk. : alk. paper)
    1. Architecture—Philosophy. I. Title.

NA2500.H379 2003
720'.1—dc21

                                              2003051206

10 9 8 7 6 5 4 3 2

for Jana

Contents

Acknowledgments   ix

Preface: Architectural Theory Is Everybody's
Business   xi

Introduction: Contours of Theoretical
Development   1

I   Underpinnings (Relevant to All Theory)   23

1   Of Architecture and Architects   25

2   Standards of Judgment and Design Justifications   39

3   The Uses of the Past   53

II   Conventions (Theory before 1800)   79

4   Images of the Ideal and Classical Design Method   81

5   The Orders: Evolving Rules for Formal Beauty   97

6   The Alternative Aesthetic: Breaking the Rules   137

7   Proportion: The Orders and Architectural Spaces   161

III	*Principles (Theory from 1800 to 1965)*	177
8	*Rational Design Method*	179
9	*Generative Planning as the Basis of Design*	193
10	*Honest Structure as the Framework of Design*	223
11	*Truth to the Medium: Using Materials*	255
12	*Decoration and the Integrity of Design*	271
13	*Restoration: The Care of Inherited Buildings*	281
14	*Design of Cities*	289
IV	**Convolutions** *(Theory since 1965)*	303
15	*Rationales beyond Rationalism*	305
16	*New Directions in Design Method*	323
	Conclusion	335
	Time Line of Treatises (by John Hearn)	337
	Bibliography	343
	Credits	351
	Index	355

Acknowledgments

There was a time when I thought this book was going to be virtually a solo production. But as it took shape and neared completion, I became gratefully indebted to a number of people for all sorts of assistance.

My students, using photocopied drafts of the text for my theory course in recent years, have provided gratifying encouragement. John Hearn, my son, read and commented on several versions of the text along the way and wrote the time line. Kai Gutschow, historian of architecture, read the first draft and gave many helpful suggestions. Anthony Serba, architect, read the penultimate draft and corrected a number of errors. I also thank Thomas Kozachek for his meticulous editing of the final draft on behalf of the MIT Press.

Claudia Funke, Rare Books Librarian at the Avery Library of Columbia University, went well beyond the call of duty in making available to me many rare original editions of treatises written before 1800. Ray Anne Lockard, Frick Fine Arts Librarian in the University of Pittsburgh, and Marcia Rostek and Margaret Gill, her assistants, have been enormously helpful in finding volumes and facilitating interlibrary loans.

For preparation of the illustrations, Debra Doty of the Frick Fine Arts Virtual Reality Laboratory provided technical assistance on numerous occasions. Kai Gutschow, Jana

Hearn, Anthony Serba, Ann Thomas Wilkins, and David Wilkins have generously contributed photographs or other visual materials for the illustrations. Elizabeth Scanlon at Venturi Scott Brown Associates, Cynthia Davidson at Peter Eisenman Architects, John Outram of John Outram Associates, and Priscilla Philippi of the Jordan Tourism Board have arranged donations of photographs. Claudia Ponton at Art Resource, Margo Stipe at the Frank Lloyd Wright Foundation, Amy Bisonnette at the Chicago Art Institute, John Ferry at the Buckminster Fuller Archive, and Fernanda Meza at the Artists Rights Society, have graciously gone out of their way to see that I got the illustrations and/or permissions I needed.

At the University of Pittsburgh, grants to pay for the illustrations were awarded from the Richard D. and Mary Jane Edwards Fund and from the Center for West European Studies. Linda Hicks, administrative assistant of the History of Art and Architecture Department, made all the administrative processes go smoothly.

Preface: Architectural Theory Is Everybody's Business

A theory of architecture resides in any notion of what a building ought to be like. The form a building takes presupposes a theory of design. The way its members are assembled presupposes a theory of structure. And the procedure followed to arrive at the design presupposes a theory of design method. This is true for structures as simple as log cabins or elaborate as palaces. In the case of vernacular buildings, theory is exercised through rote procedure rather than premeditation, but it is there nevertheless. In the case of ambitious buildings, where deliberate design choices are made at every turn—whether for the sake of structure, function, or design—the purposeful application of theory is inescapable. Even a person standing on the sidelines who articulates an opinion is necessarily taking a theoretical position. So it is, then, that architectural theory is both the property and the concern of all who build and all who evaluate buildings, either as observers or as users.

The working boundaries of architectural theory have been more tightly defined through formal treatises, written by a variety of interested professionals and laymen, as guides for both architects and patrons. Although some of the most famous and important examples have been primarily addressed to patrons and cultivated lay readers rather than to architects, all the treatises are relevant to professional practitioners. Indeed, theorists from Vitruvius on have asserted that an effectual architect needs to be equipped with a fluent knowledge of theory as well as practice. They have maintained that whereas knowledge of theory alone results in impotence to fulfill a building project, knowledge of practice alone limits one to the skills of a craftsman. So, if expertise in practice makes it possible to translate ideas into reality, it is theory that provides the conceptual awareness needed to devise a design. Such awareness is prerequisite to creative freedom. Properly consulted, then, architectural theory is not narrowly prescriptive; its purpose is to establish the range of liberty, even when that freedom is subordinated to a regulatory system. Rather than constricting with narrow dictates, theory enables and inspires.

Ideas about architecture occur in the literature of history, formal analysis, criticism, and theory. Their inclusion in all these categories of discourse, however, does not amount to the expounding of theory, because each category has its own distinct purpose. History traces developments, analysis explains, criticism interprets, and theory advocates. In the course of the last two centuries the boundaries between these various genres have become less distinct, so that a historical treatment of architectural theory must distinguish at the outset what sort of material is to be examined. Properly speaking, architectural theory is active in outlook, whereas the other types of writing are contemplative. Because theories of architecture are concerned with the way architecture ought to be, they are usually couched as apologias for a particular outlook. This book is concerned only with the literature of advocacy.

The cultural phenomenon of writing about the way buildings should be designed is peculiar to Western civilization of the last two millennia. More precisely, the continuous tradition began only in the middle of the fifteenth century, looking back to a single precedent in antiquity, from the first years of the Roman Empire. Although specifications for the format and appearance of particular types of buildings do exist in other cultures, such instructions do not have a broader relevance and do not function as guidelines for the architecture of an entire society. With the theory of architecture, then, we are dealing with a cultural concern that was limited to portions of Europe until the nineteenth century, when it spread to the United States.

Architectural theory has been expounded in numerous treatises, among which only a few have enjoyed wide and lasting influence. It is to those influential few, the authors of which are still invoked in everyday professional discourse about architecture, that this book is primarily directed. The scope of those treatises varies considerably. Some of the best-known examples attempt to be comprehensive, treating practical as well as conceptual matters. Others are more limited, focusing on discrete issues of great concern to the author.

Either way, one of the ironies of the fate of theoretical writings is that the material concerning practice remains relevant, if at all, for only a short time or within a narrow geographical compass. Injunctions pertaining to particular formulations of technical details of construction are the most ephemeral, followed by matters relating to functional use, whereas passages addressed to formal qualities and cultural significance may remain of interest indefinitely. Thus it is that even the most famous and influential treatises are now remembered and consulted only for portions of their text. From this circumstance we may deduce at the outset an important principle regarding the most durable aspect of the theory of architecture, namely that lasting theory is addressed foremost to conceptual matters, especially matters concerning design and design quality. Put another way, enduring theory is about the quest for satisfying form and cultural appropriateness in buildings. This residue of the historical corpus of theoretical treatises is the subject of this book.

The theorists included in this survey necessarily represent a personal selection from the array of established texts and themes that might be treated. Indeed, it is unlikely that any two people undertaking the same task would have chosen exactly the same treatises to represent the wisdom of the theory of architecture. Moreover, the theorists I have chosen as spokespersons for particular themes are those I judge the most memorable, most timely, or most lucid, not necessarily the first to have articulated the idea at issue. Indeed, almost any theorist can be shown to have predecessors for virtually any idea. I am more concerned with delineating issues, so my treatment is less a narrative history than a historical essay, that is, a carefully considered personal synthesis of the literary monuments of an architectural culture.

Whatever its limitations, this book has been motivated by a concern for its relevance to the present and the hope that it may be useful to working practitioners. It is meant to be a guide to the aspects of the historical tradition of architectural theory that have been widely influential in the past and remain vital today. It attempts to arrange the basic ideas in some semblance of logical order. With this armature my aspiration has been not only to make sense of the theories from the past but also to establish a means for relating current or future ideas to the theoretical tradition. I hope that the following chapters may suggest how these ideas may be useful to creators of architecture, both patrons and architects.

For the sake of simplicity, short citations of secondary literature are given in the text by author and date and refer to full entries in the bibliography.

Ideas That Shaped Buildings

Introduction: The Contours of Theoretical Development

The status of architectural theory as a *topos* of discourse in Western civilization owes much to the fact that the earliest known treatise, *De architectura,* was written in ancient Rome. Composed about 30 B.C.E. by Marcus Vitruvius Pollio (known to the world as Vitruvius), it purports to be the first attempt to write a systematic and comprehensive theory of architecture. By contrast, precedents in Greek literature, cited by Vitruvius but now lost, all appear to have been limited to narrow topics, such as theories of proportion or explications of individual monuments.

Composed in ten parts, or "books," Vitruvius's text broaches many topics. It begins with general matters: the education and professional scope of the architect and the criteria of excellence in architecture. It then proceeds to practical considerations, such as the siting of new cities and the handling of building materials. Aesthetic and functional issues are treated in the detailed prescriptions related to the design of three building types: temples, amphitheaters, and houses. Finally, it deals with technical matters involving machines used for construction or warfare, timepieces, and the handling of water. Out of all this, about one third of the text touches upon still-relevant issues of architectural theory. Much of this third is addressed to the peripteral temple—exalted as an architectural ideal—and focused upon the rules of its columnar orders.

Because we do not know how Vitruvius's treatise was valued by his contemporaries and know virtually nothing of the influence it may have exerted in his own time or later in antiquity, its meaning and value in the Roman context cannot be assessed. Its importance for us lies in what it has meant to subsequent times. Although we know that Vitruvius was read intermittently throughout the Middle Ages, his example did not inspire anyone during those centuries to set down theories about the design and construction of buildings. Indeed, nearly a millennium and a half would pass before someone would again compose a treatise of this sort. Since then, readers have been both enthralled by the virtues of this treatise and vexed by its defects. However mixed the response, Vitruvius's text has always held the status of archetype, influencing the way the theory of architecture has been posited even to the present day.

AFTER VITRUVIUS IN ANTIQUITY AND THE MIDDLE AGES

No subsequent ancient theoretical texts are known to have existed. Certainly the elaborate architecture of the later Roman Empire, of Byzantium, and of Western Europe in the Romanesque and Gothic eras was based on a highly developed theory of architecture, but this theory was not formulated in treatises. By whatever means it was transmitted, this lore was restricted to professional circles and not written down for others to read. Throughout this long period copies of Vitruvius are known to have been available and read, but they were not used to guide the design of architecture, and they did not inspire the composition of new versions of written theory.

THE RENAISSANCE TRADITION

That the writing of architectural theory was revived in the Italian Renaissance is due to the coincidence that Vitruvius was seen to serve a particular fifteenth-century need, which was the cultural urge to revive the antique tradition in architecture. Even so, were it not for the solemn respect he commanded from Renaissance scholars, his work would have fallen into oblivion. But as it turned out, when a remarkably complete and pure manuscript text of *De architectura* was discovered in the monastic library of Saint-Gall (Switzerland) in 1414, the feverishly transcribed chapters were posted book by book to Florence, where they were eagerly awaited by the community of humanist scholars. From that time Vitruvius was regarded as the presiding spirit of the realm of architecture. His continued importance as a writer of architectural theory was assured, however, only by the composition, in Florence, of a treatise of similar format, *De re aedificatoria,* by Leon Battista Alberti, begun in the 1430s and labored over for the next two decades.

Written in Ciceronian Latin in order to project the gravity ascribed to ancient literature, Alberti's treatise of ten books was at once both an homage to Vitruvius and a rebellious reaction. Alberti attempted to reconcile a thorough study of Vitruvius with his own precocious empirical investigation of surviving Roman architecture (spanning several more centuries than the examples Vitruvius knew), combining this synthesis with a conscientious compilation of practical lore. Alberti sought thereby to adapt the issues discussed by Vitruvius to the architecture of his own time. His overriding motive was to justify and facilitate a revival of the antique manner in architecture. In that connection, Vitruvius's prescriptions for usage of the classical orders in peripteral temples were dislocated from their original specific applications and given a new and more general emphasis. For, however Vitruvius's treatment of the orders may have been seen in his own Roman context, Alberti interpreted it as the pretext for creating an entire idealized architecture, with the result that the columnar orders became the focus of subsequent theoretical writing in the sixteenth century.

Alberti presented his treatise to Pope Nicholas V (Vitruvius had dedicated his own to Caesar Augustus) about 1450. He completed it shortly before Gutenberg's movable type could have made mechanical reproduction possible, and it was transmitted in manuscript copies until 1485, thirteen years after Alberti's death, when—still in Latin—it was finally printed. A translation into Italian did not appear until 1550, so for a full century the readership of this treatise was limited to elite intellectual circles. It is a prodigious work, admirable for the quality of the author's research and thought. From the outset, it enjoyed wide repute among the intelligentsia and commanded enormous respect, largely due to its very existence as the first treatise on the theory of architecture since antiquity. But because it had several rivals by the time it was broadly accessible, it was not widely read within the architectural profession and never exerted the influence one would normally expect from such a groundbreaking effort. Its almost inestimable importance, then, lay in the precedent it set for future theorists.

Among the rival treatises were printed editions of Vitruvius, translated into Italian, the best being those, respectively, of Fra Giovanni Giocondo (1511) and Daniele Barbaro (1556). But their effectiveness was blunted by a concurrent sea change in the formulation of architectural theory, brought on by the appearance of treatises dominated by images, in which the text, now written in the vernacular, did little more than explain the illustrations. This new type of treatise actually established architectural theory as something requisite for the art of building. Although based on experiences acquired in the rich artistic ferment of Rome, where the new St. Peter's was rising, most of the treatises were published in Venice by men from that general region, alongside Italian translations of Vitruvius and Alberti. Indeed, Venice, then the publishing capital of the world, was the principal generator of architectural theory for much of the sixteenth century.

Sebastiano Serlio, the first of these new authors, produced his treatise in installments, one or two at a time. Though he probably originally projected ten books, only five were published in his lifetime. The whole became known as *Tutte l'opere d'architettura* when the parts were collected in one volume in 1584. In the long run, the earliest two mattered the most, namely Book IV, on the orders (1537), and Book III, on antique Roman architecture (1540), and the way they were influential was of the highest importance. The illustrations included not only the canonical form of each of the five orders but imaginative variants as well, thereby enlarging the range of possibilities for using the orders in architectural design. The explicit renditions in the drawings also made the illustrations paradigms for imitation outside Italy. Similarly, the scale drawings reconstituting the great monuments of Roman architecture transmitted for the first time the actual designs of ancient buildings—rather than just verbal descriptions, as in the past—to people unable to travel to Italy. These visual materials incidentally also provided for the first time illustrations of a coherent body of historically related buildings, the indispensable prerequisite for the creation of histories of architecture. More influential in matters of style was a narrowly focused treatise, the *Extraordinario libro di architettura,* published in Venice in 1551, in which Serlio set out schemes for fifty rustic and urban doorways. In it he exploited numerous ways in which the canonical regulations of the orders could be creatively broken, providing a virtual handbook of mannerist design.

Other highly influential illustrated treatises were Giacomo Vignola's systematization of the orders (published in Rome, 1562) and the four books by Andrea Palladio (issued in Venice, 1570). Vignola's *Regola delli cinque ordini d'architettura* presented in 32 plates all five orders in various situations: with and without pedestals, with flanking arches, and aligned in colonnades. All the situations were rendered in a consistent method, devised to achieve correct proportions while using only multiples or fractions of a unitary module, the radius of the column shaft. It became in time the most widely disseminated and probably the most used handbook on the orders ever produced. Palladio's *Quattro libri d'architettura,* valuable for its treatment of the orders and detailed drawings of ancient Roman monuments, even more importantly inaugurated the practice of including designs of the author's own architecture. His designs, particularly of rural villas, were susceptible to widely inventive adaptation and so opened up new horizons for the conception of architectural formats. More widely disseminated even than the books of Serlio, these treatises helped to sustain the vogue for antique classicism and to transmit it throughout Europe and to North America.

In the two centuries that followed, scores of other treatises were produced, in northern Europe as well as Italy. Five of them, cited here, were newly ambitious in scope, with both detailed texts and copious illustrations. Published just earlier than Palladio's was the first architectural theory written by a non-Italian, Philibert de l'Orme's *L'architecture*

(Paris, 1567). Heavily influenced by Serlio, whom he credited with introducing classicism into France, de l'Orme treated a wide variety of mannered versions of the orders and even introduced a new, "French," order into the canon. Back in Italy, Vincenzo Scamozzi, a follower of Palladio and admirer of Serlio, attempted to set out a densely detailed treatment of all the issues raised by Vitruvius and his own Renaissance predecessors. The result, *L'idea della architettura universale* (Venice, 1615), demonstrated, however, that a little more than a little is by much too much. His treatise, never completed as planned, was ultimately influential only as a compilation of material on the orders and their imaginative application to schemes for Vitruvian houses, imaged as Renaissance palaces.

Three French treatises written between the middle of the seventeenth century and its last decade marked the definitive shift of dominance in architectural theory from Italy to France. Roland Fréart de Chambray, in *Parallèle de l'architecture antique et de la moderne* (Paris, 1650), systematically compared the five orders as employed in ancient monuments to the prescriptions of all his Renaissance predecessors. He disapproved of the liberties taken with the antique tradition by the latter-day theorists and upheld the authority of antique usage over modern interpretation. So began the controversy between the ancients and the moderns over the use of proportion in the classical orders. This treatise was followed by François Blondel's *Cours d'architecture* (Paris, 1675, 1683), and Claude Perrault's *Ordonnance des cinq espèces de colonnes* (Paris, 1683). Blondel took a conservative position, upholding the authority of ancient architecture as the model for proportions in the orders, whereas Perrault advocated reliance upon the visual judgment of the architect, maintaining the modern position that no objective authority for proportion exists.

The ultimate impact of such treatises was that a kind of discourse primarily intended to guide architects in making designs also became the substance for academic disputations. The only matters all the theorists could agree upon were that the central concerns of architectural theory are the formats of the orders, their imaginative variation, and the proportions applied to them. Broadly speaking, then, except for some technical treatises, the issues shaping the theory of architecture from the fifteenth to the eighteenth centuries were those begotten by Alberti's obsession with reviving the classical aesthetic of antique Roman architecture. In turn, the limits implicitly imposed by Alberti's motivation honored the parameters that had already been established in the first place by Vitruvius. In other words, a lot of intellectual energy went into the development and propagation of a subject that had been instigated in the fifteenth century by a narrowly focused cultural impulse. But the scope of architectural theory did not remain narrow.

THE BRIDGE TO MODERNITY

Broadened perspectives on the theory of architecture came with the radical transformation of European life and culture that began around 1750 and continued until the 1830s. No longer the fountainhead of artistic culture and its formative theory, Italy gave way to France and England. During this period, revolution in all spheres of life and thought brought every verity under critical review. In architecture the fundamental changes occurred in the context of a phenomenon that at first appears not to have been radically new, namely the neoclassical style, which would seem to have been just one more in a series of revisions of the classical tradition. But neoclassicism was employing a familiar vocabulary of forms in what actually turned out to be a fundamentally new syntax of creative expression. Within the framework of this movement, a number of theorists contributed strands to what became a complexly interwoven tapestry of new ideas. As individuals, these authors were not intellectual giants, and none achieved the heroic historical stature imputed to the Renaissance figures already cited. Some, however, deserve to be identified with the concepts they introduced.

Marc-Antoine Laugier was a former Jesuit priest and hanger-on in social-cum-intellectual circles of Paris. His *Essai sur l'architecture,* first published in 1753 and reissued with additions in 1755, was substantially inspired by a little-known work of 1706 by another priest, Jean-Louis Cordemoy. Whatever it lacked in originality, Laugier's treatise happened to be the right sort of presentation in the right place at the right time to capture wide attention in what had become the most important center of architectural activity in Europe. It advocated the use of pure versions of the orders in rationally composed buildings, parallel in the clarity of their structural expression to the Gothic cathedrals. The implications significant for the future were the rational conception of a building in terms of its structure rather than its formal image and the incipient displacement of the ideal of the classical temple by that of the Gothic cathedral.

Perhaps the first theorist to assert that architecture need not employ the orders was Jean-Nicolas-Louis Durand. A full-time professor of architecture, Durand published the first treatise illustrating world architecture on a comparative basis. Titled *Recueil et parallèle des édifices de tout genre* (Paris, 1800), its most remarkable aspect—besides being a landmark of scholarship—was that it implicitly placed Western and non-Western cultures on an equal standing, presenting examples by building type. The accomplishment that secured his place in this historical sequence of theoreticians, however, was *Précis de leçons d'architecture* (Paris, 1802–1819). The remarkable feature of this treatise was that it presented for the first time an explicit design method, set out in orderly stages.

Another important step in the direction of modernity was the novel definition of architecture as having the nature of a language, devised by Antoine-Chrysostome Quatremère de Quincy. His most important ideas about architecture were published in *De l'architecture égyptienne* (Paris, 1803) and the *Encyclopédie méthodique,* the numerous volumes of which appeared in Paris between 1788 and 1823. An energetic scholar, politician, and finally bureaucrat who enjoyed independent means, he was motivated to write about architecture both to satisfy a need to articulate certain issues and to enunciate a belief in the social value of culturally expressive buildings. He regarded architecture as the product of human rationality and its evolution as the result of rational application.

Quatremère de Quincy was one of the sources of inspiration for Gottfried Semper, the first German theorist to gain wide notice. His treatise *Der Stil in den technischen und tektonischen Künsten oder praktische Aesthetik: Ein Handbuch für Techniker, Künstler, und Kunstfreunde* was extraordinary for asserting that the formal characteristics of buildings, a legacy of antiquity, had been aesthetic rather than structural in origin. This highly intellectual effort, which followed numerous pamphlets and published lectures in which his ideas were developed, was projected to consist of three volumes, only two of which were actually written and published, in Frankfurt, 1860 and 1863. It sought to explain architectural forms as adaptations in remote antiquity from the crafts of textiles, ceramics, carpentry, and masonry. For instance, a connection or border in a structure was interpreted as equivalent to a textile seam; an interlaced screen wall to a weaving.

Semper's theory never dealt with how a building should be designed, but his most influential ideas ascribed primacy to chromatic decoration as the meaningful factor in monumental architecture and to space as the formal determinant of architectural planning. The latter he imputed to the technique of masonry, which readily produced first the arch and then the vault. Although Semper was preeminent among German—and only German—theorists in his own lifetime, his sphere of influence widened at the turn of the twentieth century when Dutch and German admirers came to play a formative role in the development of modernism. Yet he stands outside the mainstream of theoretical development, which focused on rationalism.

Architectural rationalism entered new territory when it ceased to say that a desirable model should be merely *similar in character* to a Gothic cathedral and simply pointed to the Gothic cathedral as the ideal. The shift was prompted more by external cultural changes than by a shift of taste on the part of theorists. The prestige of neoclassicism had been severely damaged with the fall of Napoleon, its latest and most powerful benefactor. The romantic reaction to Enlightenment secularism had fostered a resurgence of Christianity and, in England, a reaction to eighteenth-century, low-church Protestantism—which typically had been practiced in classicizing churches. Thence came a renewal of the Catholic roots of Christian worship and the Gothic architecture that had developed to house it. Moreover, England, emerging as the dominant power of Europe, celebrated its ascendant nationalism with recognition that its two greatest secular institutions, parliamentary government and university education, had both originated in the Middle Ages in Gothic settings. Even in France, where classicism in architecture was never eclipsed, the genius of French culture was imputed to its medieval past and to the Gothic cathedrals. So it was that the Gothic cathedral came to displace the classical temple as the ideal in architectural theory.

Enter Augustus Welby Northmore Pugin, a Roman Catholic architect of Protestant heritage, a Frenchman working in England, who probably did more than any other single individual to displace the classical temple with the Gothic cathedral as the ideal of architectural theory. His illustrated pamphlet *Contrasts* (London, 1836) envisioned a number of scenes in the fifteenth century and juxtaposed them with their counterparts in nineteenth-century industrial England, always denigrating the latter. Its wide circulation enhanced the prestige of Gothic in the popular imagination and awakened the notion that good architecture, Gothic or otherwise, could both embody and reinforce social virtue. It also implied that, as designer, the architect could be the promoting agent of this virtue. Pugin's second treatise, *True Principles of Pointed or Christian Architecture* (London, 1841), was a transcription of earlier lectures on Gothic architecture. He explained every feature of Gothic architecture as functionally inspired, thereby exalting Gothic as the embodiment of the rational ideal. Neither of these works went far enough to enunciate a complete doctrine of architectural theory, but they were enormously influential in preparing the way for the greatest theorists of the nineteenth century, John Ruskin and Eugène-Emmanuel Viollet-le-Duc.

THE FORMATION OF MODERNITY

John Ruskin, an English aesthete whose sensibilities were cultivated on Gothic architecture in general and that of northern Italy in particular, began his career as theorist with *The Seven Lamps of Architecture* (London, 1849) and enhanced it with *The Stones of Venice* (London,

1851–1853). Taking Gothic architecture as his main source of inspiration, he devised a wholly new format for a comprehensive treatise, altogether ignoring Vitruvius. Involving patron, architect, and workman in his theory, he extended Pugin's inference of moral expression in Gothic to embrace the morality (read honesty) of a building—its structure, use of materials, quality of facture, and cultural appropriateness. Even more than with Pugin, Ruskin's architect becomes, through good design, an agent of social improvement. Of Ruskin's two titles, the earlier tome is the more systematic and comprehensive, but the much longer, later work probably had even more exposure. Influential also in Europe, Ruskin was, in the English-speaking world, easily the most widely read commentator on aesthetic matters in the nineteenth century.

Eugène-Emmanuel Viollet-le-Duc, on the other hand, was the real father of the theory of modern architecture. He was at once the most comprehensive and systematic of all the importantly influential theorists writing since Alberti. Yet his thought was dispersed among so many different titles that only someone who made a point of reading his entire oeuvre would have been likely to encounter all his important ideas. The most widely read was his *Entretiens sur l'architecture* (known in English as *Discourses on Architecture*), a collection in two volumes (Paris, 1863, 1872) of lectures he had delivered at the École des Beaux-Arts. In these chapters he set out a history of architectural principles and a rational conception of planning, structural composition, and use of materials. He also explained how style should emanate from the use of rational methods and suggested metaphors that can be used to inspire unprecedented architectural designs. Similarly important, his *Histoire d'une maison* (Paris, 1873)—known in English as *How to Build a House*—set out in meticulous detail his theory of design method. This procedure, adapted from

Durand and the Durand-influenced practice of the École des Beaux-Arts and much elaborated, is the same method still largely taught in architecture schools today. In addition to theory for the production of new buildings, Viollet-le-Duc was among the first to devise a concerted doctrine for architectural restoration. Several other titles, some of which will be cited later, contributed to the continuing theoretical discourse.

A new, albeit limited, focus for theory was introduced by Andrew Jackson Downing, a modest architect working in upstate New York. His *The Architecture of Country Houses* (New York, 1850) was nominally only a handbook for designing a freestanding house, either in the country or in a spacious suburb. But the completeness with which he addressed the subject raised it to the level of theory, making it the first treatise of importance by an American and one of the first ever to be devoted to modest architecture. Other than in a scattering of American journal articles, domesticity in architecture had not been the focus of theoretical attention. Acutely aware of the house as a distinctive building type, Downing concerned himself with providing for the domestic comforts of ordinary people.

Some of the issues articulated by Downing were also expressed on the other side of the Atlantic by members of the Arts and Crafts movement, instigated by Ruskin but led by William Morris. These concerns were translated into architectural principles as programmatic planning, honest use of materials, painstaking craftsmanship, and formal integrity, most notably represented in Philip Webb's Red House at Bexleyheath, Kent, 1859, and later in the work of W. R. Lethaby, C. R. Ashbee, and C. F. A. Voysey. The connection to architectural theory came when Hermann Muthesius, then a cultural attaché of the German embassy in London, was asked to write a report on English housing for the German government. What he produced instead was a substantial monograph, titled *Das englische Haus,* published in Berlin in 1904–1905 and later translated into English. In the German original this volume had the effect of a theoretical treatise, exerting considerable influence upon architects of the Art Nouveau movement in Germany, Holland, and Austria.

Meanwhile, the introduction into architectural theory of city planning from an artistic point of view, which had been initiated by Laugier, was taken up on a continuing basis near the end of the nineteenth century. The most conspicuous early contributor was Camillo Sitte, an architect and teacher in Vienna. His *Der Städtebau nach seiner künstlerischen Grundsätzen* (known in English as *City Planning According to Artistic Principles*), published in Vienna in 1889, had an enormous international impact. Curiously, his most pervasive influence was probably on site planning for complexes of related buildings rather than on city design itself. More influential in the latter field was Ebenezer Howard, whose *Tomorrow, a Peaceful Path to Real Reform* (London, 1898) was reissued to great acclaim in 1902 as *Garden Cities of To-morrow.* This was the treatise that established principles for the design of suburbs. And Tony Garnier, in *Une cité industrielle* (Paris, 1917), provided an organic model for the zoning of the various components of a city—industrial, residential, civic, and commercial—in an informal, asymmetrical arrangement determined by the topography and geographical features of the site. Between the world wars, the design of cities was taken up as a topic of architectural theory by both Le Corbusier and Frank Lloyd Wright. Both treated it as an aspect of modernist theory.

MODERNISM

Although Viollet-le-Duc proved to be incapable of designing a modern architecture himself, his theory inspired most of the great innovative architects of the next generation, especially those who created the international movement we know as Art Nouveau. And although his theory was of fundamental value to the next two generations after *them*, other theoretical sources of inspiration were also crucial to the development of a truly modern architecture. Composed as manifestos, polemical in tone and narrow in focus, they contributed ideas for a radically new appearance of architecture. Adolf Loos's essay *Ornament und Verbrechen* (known in English as *Ornament and Crime*), published in Vienna in 1908, anathematized decoration as decadent and immoral, prescribing instead the austere plainness that later came to characterize modern design. Paul Scheerbart, a poet and social visionary in Berlin, focused on the physical merits of glass and other glazed materials in *Glasarchitektur* (1914), analyzing the potential psychological, sociological, and aesthetic advantages of structures sheathed entirely in transparent or translucent material. And the expressionistically mechanistic visions of Antonio Sant'Elia, presented in drawings for an exhibition of the Città Nuova (Milan, 1912–1914) and in his *Manifesto dell'architettura futurista* (*Manifesto of Futurist Architecture*) of 1914, paved the way for fundamentally new shapes and configurations in post–World War I architecture. Together, these leaps of the imagination gave added impetus to the epoch-making principles enunciated by Ruskin and Viollet-le-Duc.

Numerous writers could claim to have contributed to the modernist theory of architecture. Otto Wagner's *Moderne Architektur,* published in Vienna, set out most of the principles previously enunciated by Viollet-le-Duc, but without crediting sources. Initially issued in 1896 and revised and reissued in three successive new editions in 1898, 1902, and 1914, it promulgated in the German-speaking world the ideas that were already abroad in French and

English. Success in propagandizing the movement was also enjoyed by Walter Gropius on behalf of the Bauhaus, in Dessau, especially in *Idee und Aufbau des staatlichen Bauhauses Weimar* (1923). In America the movement was promoted by Philip Johnson and Henry-Russell Hitchcock in *The International Style,* written to accompany an exhibition they curated at the Museum of Modern Art in 1932. But pride of place belongs to Frank Lloyd Wright and Le Corbusier. Although Wright was older and defined his theoretical position in print earlier than Le Corbusier, the elaboration of his ideas in books actually came later, at several points in his career after he had been upstaged by his European rival and junior. Both authors devised a streamlined and logically extended version of Viollet-le-Duc's rationalist theory (with Ruskin in the backround), with the important exception that each based his theory and his architecture on only one of the Frenchman's metaphors: Wright fixed on the organism, Le Corbusier on the machine.

Wright's theory was set out in a series of essays in a professional journal, *Architectural Record,* beginning with "In the Cause of Architecture" in 1908 and continuing in 1927–1928 and again in 1952. Other statements were set out in *An Autobiography* (New York, 1932) and several additional books—with overlapping messages—through the 1950s, especially *The Disappearing City* (1932) and *The Natural House* (1954), all published in New York. His ideas did not have an impact in proportion to his reputation as an architect, due to their perceived conflicts with European modernism, but more recently they have acquired a currency unprecedented during Wright's lifetime. Le Corbusier, on the other hand, published one book on architecture, *Vers une architecture* (Paris, 1923), and one on city planning, *Urbanisme* (Paris, 1925), both exerting considerable impact. The former, translated into English as *Towards a New Architecture* (London, 1927), became the single most influential treatise of the twentieth century and still commands attention and respect in architecture schools. The latter, translated as *The City of To-morrow* (London, 1929), was much heeded but often to ill effect. He also published two volumes devoted to his attempt to create a universal system of proportions for architecture, both under the title *Modulor* (Paris, 1948 and 1955), neither of which exerted the desired influence.

The initial introduction of most of these modernist theorists to students and practitioners of architecture alike probably occurred in their reading of Sigfried Giedion's *Space, Time and Architecture: The Growth of a New Tradition* (Cambridge, MA, 1941, followed by numerous reprints and new editions). Issued by Harvard University shortly after Walter Gropius had been installed there as head of the Graduate School of Design, it interpreted the history of Western architecture in terms of evolution toward modernist theory. Readers of this book were thereby enticed to look into the actual theoretical writings, especially those by Europeans.

Modernist theory received further development after World War II in connection with three movements: new brutalism, high tech, and neomodernism. The first logically extended yet again both Ruskin's and Viollet-le-Duc's concern for the honest, or rational, design of structure and use of materials that had already been enlarged in modernist theory. High tech has been centered on the conception of radically direct structural solutions to serve as the basis for the creation of a design. Neomodernism permits a single planning factor—aesthetic or technical—to dominate all others during the planning process, usually with the result that the building acquires a strikingly innovative image. The theory of all three movements has been promulgated not through treatises but in articles in professional journals that introduced provocative new buildings. None of the three seriously challenges any of the basic values or planning assumptions of modernism: they merely rearrange the priorities or magnify one or two of the principles so that they dominate the rest.

Given the increasingly global nature of journalism, through which developments in architecture have been publicized as they occurred during the past half-century, few theoretical innovations have been introduced in treatises. Instead, new ideas have been mostly developed in the course of designing specific buildings and promulgated, in scattered fashion, in the explanatory accounts of the architecture. That change helps to explain why some new theoretical approaches from recent decades cannot always be attributed to a particular theoretical text. Indeed, in some cases the buildings themselves serve as nonverbal representations of theory. This has especially been the case with adjustments to modernist theory.

REACTIONS TO MODERNISM

The most fundamental reaction to modernism was articulated by Robert Venturi of Philadelphia and his associates. Labeled postmodernism by critics, it has addressed those aspects of architecture that were ignored by Viollet-le-Duc, namely the cultural meaning and contextual relationship of architecture. The message began with *Complexity and Contradiction in Architecture,* published by the Museum of Modern Art in New York (1966) with the conscious memory of its role in fostering modernism through *The International Style.* Using analytical concepts that challenged both the design verities and the deliberately ahistorical character of modernism, Venturi implicitly fostered a new mannerism in design as well as a new concern for cultural meaning in architecture and for the context in which a new building must fit. With his colleagues Denise Scott Brown and Steven Izenour in *Learning from Las Vegas* (Cambridge, MA, 1972; substantially revised in a second edition, 1977), he explored the functional satisfactoriness of vernacular architecture in the contemporary urban context and the indispensability of the cultural meaning it conveys. Easily the most influential treatises of the second half of the twentieth century, their impact on architecture, though profound, has been somewhat blunted by the plethora of vulgar misinterpretations they inspired.

Another reaction, tentatively labeled deconstructivism, occurred in the guise of an attempt to appropriate the development of French poststructuralist philosophy into the framework of architectural design. Basically this approach allows any conflicts between incompatible planning factors to remain unresolved and relieves the architect of responsibility for imposing a synthesis that would compromise the honest expression of those factors. The resulting building may therefore defy conventions of rational order in structural assembly and spatial organization for the sake of honoring the disorderly truth imposed by competing factors in the environment. In consequence, deconstructivism involves designing buildings in such a way that the user must negotiate his or her way around, in, and through a building on the basis of a series of experiential decisions, without benefit of standard indications for a predetermined path. The point is to make the user's experience existentially more vital by not allowing the configuration of the built environment to be taken for granted.

It was the Museum of Modern Art, yet again, that presented, named, and promulgated the movement, for which the exhibition catalog *Deconstructivist Architecture* (1988) may be taken as the key document. No individual architect has willingly subscribed to the deconstructivist label, largely because the embrace of irrational design by each individual is based on different philosophical and aesthetic principles. Among the architects associated with deconstructivism, Peter Eisenman has been most prominent in the intellectual formulation of theoretical issues. He has published a number of essays, but no one of them has been identified as defining the movement.

Still another reaction to the orderliness of modernism has been instigated by the use of computers in the design process. An image alteration program may be employed to reshape or distort the initial design. The computer not only can do this in a way that no human hand can reliably represent, but it can also determine the exact measurements of the resulting odd shapes. In addition, it can transmit the dimensions to laser equipment for cutting the building materials to the precise size and configuration needed. Morphing—as this practice of distortion is named—has been practiced by Eisenman, and the linkage of computer images to lasers has been employed by Frank Gehry. No particular treatise has promoted these methods.

WHAT COMES NEXT?

It is likely that developments in architectural theory will continue to reflect the basic concepts and methods of modernism, either through extensions and variations or reactions. The implications of the use of computers on the functional programs of buildings are only beginning to be understood, but they promise to be profound.

I   *Underpinnings (Relevant to All Theory)*

There are some concerns that belong to (or are implicit in) all theories of architecture. Functioning as universal issues, they transcend the typology of imperatives that animate the theory of a given historical era. Such concerns include definitions of the role of architecture—and of the architect—in society. They also extend to the education of the architect and a code of professional conduct. Other universal issues are criteria for judging excellence in architecture and explanations put forward to justify certain theoretical imperatives so as to place them beyond dispute. Such issues also include appeals to architecture of the past for paradigms of practice or for authentication of precepts, usually for the purpose of demonstrating or validating a given approach to design.

Of Architecture and Architects

THE ROLE OF ARCHITECTURE AND THE ARCHITECT IN SOCIETY

Theorists from Vitruvius on have exalted the role of architecture and the architect in human society. Vitruvius did not dwell at length on the matter, but in the context of hypothesizing an origin for architecture he offered the art of building perhaps the highest encomium it has ever received. After attributing to the discovery of fire the origin of society and language, he accorded to the invention of architecture the status of generator of civilization. From architecture, he asserted, all the other arts and fields of knowledge were descended. By implication, then, the architect is one of the prime contributors to the shaping of civilization. By defining the importance of the art of building in this way, Vitruvius raised the writing of architectural theory above the level of technical manuals to that of intellectual discourse bordering on philosophy. Subsequent theorists had to subscribe to similar characterizations in order to maintain the same lofty status for their treatises, but their different circumstances prompted them to employ somewhat different formulations.

Because Alberti's mission in writing his treatise was to revive the antique tradition, it was necessary for him to make classical architecture important to others as well. Hence for him the role of theory had to be one of advocacy—as it has remained to this day. For that reason Alberti felt impelled to cite the benefits to society of beautiful, well-planned buildings: they give pleasure; they enhance civic pride; they confer dignity and honor on the community; if sacred, they can encourage piety; and they may even move an enemy to refrain from damaging them. By the same token the architect through his work bestows benefits: he is useful both to individual clients and to the public. Through the design of military machines and fortifications he may be more useful to the defense of society than the generals; and as an artist and theorist he is an ornament to his culture.

For as long as the classical tradition reigned as the sole desirable mode for architecture, these assertions did not need to be restated or defended. But near the end of the eighteenth century, when a theorist such as Quatremère de Quincy could assert that the orders need not necessarily be the basis of design, a new way of defining the role of architecture became appropriate. Quatremère saw architecture as a mode of expression, parallel to language and similar in nature. Like language, it is not only a means whereby human society is formed but is also a cause of its formation. Like language, architecture evolves and with that evolution comes to serve a progressive social purpose. Hence architects and architecture can be the instrument of social improvement.

That outlook got a new spin when Gothic became the conceptual ideal. Pugin, for instance, cited this one particular style of building, the medieval architecture of the pointed arch, as not only evocative but also supportive of a virtuous society. The medieval architect, by implication, had been the instrument of that virtue. Ruskin, imputing similar virtue to Italian Gothic, maintained that good architecture inspires the citizens who have incorporated it into their daily lives, because it expresses and at the same time reinforces the highest values of their society. It contains the most palpable evidence of their historical experience, endowing the surrounding landscape with the cultural meaning that makes nature poetic. Moreover, it manifests the inner spirit of a people, witnessing to their distinctive identity. The architect assumes the burden of realizing all these important missions. When he is successful, he has contributed to and improved his society.

For Viollet-le-Duc, who preferred to involve himself in architecture without benefit of metaphysics, the architect provides rational designs to meet practical needs. Architecture, for him, is the product of logical analysis, providing for a functional need with a suitable structure while employing appropriate materials. His views are akin to Ruskin's but without the romantic sentiment. Together the two theorists provided the basis for a magnified esteem, current during the early decades of the twentieth century, of the social value of good design and the architect's role in creating it.

Paul Scheerbart, envisioning in 1914 a virtually transparent architecture with curtain walls of glass set in minimal ferroconcrete frames, offered one of the most radical assessments. He recognized that while living and working in transparent buildings a person would have to shed the sense of being cocooned that traditional architecture provides. That person would also have to be willing to function with the environment in full view, and in full view of those on the outside. Such an alteration of circumstances would require nothing less than a fundamental change of behavior and a modification of prevailing notions of privacy. It would radically redefine the way people had related to architecture for more than two thousand years. For Scheerbart, then, architecture is capable of playing a role in society that would profoundly change how people live and relate to each other. He had, on the other hand, no particular notion of the architect's place in all this other than to assume that the designer can and will recognize and take advantage of all the new opportunities presented by modern technology.

Frank Lloyd Wright, Walter Gropius, and Le Corbusier shared an exaggerated notion of the profound effect that good architectural design and the architect who created it could have on society. For Le Corbusier it was largely a case of solving problems to create a more healthful and efficient built environment. To a considerable extent he subscribed to the same notion as Scheerbart, namely that through spare, lean domestic design one could correct the indolent, materialistic inclinations he deplored in nineteenth-century society and perceived in its architecture. He was fully aware of the implications for lifestyle that are inherent in his architectural design, and he tended to idealize the impact that an architect of such inclinations could exert upon his society. His urban design schemes, centered on widely dispersed glass and concrete towers and surrounded by long ribbon buildings of similar construction, were abstractions based on generalized concerns for physical health and circulation and little else. They were environments to be shaped by a single intelligence, granted total control over a large area.

Gropius's notions were nearly the same; indeed, he and Le Corbusier both trusted in modern industrial technology to sweep away the ills of the past, especially the horrors of the nineteenth-century industrial city. More than the other two leaders of modernism, however, Gropius put his faith in the creation of material environments in which all artifacts, not just the architecture, would be well designed. They would not only be tasteful and efficient; they would also be industrially produced, and in a manner that would make them economically available to most of the population. He regarded the function of an architect as that of a social benefactor.

Wright, having early imbibed from Japan the Zen Buddhist concept of the oneness of humankind with nature, was always more concerned than the other two pioneers of modernism with using architecture to help people establish a philosophically healthier relationship to nature. Toward this end he devoted special concern to the siting of his rural buildings in nature and also to designing the natural environment surrounding his urban buildings. He regarded his architecture as capable of helping people adopt a saner lifestyle, and as an architect he thought of himself as the one who would show the way. His Broadacre City project—made with the Taliesin Fellows in the mid-1930s—integrated the amenities of both city and country in a thinly populated regional plan. The architect of such a community would implicitly both design and control the environment. Consequently, just as Plato's republic was to be headed by a philosopher-king, Wright's Broadacre City would have to be governed by a philosopher-architect.

Of the three, it was Le Corbusier whose ideas about the role of the architect enjoyed the greatest influence, especially in the area of city design. Conceived with altruistic motives for housing the many, his urban schemes were dominated by a concern for providing healthful environments, light and airy, in which circulation by modern modes of transportation would be maximally efficient. Through such improved design he thought it would be possible to transform urban life for the better.

As it turned out, Le Corbusier's exalted aspiration for the role of the architect signaled the high-water mark of the modernist movement's professional ambitions. The apartment tower schemes constructed according to his model ended up exerting upon the occupants an impact exactly opposite from the one he had imagined. Not only did the structures not revitalize their alienated and dehumanized occupants, but they even atomized the very communities they were meant to unify. In acknowledgment of their failure, the dramatic intentional demolition of such a complex in St. Louis in the 1960s did more than any other one event to deflate the exalted regard for the architect and the social role of architecture that modernism had fostered. Since then, statements on those twin themes have been little more than asides interpolated into the explanations of designs in monographs and professional journals.

Nowadays the professional is more likely to present him- or herself as a nonintrusive interpreter of the client's needs, functioning principally as a facilitator for their realization. If the reality of performance is more active than that, it is one in which the designer's creative freedom is exercised more with the way the structure is formulated than with the way the building is to be used, that is, with the means rather than the ends. If the present-day architect does not still claim to improve society through good design, he or she may nevertheless produce an unanticipated new cultural icon in the course of developing a radical structural solution to the practical needs of the client. Be that as it may, the diminution of the role of the architect in architectural theory is real, and it has been accompanied by a parallel diminution in both the advocacy and the comprehensiveness of architectural theory itself.

THE EDUCATION OF THE ARCHITECT

Vitruvius regarded the architect's ability as so central to the enterprise of building that he made the architect's education the point of departure for his entire treatise. He certainly expected that the training would be practical as well as intellectual, each of those aspects being equally necessary

UNDERPINNINGS (RELEVANT TO ALL THEORY)

as well as indispensable to the other. The practical he felt no need to describe, whereas the intellectual he discussed in considerable detail. At another point in his text he expressed pride in his education and gratitude to his parents for having provided it. So the curriculum he delineated in the opening book may have been pretty much what he had received and found useful in his own career.

The subjects he prescribed are not far removed from a liberal arts curriculum in present-day institutions. They include eleven disciplines. Drawing is needed in order to make sketches. Geometry helps one to employ a rule and compass in making a design and also to figure proportions. Optics is useful to determine the quality of light in buildings. Arithmetic is needed to calculate costs and dimensions. History helps one to explain features of famous buildings to clients. Philosophy provides the basis for cultivating personal virtues. Physics is needed to understand the laws of nature. Music, as an intellectual rather than a practical pursuit, helps one to acquire mathematical theory (related to acoustics) and to tune weapons. Medicine is useful in judging the health conditions of building sites. Law informs one about regulations related to building. And astronomy helps one to understand the harmony of the universe. Although each of those subjects is individually important, he recognized that each informs the others as well. He was quick to admit that he was no scholar and that one need not be an expert in any of the subjects. Rather, he felt it important to grasp the principles involved in the various disciplines so that they can be employed in a pragmatic way.

It is hard to fault such a curriculum and general outlook for the education of an architect. The difference in concept between this and what is prescribed today is not great, even if the particular subjects are not the same, but ironically the similarity probably has little or nothing to do with the fact that Vitruvius articulated its scope. It has more to do with the gradual return to a cultural situation in which a holistic view of the needs of society combined with the technological demands of construction is roughly parallel to that of ancient Rome.

From Alberti's standpoint, such a curriculum could not be provided in one institution or cultural circumstance. Functioning in a context in which the medieval curriculum of the seven liberal arts still survived virtually intact, Alberti posited a prospective architect closer to the realm of the scholar than to that of the builder. Indeed, in writing his treatise he was carrying on a campaign to gain acceptance of the visual arts as pursuits belonging to the intellectual realm. For him it was important to gain recognition for the architect as a scholar and gentleman rather than merely the craftsman he had long been in Italian society. Thus did Alberti get cornered into asserting a greater importance for theory than practice in the architect's education and regarding his profession as more that of an artist than a builder.

Alberti's outlook prevailed, with two telling consequences. The most direct is that for as long as the classical tradition dominated in European architecture, the education of the architect was more artistic and theoretical than practical. Official academies were eventually founded in the seventeenth century to propagate exactly this regimen, and they dominated the preparation of young architects for at least two more centuries to come. The less direct consequence was that, lacking a venturesome technological training, European architects did not develop any important structural innovations during the era when this philosophy of training prevailed. Although rich in formal invention within the rubric of classicism, their practice remained largely static in matters related to technology.

Viollet-le-Duc is the theorist who wanted to bring the education of the architect into the modern age. The chronology of his writings on the subject does not correspond with the order of their applicability to the development of an architect, so it is the latter sequence that will be followed here. The education of a child who shows interest or capability in matters visual should, he thought, be centered on drawing. Discussed in his last work, *Histoire d'un dessinateur, comment on apprend à dessiner* (Paris, 1879), drawing is to be pursued not for the sake of developing an artistic talent but to help a child learn to see what he looks at and to analyze what he sees. The point is that through the exercise of independent analysis of things not encountered before one develops an active rather than a passive intellect, fostering in turn a problem-solving outlook. While pursuing a higher education, Viollet-le-Duc explained in *Histoire d'une maison* (Paris, 1873), the prospective architect should work in a professional office—much like today's intern—and even on a construction site, if possible, in alternation with academic activities. Moreover, he explained in the same treatise, design should be developed step by step in accordance with a definite rational method. Fundamentally, as he argued in the two volumes of *Entretiens sur l'architecture* (Paris, 1863, 1872), academic training should cease to be addressed wholly to the artistic side of architecture but should be balanced with the technological concerns of engineers.

Viollet-le-Duc's negative view of an art-centered architectural education was directed toward the official academy, the École des Beaux-Arts, where, ironically, he had been teaching just before the *Entretiens* were published. His opinion was that the only original works in building in France at the time were the undertakings of engineers. By the early twentieth century his position had been adopted by numerous universities, especially in America, and their curricula began to resemble more and more a combination of the formulas of Vitruvius and Viollet-le-Duc.

In the 1920s the Bauhaus, under the direction of Walter Gropius, emphasized even more strongly the practical aspects of training. Before proceeding to a professional level of architectural education, students were required to master all sorts of practical skills related to building, both in institutional workshops and in formal apprenticeships. The requirements stipulated in Gropius's booklet *The New Architecture and the Bauhaus* (Cambridge, MA, 1965) certainly exceeded the level of practicality that elitists like Gropius would themselves have tolerated as students, but they served to advance a strong case for the inclusion of practical training in architectural education. A certain amount of this carried over into the curriculum he imposed upon the Graduate School of Design at Harvard, which spread from there to architecture schools throughout the United States.

Architectural training today increasingly tends to emphasize technological training, largely in response to the demands of senior partners in firms hiring new graduates. Many employers take for granted a familiarity with CAD—computer-aided design. What they do not take into consideration is that education is not the same thing as job preparedness, and that the more beginners are educated in analytical thinking, the more readily they acquire practical skills and become effective in office procedure.

THE SCOPE OF THE ARCHITECT'S ACTIVITY

The range of activities considered the proper work of the architect has varied considerably over time, generally developing in the direction of greater specialization. For Vitruvius's architect, the creation of all types of buildings was to be accompanied by the making of timepieces and the construction of machinery. In other words, his architect was fully the equivalent of both the civil and mechanical engineer of our time as well as the architect; he was expected to be able to devise military structures and machines in addition to civil facilities. Regarding the built environment alone, Vitruvius specified four activities that involved special expertise. Laying out new cities required a mastery of health, safety, and security issues. Constructing ceremonial structures required a mastery of the orders. Constructing amphitheaters required a mastery of acoustics. Constructing houses required a detailed knowledge of functional layout and techniques of decoration. In sum, such a professional had to be both intellectually flexible and technically accomplished.

Alberti's architect, concentrating upon art and theory while still conversant with engineering, would, in actual practice, mainly design buildings and monuments. To be sure, he would regard military fortifications as his responsibility, and perhaps also the machinery involved in his construction projects, but the mechanics would be largely left to the builder. As the scope of the architect's activity became narrower, a division between the architect and engineer developed that continued to widen during the next three centuries, reaching a climax in Scamozzi's art-centered definition of the profession. Ironically, as that gap widened, architects were becoming involved in the artistic aspect of exterior environments—notably great gardens and parks, city squares, and avenues. Even so, the artistic orientation of the profession continued to dominate through much of the nineteenth century, and the issue of its relative appropriateness still persists.

Viollet-le-Duc advocated a greater overlap between the activities of the architect and the engineer, but in his theoretical construct the two professions remained separate. His architect is concerned almost entirely with the design and construction of civil buildings. It remained for the visionaries of the early twentieth century—such as Scheerbart and Sant'Elia—and the first generation of modernists—such as Tony Garnier, Le Corbusier, and Wright—to expand the scope of the architect's activity, if only in theory, to city and regional planning. Meanwhile, treatises composed under the influence of England's Ruskin-inspired Arts and Crafts movement, such as Hermann Muthesius's *Das englische Haus* (Berlin, 1904–1905), justified expanding the architect's purview to matters smaller than the design of a single building—including specific features of the interior such as furniture, rugs, wallpaper, and even dishes and cutlery—in the interest of promoting design of the total environment. This concern was adopted by Gropius for his Bauhaus curriculum and was promulgated by his theoretical propaganda on behalf of the school. Manifested in furniture design, it has persisted in the practice of some high-profile architects until the present.

It is hard to imagine what more anyone would have ventured to add to the role of the architect. Perhaps not surprisingly, such comprehensive ambitions have subsequently dropped out of theoretical writings. Nevertheless, any major architect asked to take on a large-scale assignment is more likely than not to accept it and to regard it as justly included within the competence of the building professional.

THE PROFESSIONAL CONDUCT OF THE ARCHITECT

The matter of professional behavior has been of concern to several of the most prominent theorists. Vitruvius opined that so many insufficiently trained and unscrupulous individuals put themselves forward as architects that it is of the greatest importance for a serious practitioner to be circumspect in all aspects of his professional conduct. Regarding commissions he advised that rather than pressing for engagement one ought to wait to be asked, even to be approached by a prospective client more than once. He cautioned that the client's ability and willingness to meet the financial obligations of the project should be carefully scrutinized. At the same time, he held the architect strictly responsible for making a realistic and accurate cost estimate. He even proposed that cost overruns of more than one quarter of the total amount should be deducted from the architect's compensation.

Alberti likewise advised the architect to be cautious in acquiring clients and to conduct himself with the greatest probity. Moreover, he warned, it is extremely important to be certain that a design is right before beginning construction, in order to avoid undue expense in correcting flaws. Toward that end he recommended examining the design in great detail and building a scale model so that both architect and client could study the scheme carefully before making a final commitment.

Ruskin's overriding concern regarding the architect was that he exercise his scruples to the utmost in order to produce the highest-quality building possible within the limits of the commission. He was particularly concerned that the architect should specify the best materials affordable and see that they are worked with the greatest degree of skill. The architect should cut no corners with regard either to materials or labor and should especially avoid industrially produced elements that imitate highly crafted handwork. The overall implication was that the architect is fully responsible for the finished product and that careful supervision of the construction is virtually as important as the design itself.

Twentieth-century theorists have been less explicit about professional conduct and ethics, but not because these matters have been regarded as unimportant. To the contrary, the stipulation of injunctions has undoubtedly come to seem unnecessary in theoretical contexts because guidelines are spelled out by professional organizations and conduct is strictly circumscribed by legal regulation. Within the limits of practicality, however, general theories of modern architecture still subscribe to Ruskin's aspirations of diligence in performance.

Standards of Judgment and Design

Justifications

STANDARDS OF JUDGMENT

Immediately after his opening passage on the education of the architect, Vitruvius introduced a feature that definitively established, then and forever, the difference between a theory of architecture and a building manual. That feature is a set of criteria for judging the quality of a building. It is one thing to stipulate how a building *can* be built, or even how it *should* be built, and quite another to create an apparatus for determining whether or not it *was* built well—that is, a means of judging its quality. By quality Vitruvius did not just mean how soundly a structure was built or how aptly it fulfilled its purpose. He also (especially) meant its visual quality, its beauty. Although the criteria he established suffice to analyze and assess a building, they do not preclude the substitution of different but equally efficacious criteria. So, if his system is valuable for its own sake, its greater importance is that it makes of architecture a phenomenon worthy of contemplation, discussion, and evaluation. In a phrase, it elevates buildings into architecture and raises architecture to the level of all the other human activities that are regarded as aesthetic—such as poetry, music, and painting. The particular system he set out may, even now, be used to judge buildings of any architectural tradition, but it is particularly attuned to architecture that employs the classical orders.

What are Vitruvius's criteria of judgment? The categories are order, arrangement, eurythmy, symmetry, propriety, and economy—all of them abstractions intended to characterize concretely the physical aspects of a design. Order means that the building must make visual sense, of course, but more profoundly it pertains to the plan and how well the various spaces serve their respective purposes, and the whole its basic mission. As expressly regards classical architecture, Vitruvius associates order with mensural consistency, achieved by applying a module taken from a dimension of a specific member to all aspects of the whole. Arrangement overlaps with order regarding the functional efficacy of a plan, but it is primarily concerned with the beauty of the composition of the plan (and, by implication, that of the elevations and the massing of the whole). This is the category under which building begins to become art.

Eurythmy and symmetry are related categories for judging the beauty of the design. Eurythmy is the right relationship, proportional as well as formal, of all the parts of an individual element, such as a column. Symmetry, on the other hand, is the right relationship of all the individual elements to the composition as a whole. For Vitruvius a right relationship is one based on adherence to a proportional system. Indeed, for him symmetry is never the bilateral correspondence we impute to the term today. Rather, his symmetry, the most important aesthetic quality in a building, is the harmonious correlation of proportions throughout a design.

Propriety is making the design correspond exactly to the usage traditional for a particular type of building. That means not only getting the form right but also selecting the right category and degree of decor. This is the quality that reins in any tendency to overdo or underdo whatever is appropriate for a particular situation. In a word, it is good taste. Finally, economy is the quality that Vitruvius defines as the proper management of materials and site with regard to both cost and good judgment. According to the factors he mentions, it could more readily be termed the skillful execution of the project or the degree of finesse appropriate to the project. Oddly, he does not seem to relate it to the concept of economy of means—the right amount of structure and material for the circumstance.

For Alberti, beauty was the overriding criterion of excellence in a building. Indeed, he regarded it as inseparable from suitability for use and hence an aspect of utility. Because he gathered the virtues under that one conceptual umbrella, he had to develop an approach different from Vitruvius's code of six key qualities. He opted instead to use several questions inherent to criticism. The first—How well was it conceived?—pertaining entirely to the architect, comprises the intellectual input: "choice, distribution, arrangement, etc." The second—How well was it executed?—addresses the issue of workmanship: "laying, joining, cutting, trimming, polishing, etc." The third—How good are the qualities determined by nature?—comprises all the external factors: "weight, lightness, density, purity, durability, etc." A fourth—How does all this add up?—is meant to assess the integration of all the factors. This combinatory quality he found hard to define, even to name, for he deemed it virtually ineffable; but its effect, he averred, would be recognizable to anyone.

To this set of critical questions about the building he added one more—What are the benchmarks of excellence?—by which he meant the degree to which the design follows the rules of nature as regards "number, outline, and position." Under this rubric he was concerned about the extent to which the number and arrangement of components, the use of proportion, and the generation of forms correspond to their equivalents in nature. After observing the naturelike virtues of a design, he recommended that one survey the absence of the kind of faults that occur in nature, by which he meant "anything that is distorted, stunted, excessive, or deformed in any way."

Critical codes employing these or similar questions were conceived primarily for the purpose of evaluating formal architecture composed primarily as an aesthetic image. For that reason Alberti's criteria, or versions of them, were useful for as long as the taste for architecture of the classical tradition prevailed. But when the classical ideal was replaced by the Gothic, the criteria needed to be substantially revised. The person who effected that change was John Ruskin.

Ruskin's *Seven Lamps of Architecture,* more than any other treatise, was organized entirely around criteria of evaluation. Like Alberti, his dominant concern was beauty. The distinctive aspect of his treatment of the issue was that he explored other kinds of beauty in addition to comeliness. In this respect Ruskin undoubtedly owed a great deal to his great Renaissance predecessor, whose text touched upon some of the same sociocultural issues. The difference is that Alberti had simply enunciated his criteria as pronouncements, whereas Ruskin justified his with reasoned argument and analysis, making them his principal topics. Unlike Alberti, Ruskin was not interested in authenticating regulatory procedures, nor did he concern himself with envisioning a new architecture of the future. Rather, he was content to spell out what was satisfactory regarding the architecture of the past as a source of inspiration to the creators of architecture of the future. Perhaps part of his appeal to architects was that he identified various types of satisfactoriness in architecture in general and left it to them to discover how these virtues could be incorporated into their own work.

In Ruskin's treatise the seven "lamps" of the title are the criteria of excellence. The first, designated "sacrifice," deals with the positive effect in a building of the expenditure of unstinting care, in the form of support by the patron and effort by the architect and workmen. This involvement may be manifested in generous size, lavish materials, and painstaking execution. The same virtues can be equally evident at descending levels of project importance and cost; indeed, it is crucial, Ruskin thought, to make the degree of expenditure commensurate with the scope of the project. In this perspective utter simplicity can be as effectual as sumptuous grandeur.

The criterion of "truth" concerns the expression of honesty in a building, regarding both materials and structural composition. One of Ruskin's most enduring dicta is that one material must never be camouflaged to look like another, most especially when the material imitated would have been the more expensive. More fundamental to later theory and practice, though, is the principle that materials should only be employed to perform tasks consonant with their inherent properties. Structure should be composed so as to express how the building is put together. This does not mean that all structural elements should be in view, but that the building must not appear to be constructed differently from the way it actually is.

The criterion of "power" distinguishes between two modes of vivid aesthetic expression, the sublime and the beautiful. These modes are not mutually exclusive and both can be present in a given building. More generally, however, one mode or the other will be recognized as the signal virtue. The sublime impresses with its forcefulness, due to such qualities as great size, stark simplicity, overwhelming muchness, dramatic play of light and shadows, and rugged strength. Beauty, on the other hand, charms with such qualities as harmony, grace, delicacy, and refinement.

Incorporation of this duality into the theory of architecture was perspicuous on Ruskin's part, but modern theorists have ignored it, implicitly relegating it to the dustbin of history despite its timeless relevance.

The criterion of "beauty" treats the ways in which ornament can be effective in the design of a building and also the ways in which it can detract. Ruskin's acquaintance with formidable numbers of specific examples led him to form strong opinions, which limited their efficacy to the taste of his own historical moment. Indeed, the one regulatory imperative in the treatise is his codification of types of ornaments and the ways they ought to be used on buildings. These are permutations and combinations of the qualities of mimetic naturalness and abstraction, color and monochrome, plasticity and flatness, proximity and distance. Arguably still applicable, these dicta fell from grace when ornament was rejected from modernist theory, making Ruskin seem more old-fashioned than he actually was.

The criterion of "life" focuses on the distinction between the vitality evident in expert handwork in historical architecture and the flaccid quality of manufactured ornament of the industrial age. Ruskin's emphasis on the merit of the minute variations that give handwork its characteristic brio provided impetus in England to the incipient Arts and Crafts movement. The prestige still attributed to the quality of handcraftedness is one of his most lasting legacies.

The criterion of "memory" stresses the poetic and inspirational value of buildings from past ages in both the city and the rural landscape. Ruskin's celebration of their salutary effect did much to instigate the modern taste for historical architecture as well as for the preservation of a historical mix in the urban environment, both of which are distinctive characteristics of the modern age. His negative sentiments concerning restoration, on the other hand, have served as a restraining influence. They remain vital in debates over the best way to deal with specific situations in preservation.

The criterion of "obedience" concerns the importance of honoring and maintaining national traditions in architectural practice. Ruskin denounced the cultural irrelevance of designing buildings in exotic modes and deplored their deleterious effect upon the architectural environment. On the other hand, he did not favor static adherence to a particular historical moment of a national tradition but encouraged its continued evolution. He saw in such continuity the only way for a culture to remain true to itself. Meaningless to modernism, this tenet contributed considerable weight to postmodernist theory, as an antecedent authority.

Ruskin's predilection for Christian architecture of the late Middle Ages and early Renaissance led him to posit the evaluation of architecture much more in historically cultural terms than had the theorists of the pagan classical tradition. Yet, like them, he couched his criteria in aesthetic terms, not recognizing that other desiderata in the modern age were competing for equal status as concerns of critical judgment. Because he was an analytical observer and not a designer of buildings, he did not discern that new planning assumptions would change the way buildings are evaluated and vitiate the need for an evaluative code in the theory of architecture. But Viollet-le-Duc was about to show how to do it.

Viollet-le-Duc saw the historical traditions of architecture first and foremost as having created rational solutions to design problems, not compositions prompted primarily by aesthetic impulses. The extent to which buildings are beautiful, he opined, is the extent to which the special problem each confronted was solved in an optimal way. Hence, for him, there was no need to evaluate the beauty of a building as an independent quality; beauty was simply the outcome of a rational analysis. So it is, then, that in his theoretical writing critical evaluation was addressed first to the interrelationship of the functional program and the structural design. The style of a design was thus interpreted as the by-product of this relationship. Style, he held, is something a completely rational scheme achieves by virtue of its correspondence to the needs of the project. The historical styles, on the other hand, are simply artificial intellectual constructs devised after the fact for purposes of formal classification.

DESIGN JUSTIFICATIONS: THE AUTHENTICTY OF ORIGINS IN NATURE

To hypothesize how the first structure may have come into being is to identify the principle a theorist believes has animated the conception of architecture from the beginning of time. Vitruvius saw the first structure as a response to the needs of people who had come together in sociability following the discovery of fire. He recognized from the outset that there were different responses to the need for shelter, some people piling up leafy branches, others digging caves, and still others using logs. Indeed, the materials used and the resultant form, he surmised, were factors determined by geographical variations in climate, topography, and availability of materials. Thereby did he explain the distinctive formats of vernacular architecture in the different parts of the world that were in his ken. He regarded them all as having been determined by the laws of nature and the inherent qualities of available materials.

He attributed the evolution of a mature architecture from these beginnings to a gradual progression of little improvements made from one building to the next, innovations that had been noted, remembered, and subsequently incorporated into new structures. Most importantly, he hypothesized for prehistoric Greece and Italy rude structures that could serve as germinal prototypes for the architecture of the classical orders. Drawing such a connection, it was important to him to be able to assert later in his text that the orders had been formulated in wood, employing a technology peculiarly appropriate to wood, and only afterward, for the sake of permanence, translated into stone. The value of this assertion was that he could justify the compositions of the Doric and Ionic orders, respectively, as having evolved from responses to nature and natural conditions, hence irrefutable as canonical formulations. In this connection it is significant that his account of the invention of the Corinthian capital hypothesized an imitation of natural and human-made objects, in a composition that had been fortuitously assembled and also discovered by chance in a natural setting.

Indeed, it was so crucial to Vitruvius to justify the orders with an origin in nature that he inserted a different but related argument into his explication of their mature formats. He drew a parallel between the elaborate system of proportions inherent in the orders and the natural proportions of the human body. The implicit justification was twofold. Because buildings are constructed for the sole purpose of being used by people, their relative measurements should be coordinated in a manner like those of people; second, because the incorporation of a system of proportions is parallel to an example in nature, its validity is beyond contention. The conclusion to be drawn is that both the basic composition and the proportional system of the orders are derived from responses to nature itself, an absolute standard that cannot be questioned. Vitruvius did not need to justify any further his implicit assumption that all buildings of great dignity, both sacred and civil, should employ the orders.

Ever after, when a theorist has needed to justify the forms of architecture, he has resorted to an argument based on the irrefutable authority of nature. Because Alberti took for granted that good architecture should employ the orders, he had no need to discuss the primitive hut or parallels in nature. And as long as theorists were happy with the way the use of the orders was evolving, they, too, could dispense with explanations. But by the middle of the eighteenth century, when Laugier wanted to break away from that evolution and return to the purely structural use of the orders in the manner of ancient Greece, it was necessary to return to the argument from nature.

Eager to promote directness and simplicity in the formulation of structure, Laugier posited a description of the primitive hut that made it the archetype of the classical temple, with tree trunks as columns, horizontal branches as entablature, and slanted branches as pediments and sloping roof. In the revised edition of his treatise, published two years after its initial appearance in 1753, he included a frontispiece in which this structural description was forthrightly illustrated (fig. 2-1). The image added considerable weight to his assertion that all the grandeur of the architecture of the orders was descended from this primitive building. The point that makes his argument different from Vitruvius's is that for him the orders were virtually inherent in nature (along with human proportions), hence divine in origin and irreplaceable in architectural practice. On the other hand, given that the orders had emerged from such a beginning, there is no reason why their development should not continue, even to the extent of creating new orders. Driving this principle of the natural rightness of the orders was his passionate belief that structure should be rationally formulated and that architectural composition should always reflect the way a building is put together.

Figure 2-1
Laugier's "primitive hut," frontispiece of his *Essay on Architecture,* in the revised edition of 1755.

STANDARDS OF JUDGMENT AND DESIGN JUSTIFICATIONS

Quatremère de Quincy, in *L'architecture égyptienne,* entertained yet a different concept of primitive architecture. He did not think in terms of a single beginning but, as in the case of languages, of multiple points of origin with different manifestations. He identified three fundamentally different types of primitive buildings (the cave, the tent, and the wooden hut), which he assigned to three different kinds of cultures (respectively, hunters, gatherers, and farmers). As regards materials—stone, fabric, and wood—the three types were responses to nature, like the hypothetical primitive architecture of the preceding theorists. But in terms of their formats, they were also reasoned responses to different lifestyles. With this formulation he secularized the myth of primitive architecture, which heretofore, through its putative origin in the laws of nature, had had a link to divinity. Posited in human culture rather than nature, this explanation associated their formation with national traditions. The history of architecture, then, became the evolution of different types initiated by different kinds of societies, each with its own peculiar operating system. They all had their value, albeit unequal, and Quatremère assigned greatest value to the tradition of the wooden hut and the classical orders.

Gottfried Semper, in *Der Stil,* regarded theories of evolution of architecture from primitive archetypes as materialistic and shallow. For him the forms of the Greek orders, his favorite tradition of architecture, were not pragmatic adaptations of functional forms but the transfer of aesthetic habits from older forms of human creativity, namely, the technical arts of ceramics, textiles, carpentry, and masonry. In a process closer to linguistic development than to domestic problem solving, the transfers were related to meaning rather than function. Tensile forms in structures were ascribed to textiles; forms made of malleable material hardened by drying under sun or flames to ceramics; sticklike forms to carpentry; compression-resistant forms made of aggregate material to masonry. Decoration, the dressing of a structural scaffold, was the aspect of architecture that gave it meaning and was the precondition of monumentality. The orders, then, were justified in terms of human culture.

Once the orders had been abandoned as the sine qua non of architecture, there was no further need for the concept of the primitive hut, with its appeal to some sort of absolute, to justify architectural form. Viollet-le-Duc, however, retained it for a different reason. As he hypothesized in *Histoire de l'habitation humaine depuis les temps préhistoriques* (Paris, 1875), the invention of structure in the form of primitive shelters—particularly the primitive hut made of wood and various secondary materials—could scarcely have begun in an ad hoc manner. Instead, its inception ought to be attributed to revelation from a superior consciousness, much like the mythical gift of fire. But from that point on there was a gradual but continual process of improvement through which the traditions of the great world cultures evolved. The basic point of his explanation was to make the development of architecture a product of rational analysis, combined with openness to change. Although he readily acknowledged that change, or "progress," in material culture has an impact on social values, he was fearless in the face of the new. Thus his primitive hut was employed to justify an outlook that accepted no eternal verities, such as the orders, but sought improvement through a continual process of experimentation.

In 1914, when Le Corbusier promulgated the Domino House as a universal prototype for modern structures, he might have been seen as reverting to the primitive hut as a paradigm. But in the event he implicitly justified it as a rational conception that demonstrated what was technically possible, not as a response to natural conditions. Frank

STANDARDS OF JUDGMENT AND DESIGN JUSTIFICATIONS

Lloyd Wright took a further step away. He had no use for the primitive hut in his theory, but he regularly appealed, particularly in the *Autobiography*, to comparisons with nature to justify his structural innovations. A notable example is the rigid-core high-rise building, with its floors cantilevered from a central spine, which he likened to the branches of a tree extending from its trunk. Or, relative to the human form, he compared the fused rigid spine and hollow tube of his "Romeo and Juliet" windmill to the embrace of lovers. His oft-cited boyhood summers in the Wisconsin countryside became the pretext for finding justifications in the safe authority of nature.

Indeed, the analogy to nature in structural design remained the standard means for some twentieth-century theorists to seek unassailable justifications of their designs. Buckminster Fuller compared his use of the hexagon in geodesic domes to the geometric makeup of the units of a honeycomb. And Paolo Soleri, in his *Arcology*, cited the miniaturization of parts in the higher levels of biological species to justify the small unit spaces for individual habitation within the megastructural frames of his visionary designs for new cities. But in postmodern theory, after 1965, justification has been sought more often in human culture and technological means than in nature.

Most important theorists have appealed to the architecture of the past in order to confer authority upon their dicta. From antiquity through the duration of the Renaissance tradition, the rules for correct usage were justified in the light of august architectural precedent. Then in the nineteenth century, with a new type of appeal to the past, theorists again looked to historical architecture for guiding principles. And in the twentieth, examples from the past have served as both aesthetic inspiration and critical control.

VITRUVIUS AND THE RENAISSANCE THEORISTS

Vitruvius relied mainly upon Greek examples, taken at random from the previous five centuries, in order to give his formulations, intended for Roman use, a suitable cultural authority. He cited individual details of different buildings to authenticate his own formula for a single standard usage of the columnar orders. Alberti, intent on fostering a revival of the antique tradition in architecture, was disturbed by the lack of correspondence between Vitruvius's standard and what he had observed in Roman architecture. He was either unconcerned or unaware that most of the structures he had observed were designed and erected in the four centuries after Vitruvius's death. To resolve the discrepancy he sought justification for his own standard by citing specific instances from other ancient authors and from his own measurements among the ruins.

Later theorists of the Renaissance, such as Serlio and Palladio, likewise drew upon observations and measurements of ancient buildings to establish their own standard formulas. But they went much further in drawing upon uses of the past by systematically illustrating a coherent body of historical buildings. Without any precedent for doing so, they even reconstituted some of the buildings from ruins. With these illustrations they made ancient Roman architecture available as a source of design inspiration to anyone working anywhere. Because the illustrations were not burdened with extensive textual interpretations, they could be drawn upon at random and thus serve as an open-ended resource, which they did for centuries to come.

Serlio's book of antique architecture was the first ever to present plans, sections, and elevations of the major buildings of ancient Rome. It is difficult to exaggerate either the originality of his initiative or the importance of these drawings for professional practice and private delectation in the sixteenth century. His drawings of these monuments are conscientious representations of what he deemed to have been the buildings' original states—probably the first such effort in the history of human civilization. The illustrations are systematic in the sense that they present not only general views but also plans, sections, facades, and important details, thereby removing them from the much more limited tradition of topographical drawings (figs. 3-1, 3-2, 3-3, 3-4). In addition, the dimensions of the buildings were not approximations but measured. As diagrams the drawings were translatable, for whatever purpose, into concrete actualities, thanks to a scale provided on many of the plates and to dimensions reported in the text for the others. Although famous buildings like the Pantheon had long been well known

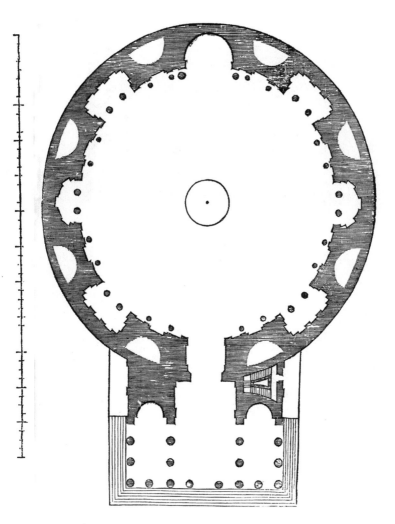

Figure 3-1
Serlio's plan of the Pantheon, drawn to scale.

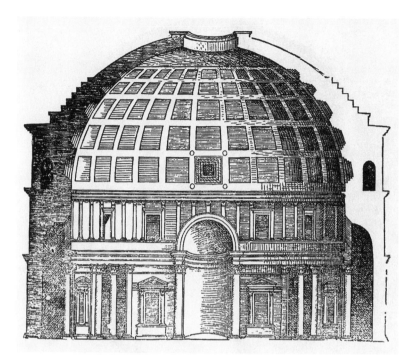

Figure 3-2
Serlio's section of the Pantheon, drawn to scale.

by repute, no amount of verbal description could convey an accurate image to those unable to visit them. In this regard the plates of details were as important as the overall schemata. Indeed, whereas verbal specifications of the columnar orders heretofore had been confined to generalized usage, Serlio's drawings clarified the full effect of actual applications. Thirty years later Palladio's drawings republished virtually the same material but presented it more precisely and in greater detail. His drawings also widened the audience for and increased still further the cultural prestige of ancient Roman architecture.

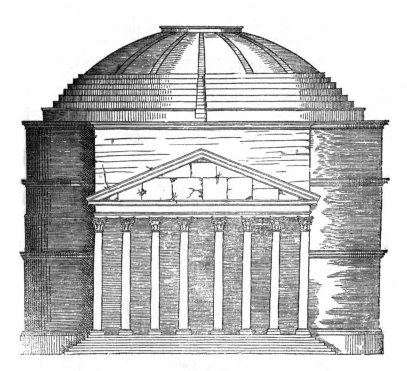

Figure 3-3
Serlio's facade of the Pantheon, drawn to scale.

LAUGIER TO PUGIN

As the factors that were to separate the modern era from all that went before began to appear, Laugier argued for the return to a purely structural use of the orders in the name of rational planning. With the purpose of discrediting the centuries-long practice of employing the orders as applied decoration, he was among the first to appeal to a historical tradition other than the classical as a model. Pointing to the logical character of Gothic structure, he urged architects to compose designs employing the orders

Figure 3-4
Serlio's detail of the original interior wall decor of the Pantheon,
drawn to scale.

but with a Gothic structural clarity. The value of this appeal would later prove to be more than just formal, because in the era of theoretical dominance by northern Europe Gothic possessed the virtue of belonging to unbroken national traditions. For that reason it retained a potency of cultural content that had long ago retreated from the classical tradition into academic abstraction. Hence, in the nineteenth century it was possible for Pugin to set up Gothic not only as a structural model for future architecture but as a cultural one as well. It remained, however, for the subsequent moment in the development of the modern era to find meaning in historical architecture that was central to the theory of architecture.

The nineteenth century brought awareness that an earlier sense of historical continuity, in which change unfolded in a continual present, had been irrevocably lost. Perhaps it was that consciousness of a separation from the past that then charged the delectation of historical architecture with the urgency of an unprecedented relevance. In all previous eras the emerging mode of architecture had made the old obsolete, thereby making only the current taste seem worth savoring. But that kind of cultural self-confidence had been lost in the course of the social, economic, and political upheavals of the late eighteenth and early nineteenth centuries. These movements did not bring with them a sure sense of how values were to be expressed in the visual arts. The feeling of being cast adrift caused knowledge of the past to seem like a cultural compass, and history became a kind of secular theology. In this context a new, didactic value accrued to historical architecture, making it a source of inspiration for architectural theory. Ruskin and Viollet-le-Duc were the first to make major use of it, but in very different ways.

Ruskin's entire system of critical evaluation was based on his deep appreciation of the aesthetic value of older architecture. His acquaintance with the period styles was broad, but his preference was focused: he loved the architecture of the later Middle Ages, not least because it was produced by a conscientiously Christian culture. Like Pugin, he found it evocative of a moral society, but as an evangelical Protestant he was not drawn to the Catholic aspect of the style. Rather, he thought he discerned in medieval architecture the efforts of honest and earnest patrons, designers, and craftsmen.

Although Ruskin harbored a fondness for the architecture of northern Europe, his wholehearted devotion belonged to Italian monuments of the Romanesque and Gothic eras. Repeatedly in his text he returned respectively to such examples as San Michele in Lucca and the Doge's Palace (fig. 3-5) in Venice, the latter being his favorite building. These buildings satisfied his taste in composition of structure, choice of materials, incorporation of color, hierarchy of decoration, variation of detail, and quality of workmanship. Indeed, no other theorist conditioned us more to admire the patina of old buildings and the layered atmosphere of ancient cities than Ruskin. It is largely due to him that we appreciate close juxtaposition of disparate historical styles in a given setting, finding poetic coexistence where a dogmatic formalist could see only incongruity. Indeed, he eloquently argued that a landscape, however well formed by nature, is devoid of poetry without the evidence in it of long-term human use and habitation, manifested by its old buildings. Hence the maintenance and preservation of fine buildings from the past is a major responsibility of any conscionable society. In all this he spoke so directly

Figure 3-5
Ruskin's favorite building: Venice, the Doge's Palace (courtesy David Wilkins).

to the concerns of his time that such sentiments now appear quaintly old-fashioned, until one stops to recognize that they speak equally to concerns of the present. Had this rich vein of Ruskinian lore been lacking in our culture, postmodernism would have been left scratching at surface gravel. (More of that later.)

VIOLLET-LE-DUC

Meanwhile, Viollet-le-Duc must hold our attention longer than anyone else, for among all theorists he undoubtedly made the greatest and most creative use of historical architecture. Indeed, from it he derived most of the principles that he thought should govern architecture. The greater part of his ideas on the subject were set down in the lectures for the École des Beaux-Arts that later became the first volume of the *Entretiens* (*Discourses*). In those essays he dealt with a large range of historical material, but in the final analysis his positive interest was focused on the Greek Doric temple, the Roman bath, the French Gothic cathedral, and the French Renaissance chateau. His negative assessments were reserved for the decorative aspects of Roman architecture, most Italian Renaissance buildings, and virtually all baroque designs of any locale.

Greek peripteral temples constructed in the Doric order possessed two supreme virtues compared to all other buildings (fig. 3-6). Viollet-le-Duc regarded their structural composition—in appearance, if not in fact—to be unsurpassed in clarity and rationality of expression. He judged the various members to have been ideally conceived to serve their respective functions in the construct. The temples were not only ideal in form but also suited to the material, the building methods, and the nature and quality of the workforce that made them. Their elemental structure—a pitched roof held up by vertical supports surrounding a rectangular enclosure—he judged to be a sublime formulation. The individual parts seemed to take into consideration their formation from the lithic material, especially the necessity of rolling the larger pieces to the building site. The block-and-tackle method, which, he conjectured, was employed to put them into place, he associated with Greek seafaring technology. And the employment of highly skilled craftsmen in all aspects of the construction he attributed to the availability of professional artisans who were freemen of a democratic society. Indeed, he found this integrated explanation so compelling that he argued, contrary to Vitruvius, that the orders had not been translated from wood into stone but manifestly were conceived from the outset in stone. Although the peripteral format was rigid, allowing no flexibility of spatial development, he regarded the Doric temple as the supreme instance of an architecture conceived in terms of structure.

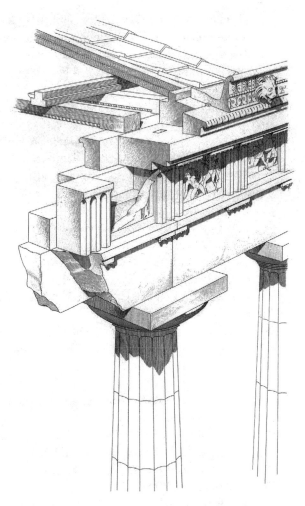

Figure 3-6
Viollet-le-Duc's structural diagram of a Greek Doric temple (*Discourses*).

Roman architecture was, for Viollet-le-Duc, almost opposite in character. Fixing upon the great baths of the third century as the highest and best realization of the Roman tradition (fig. 3-7), he regarded their format of many and varied spaces as the sophisticated resolution of disparate functional requirements into a formally coherent sequence. Each of those spaces had its distinctive structure, expressly formulated to serve the peculiar technical needs of that unit. This flexibility fostered both technological diversity and spatial creativity, involving different kinds of structural coverings, ranging beyond flat ceilings to barrel and groined vaults and domes.

The greatest virtue of this architecture was that its design derived from a functional program, with a structure responsive to specific needs of individual spaces rather than a preconceived formula. By corollary, it was more about space than form. Like Greek architecture, the character of the Roman was intrinsically related to the materials and construction methods used and the nature of the workforce employed. In contrast to the large blocks and drums of stone in Greek architecture, Roman buildings were erected of small baked bricks and mortar molded in forms. They were constructed by small armies of unskilled slaves, working under the direct supervision of professionals, in contrast to the moderate-sized Greek workshop, staffed by men of high skill. Also unlike Greek architecture, in which the stones provided the finished surface, Roman masonry provided only a structural core which needed a decorative veneer. It was precisely in this area that Viollet-le-Duc withheld approbation, for he regarded surface decor as inherently dishonest, and in this case all the more so because it was usually made up of elements from the Greek orders, which had traditionally served a structural function. Despite this flaw, he viewed Roman architecture as a supreme achievement in rational planning.

Figure 3-7
Viollet-le-Duc's plan of a Roman bath (*Discourses*).

The French Gothic cathedral (fig. 3-8), for Viollet-le-Duc, synthesized the virtues of the Greek temple and the Roman bath. Its cross-shaped plan juxtaposed tall spaces with lower aisles, which formed a processional path all around, with chapels radiating from the center of the main apse. In addition, there were usually towers flanking the main entrance, possibly galleries above the aisles, and often a crypt beneath the choir. Altogether these various spaces represented a complex accommodation of many different liturgical functions. The skeletal structure, supporting ribbed vaults above and balanced by flying buttresses on the exterior, involved coordination of shafts in response to arches in three dimensions, thereby creating a skeletal structural system in which isolated vertical elements are

Figure 3-8
Viollet-le-Duc's structural diagram of a Gothic cathedral (*Dictionnaire raisonné*).

connected by arcs and stabilized by mutual reinforcement. To realize such a system, the architect of the Gothic cathedral had to resolve a number of interrelated structural problems with an unprecedented degree of sophistication.

Gothic construction, composed of moderate-sized stones assembled by a large workforce of both skilled and unskilled workmen, mediated between the situations of Greek and Roman architecture. Like the Greek it was about form, but like the Roman it was also about space. And it seamlessly integrated the decorative arts into the structure, with more telling effect than the Greek and more honesty than the Roman. Throughout, he saw Gothic construction as a completely rational formulation, ironically employing logic to convey a mystical aesthetic effect. For Viollet-le-Duc no other architecture in human history equaled this level of achievement.

By comparison to these three architectural paragons the French Renaissance chateau as a type amounts to a more modest accomplishment (fig. 3-9). The excellence Viollet-le-Duc perceived in it was neither structural nor decorative originality but a resolutely rational approach to planning. His singling it out for praise allowed him to dwell upon the complex demands imposed by the manifold functions of domestic buildings and to hail their accommodation in a plan in which exterior form was dictated by interior needs. Accordingly, he delighted in the asymmetry of both the structural massing and the placement of openings. In addition, the virtues of this building type set up the opportunity to damn the insistent bilateral symmetry of similarly grand domestic structures of the Italian Renaissance tradition and especially those of the baroque era. His strongest objection was the extent to which functional needs were routinely compromised in a plan for the sake of formal regularity in the elevation.

Figure 3-9
Viollet-le-Duc's isometric view of a French Renaissance chateau
(*Dictionnaire raisonné*).

As a result of his analyses of historical architecture, Viollet-le-Duc asserted that principles of design as opposed to conventions of design were the fundaments of architectural theory. These principles were the application of rational methods to all aspects of planning, including formulation of structure, use of materials, and construction practice. That his analyses of historical architecture were inaccurate or at least controversial does not actually affect the validity of the principles themselves. And although his analyses represented earnest encounters with actual historical buildings, they had, by the time he wrote his essays, long been subsumed into his theoretical thinking. It is probably fair to say, then, that the lessons he articulated concerning historical architecture resulted from a symbiosis of analysis and projection of fixed ideas.

SITTE

Much narrower in range but also widespread in influence were the lessons for city planning drawn by Camillo Sitte from observations made in a variety of historical urban environments, located in Austria, Germany, Italy, France, and Belgium. Like Viollet-le-Duc, Sitte attempted to discover in his analyses a series of guiding principles, although they were addressed to urban layouts rather than the design of buildings. Whereas Viollet-le-Duc's principles were discerned in a succession of period styles, Sitte's were extracted from a series of formal categories. His categories were based on a relatively narrow range of examples, mostly city squares, dating from the Middle Ages, the Renaissance, or the baroque era.

One key category addressed the placement of statues, fountains, and monuments within a public space to achieve the optimal visual effect: preferably they are to be grouped and juxtaposed with an architectural backdrop rather than left to stand alone in the center of a large open area. Equally important to Sitte were the proportions of a square and the relationship of the principal building to the dominant axis: for instance, a tall facade should front the long axis, a wide one the short axis. He was also sensitive to the value of irregularities for adding visual interest to an urban vista. One of his more telling observations was that different portions of a major building might serve as the dominant monument for open spaces of differing size and character located on its various sides. In other cases a series of spaces of contrasting shape and size might open onto each other in a series. He underlined the value of his principles by including some examples of modern (i.e., late nineteenth-century) squares that he regarded as signally unsuccessful.

The umbrella covering all Sitte's observations, together with the principles emanating from them, was an appreciation of the picturesque. Against this predilection he had to concede that in modern construction some of the virtues he had heralded, such as charming irregularity, could become irritating vices. Ultimately he, like Ruskin, advocated a rich mix of variety and complexity, but for formal rather than cultural reasons. This principle would later have the effect of encouraging modernist architects to design without consideration of older buildings nearby, on the assumption that their new modes would eventually achieve a harmonious coexistence with the rest.

Sitte's taste was conditioned by the nineteenth-century fascination with Gothic and its penchant for the picturesque. But the aesthetic principles he derived from this context could as readily be appropriated by modernists eager to develop schemes with an organic character as by die-hard classicists with their preference for bilateral symmetry. And, paradoxically, the adaptability to large-scale complexes of his observations concerning relatively small-scale situations in urban planning made his principles as valuable to the architect as to the designer of cities. Probably few designers of government or arts centers and academic campuses thereafter were totally free of his prescriptions.

The tract writers, especially Antonio Sant'Elia, reacted sharply to the history consciousness that attended the speculations of nineteenth-century theorists. Their passionate embrace of the technological progress that was anticipated in the early twentieth century encouraged them to reject all aspects of past architecture (fig. 3-10). In its place they

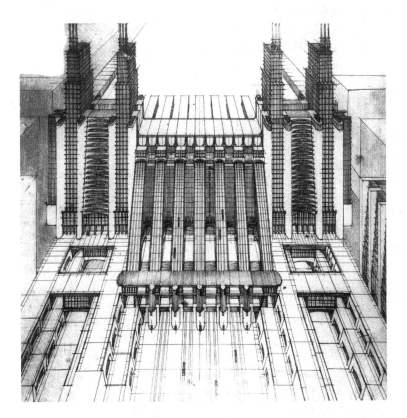

Figure 3-10
Antonio Sant'Elia's vision of a rail terminal for a futurist city (courtesy Musei Civici, Como).

espoused an ahistorical approach to architectural design that could be applied anywhere at any time, never representing any particular era or place. If they succeeded in creating a truly universal architecture, transcending period and locale, it was also one that belonged nowhere in particular. And although it often conveyed the spirit of optimism that accompanied the advent of modernism, the effect was also one of an alienated and alienating presence. This downside was not foreseen by the pioneers of modernity, although it was recognized as such by philistine detractors almost from the beginning. Only several decades following its adoption, when its resistance to assimilation in the urban environment was abundantly clear, did its ahistorical nature become fully apparent. Even so, some of the greatest figures of the modern movement recognized the indispensability of historical architecture to their own creative enterprise. Among those who did were Le Corbusier and Wright.

LE CORBUSIER

Prior to the reconsideration of the tenets of modernism in the second half of the twentieth century, it is unlikely that a high proportion of the readers of Le Corbusier's *Vers une architecture* had particularly noticed the chapters toward the end of his treatise that deal with historical architecture. To be sure, those passages about poetic artistry in buildings of the past contributed almost nothing to his influence on others. For, ironically, his modernist guidelines, eagerly assimilated by progressive architects everywhere, did not address the very quality that made his own architecture so superior to the workaday level of modernism as it came to be widely practiced—namely, its poetry.

Le Corbusier's lessons from historical architecture were drawn at random from his experiences during an extended journey from his native Switzerland to the Mediterranean between his student years and beginning of his practice. He proceeded via the Balkans to Istanbul and Athens, then visited Rome, Pompeii, and Paestum. The majority of his observations were addressed to ancient sites, but he also reflected upon Byzantine, Romanesque, Renaissance, and baroque monuments. Nothing in his analyses was systematic, and he did not even pretend to derive any principles from them. Rather, he reported his responses to delimited aspects of buildings, often a single feature or detail that appealed to his imagination. The responses cannot be codified to offer purposeful inspiration to others; they largely served to alert aspiring architects that the pursuit of beauty in the designing of buildings, however elusive, should not be ignored, for it is indispensable to great architecture. The value of historical architecture for Le Corbusier, then, was that by example it demonstrated the most accessible means of transcending the matter-of-factness of modernist design principles.

WRIGHT

In none of his writings did Frank Lloyd Wright explicitly discuss what might be learned from studying the architecture of the past. Regarding European architecture, especially that of the Renaissance on, he was almost entirely negative. Having seen little of it other than in Berlin and Florence, he was mostly parroting the views of Violletle-Duc, whose works he had read and heeded. He did, however, express great admiration for traditional Japanese architecture, meaning medieval Buddhist complexes, which he had first seen in replica in Chicago at the Columbian Exposition of 1893 (fig. 3-11) and, later, on trips to Japan. No specific building in Japan was cited, but he made clear

Figure 3-11
Frank Lloyd Wright's architectural inspiration: Japanese Buddhist architecture, represented by the teahouse at Ginkaku-ji, Kyoto (FH).

UNDERPINNINGS (RELEVANT TO ALL THEORY)

in his *Autobiography* that the Buddhist tradition inspired several key principles of his architecture. This Japanese element served two purposes at once, the first being his perverse urge to reject what others embraced and to espouse what no one else in the West had thought to seek out. The second was to reinforce his dedication to the concept of organic planning, which he had adopted from Viollet-le-Duc.

The principles he discovered in Japanese architecture began with the intimate interrelationship of interior and exterior, amounting to what he called the abolition of the box (fig. 3–11). By corollary they extended to the design of the natural environment around a structure, even to the borders of its site. The siting of the building should, if possible, make it seem to be a natural and inevitable feature of the landscape, placed in it rather than on it. The building should be constructed of materials that bespeak the earth—unpainted wood, rough-cut stone, brick, slate, and the like—and they should be incorporated into the structure in such a way as to enhance, and certainly not deny, their natural qualities. Moreover, they should be used in the same way on the interior as they have been on the exterior, avoiding all artificial finishes. They should be assembled in such a way as to integrate the parts, making the structure appear continuous, without a blatant beginning or end. Indeed, where feasible, the interior spaces should merge one into the other in an analogous manner. Finally, the harmony of the architecture should bespeak the harmony of its occupants' existence in nature. By implication, if the clients did not already possess that grace, the architecture would help them to acquire it. Although this program was never spelled out in one systematic explanation, its components suffuse all Wright's writings.

Robert Venturi appealed to historical architecture in order to articulate a critique of modernism. Drawing upon the full range of the history of architecture, but with emphasis on Italian mannerist and baroque buildings (fig. 3-12), he attempted to establish a set of principles that could validate the accommodation of all sorts of variables in design schemes. He was not, in fact, rejecting the technology of modern building methods, the use of modern materials, or even modern design methods. Indeed he was addressing only the design assumptions inherent in the modernist embrace of stark minimalism and the mimesis of technology. As with Sitte, his choice of examples was chronologically and geographically random. His purpose was to illustrate design characteristics, deemed to belong to aesthetic categories, that had been and still could be employed at any time or place.

Venturi's aesthetic categories were all versions of complexity, and particularly intended to undermine what he regarded as the modernist tendency to think in terms of simplicity and universality, as if one way of doing things could be appropriate to all situations. He was eager for architectural design to accommodate a number of variables at once, for instance, limitations imposed by the site, factors relating to the cultural setting, or details of the function. Underlying all this was a discomfort with what he took to be a naive willingness to follow a program of design principles as if they were dogma. He wished instead to promote a sophisticated openness to all sorts of inclusions, trusting aesthetic judgment to carry the day. His historical examples were mostly buildings in which some sort of peculiarity made them interesting to contemplate.

What Venturi admired raised issues of complexity and contradiction: toleration of ambiguity in the design

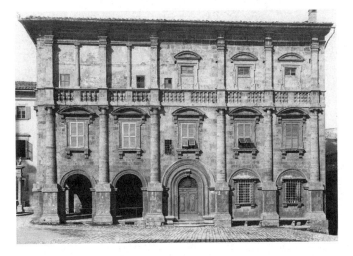

Figure 3-12
Venturi's inspiration: Palazzo Tarugi, Montepulciano (© Alinari/ Art Resource, NY).

as a whole, inclusion of double-functioning elements, accommodation of exceptional demands, adaptation to odd circumstances, acceptance of discordant juxtapositions, retention of inconsistencies between interior and exterior, and creation of a viable whole out of disparate parts. While he ostensibly articulated these issues as a means of making modernism more responsive to circumstances of the real world, his discussion of examples in the various categories had instead the unintended effect of encouraging gratuitous quotation of historical elements in modern designs. Although Venturi employed a certain amount of quotation in his own designs, endowing them with a witty sophistication, in the work of others a facile mimetic adaptation was often mistaken for application of the conceptual principle.

A positive side effect of Venturi's approach was the inference that modern architecture should be responsive to existing buildings, thereby fostering the principle of contextual sensitivity. This concept reverses the nineteenth-century notion that if juxtaposition of diverse historical styles makes an attractive, picturesque cityscape, modernist buildings will eventually also blend into the mix on a similar basis. Venturi's postmodernism acknowledges that the consciously ahistorical nature of modernist architecture prevents its ever being harmoniously assimilated. Thus the historicizing component of his contextualism is meant to redeem modern architecture from its alienated and alienating disposition.

II *Conventions (Theory before 1800)*

As the conduit to freedom in the design process, the theory of architecture sometimes serves its purpose through the liberal route of enabling principles and sometimes through the conservative route of regulatory conventions. Conventions provide a framework of limits within which creativity can be expressed. No convention has been observed for a longer time or with greater devotion than the canon of the classical orders of ancient Greece and Rome. For as long as two and a half millennia the Doric, Ionic, and Corinthian orders of both cultures—as well as the Tuscan and composite of Italy—have possessed their distinctive assemblages of components. The expressiveness of these assemblages has been subject to continual evolution, even to aesthetic revision, and their compositions to considerable adjustment. At the same time, the parts of the orders have retained their distinctive formats, and use of the orders has always been governed by rules of proportion, which extended in turn from the orders themselves to the other parts of buildings. The purpose of the following chapters is to characterize the central issues of the classical tradition of the columnar orders and to trace the major stages of its evolution after antiquity.

4 *Images of the Ideal and Classical Design Method*

An architectural design may begin with a generalized image of the building desired—which can include interior features as well as exterior—and proceed to accommodate the programmatic functions inside the structure as best they may fit. Or, by contrast, it may begin by determining how the functions ought to be accommodated on the interior and proceed to generate a design that will fulfill the requirements. Although this inside-out approach has been preferred by most forward-looking planners throughout the twentieth century, the outside-in version prevailed from antiquity right up to the modern era (even occasionally in modernist architecture as well). This is the architecture of the ideal image, issuing from a venerable theoretical tradition that deserves to be respected and appreciated alongside the currently favored option.

In theoretical writing, the architecture of the ideal image begins with Vitruvius. The heart and soul of his prescriptions for building—the explication of the orders—is set in the context of a discussion of the building type that actually spawned the orders, namely the peripteral temple (fig. 4-1). It is important to recognize that Vitruvius's peripteral temple embodied a Greek rather than a Roman format, one rarely employed in Rome until after his

Figure 4-1
The classical ideal, represented by the temple of Hera II, Paestum
(FH).

lifetime. He was therefore adopting as an architectural ideal
a format that to him was both foreign and relatively ancient.
Its value to him was that it was the format to which other
building types were related by virtue of their having employed the orders for part of their structure or decor or
having borrowed some version or aspect of the peripteral
temple's plan. Although Vitruvius discussed the amphitheater and the private house in almost equal detail, the amphitheater was of interest mainly as a pretext for explicating
a geometric technique for regularizing a plan, the house for
working out a program of functional considerations. Although all three were well established as conventional types,
it was the temple that served as the paragon of beauty in architecture and had accordingly acquired the status of ideal.

The message was not lost upon his later readers, who
made further assumptions about ideals based upon that

paragon. Renaissance theorists assumed that the orders should be regarded as indispensable to the design of beautiful buildings, indeed the sine qua non of dignified architecture. They considered the regulations for the orders as doctrine no accomplished architect could fail to master. The format of the peripteral temple itself was not useful to them, but it could be taken provisionally as an ideal prototype because it had nurtured the orders. Its format was hard to absorb because there were not many to be seen in Italy among surviving Roman ruins, which the Renaissance theorists were aware of, having surveyed Roman architecture for themselves. They also recognized that the peripteral temple could not be readily adapted to the building types already established in their own culture.

Accordingly, they instinctively sought in Roman architecture other exemplars that could serve as prototypes. The applied orders (with columns not freestanding but embedded in a wall or other structure) could be more readily assimilated. As models of that usage, two prominent Roman monuments served admirably: the Colosseum exterior (fig. 4-2), with its superposed ranks of different orders, was appropriate for multistory facades; and the triumphal arch, especially that of Constantine (fig. 4-3), was appropriate for grand fronts and transition points of interiors. Alberti memorably employed the stacks of orders for the Palazzo Rucellai in Florence (fig. 4-4) and the triumphal arch motif (combined with the temple front) for the church of Sant'Andrea in Mantua (fig. 4-5). As a model for the freestanding orders, the prostyle temple, with its columnar porch approached by monumental stairs, was more useful than the peripteral format. Exemplars still standing in a complete state were the Temple of Fortuna Virilis at Rome and the Maison Carrée at Nîmes, providing paradigms that could be readily adapted as the entry feature on any grand building, as occurred first with Antonio da Sangallo's

Figure 4-2
The paradigm of superimposed orders: Colosseum, Rome (© Alinari/Art Resource, NY).

Medici villa at Poggio a Caiano. Vitruvius's conceptual ideal, then, could be honored through substitution and variation.

From the tradition of Roman architecture Alberti identified yet another architectural ideal, one that would have extraordinary appeal and durability in Western architecture thereafter: bilateral symmetry. The Renaissance concept of symmetry was substantially different from Vitruvius's, and much simplified. Whereas Vitruvius had regarded symmetry as the harmonious relationship of all the parts to one another and to the whole—a perfectly calibrated proportional system—Alberti defined symmetry to

Figure 4-3
The paradigm of the triumphal arch: Arch of Constantine, Rome
(FH).

mean the balance of parts identically arranged with reference to a central axis. As he put it,

> So agreeable is it to nature that the members on the right side
> should exactly answer to the left . . . [that] the very first thing
> we are to take care of must be that every part be disposed with
> an exact correspondence as to the number, form, and appear-
> ance, so that the right may answer to the left, the high to the
> low, the similar to the similar. . . . Even statues, pictures, or
> any other ornaments of that sort with which we embellish our
> work must be so disposed as to seem to have sprung up natu-
> rally in the properest places and to be twins. (*De re aedificato-*
> *ria* IX.7; translation attributed to James Leoni, 1726)

IMAGES OF THE IDEAL AND CLASSICAL DESIGN METHOD

Figure 4-4
Renaissance superimposed orders: Palazzo Rucellai, Florence, by
Alberti (© Alinari/Art Resource, NY).

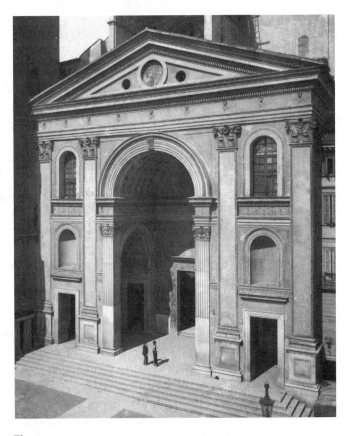

Figure 4-5
Renaissance triumphal arch-cum-temple front: Sant'Andrea, Mantua, by Alberti (© Alinari/Art Resource, NY).

The lack of clamor with which he introduced this definition, inserted into the category of "arrangement" and subordinated to it, suggests that it may have been a received notion and not of his own invention. Nevertheless, his statement did introduce into the written theory of architecture the definition of symmetry that is still current, namely the mirror-image arrangement of parts along a central axis,

IMAGES OF THE IDEAL AND CLASSICAL DESIGN METHOD

and it entered the theoretical tradition as an inseparable aspect of the classical ideal.

If Alberti, and to a lesser extent Serlio, reinforced Vitruvius's exaltation of an ideal image by adopting various Roman monuments as guiding exemplars, Andrea Palladio reinvigorated the concept by unconsciously creating several new ideals, each firmly rooted in the antique models. Palladio's attempt to revive the authentic classical tradition created a context in which he was able to conceive and exploit a number of bold inventions. Almost all of them occurred in his designs for houses. For all their subtle formal variations, Palladio's town palaces were basically a refinement of the traditional urban house with flat street facade and inner courtyard, which had evolved from the time of the Middle Ages to the Renaissance. But the rural villa, taking the place of traditional farmhouses and feudal strongholds, introduced a major new building type into the repertory of Western architecture.

Centered on a great hall, the most conservative feature still remaining in Palladio's designs, the villas are concentrated into a massive block with a suite of rooms abstractly arranged around the hall, without an explicit functional program. They are composed without the customary apartments or room sequences that still governed the composition of English country houses or French chateaus. Moreover, the proportions of these rooms, whether square or oblong, are fixed according to one of the three proportional formulas—based, without attribution, on Alberti's system of ratios—that determine the length, breadth, and sometimes the height. The end result is a spatial ensemble predicated upon formal coherence rather than functional convenience. They are useful buildings, but buildings in which beauty is allowed to be the dominant desideratum.

The rural villa was a working farm as well as the seat of a cultured gentleman. It necessarily included a barn, stables, and storage rooms for equipment and crops. Making a virtue of necessity, Palladio incorporated all these outbuildings into an integrated ensemble along with the residence itself (fig. 4-6). This task was accomplished by disguising these functional structures behind classical elements. The connections between the villa and the major outbuildings were realized with colonnaded or arcaded loggias, sometimes straight and sometimes curved in a great arc. In the treatise, these compositions always conform to Alberti's bilateral symmetry. On occasion the composition is doubled to make the ensembles identical on both the front and the back, and on the sides as well. The underlying similarity among all the elaborate estate compositions is that any complex facade consists of five parts—the central block, the two connecting wings, and the terminal pavilions. This five-part composition was to become the formula for almost all subsequent monumental complexes and joined bilateral symmetry as a dual ideal for designs formulated in the classical tradition, regardless of whether they were for palaces, government centers, or cultural institutions.

The spatial implications of these ensembles were profound. The central axis, reinforced by the dependent wings, established a strong frontal focus for the composition as a whole (fig. 4-6). The disposition of the wings shaped a spatial zone along this axis. If the wings were curved or projected forward, the enclosure formed a shaped exterior space inseparable from the rest of the complex ensemble, in which shaped space and formal mass were integrated. A number of these ensembles were also hierarchically arranged in grade level on the site, with the central block at the apex, thereby enriching the spatial composition with vertical variation. These compositions ultimately served as prototypes for palace-and-garden or public-building-and-piazza complexes in all sorts of situations. Indeed, the

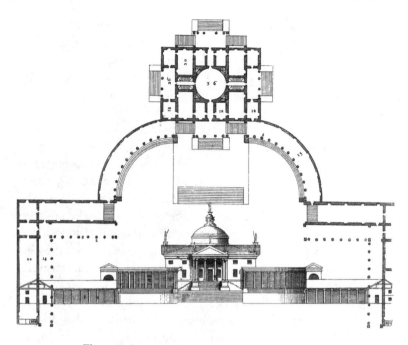

Figure 4-6
Exterior architectural space vertically and horizontally shaped:
Villa Trissino, by Palladio.

great compositions of the baroque, rococo, and neoclassical eras would have been virtually unthinkable without these precedents.

One more specialized but highly evocative example of the interrelationship of space and structure is the house known today as the Villa Rotonda, built around 1550 (fig. 4-7). Designed with four identical porticoes reached by broad stairways, the four axes meet in the central rotunda. Culminating in a dome at the top of the house, the center of the rotunda converts the four horizontal axes into a single vertical one. Thus the exterior is brought into a forceful relationship with the interior. But this relationship also works

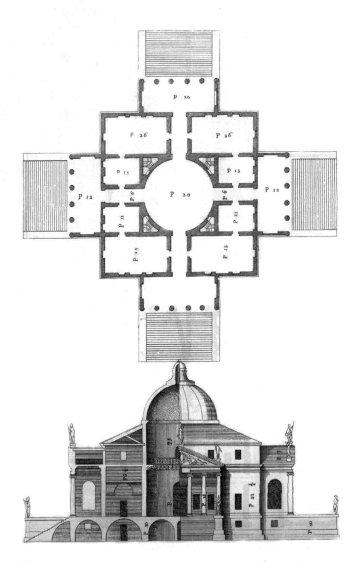

Figure 4-7
Interpenetration of a building and its exterior environment: Villa
Rotonda, by Palladio.

IMAGES OF THE IDEAL AND CLASSICAL DESIGN METHOD

in the same fashion in reverse, from the inside out. From the porticoes, each of the broad stairways is flanked by projections of the raised podium, thereby thrusting the four axes far beyond the house, powerfully rooting the architecture in the landscape. Although this particular composition was not susceptible to as many formal variations as the others, it became the most frequently imitated design in the treatise, not only for grand residences but also for government buildings, of which American state houses and county courthouses are familiar examples.

Palladio's great contribution to the ideal images of architecture, conveyed to the world through Book II of the *Quattro libri,* lay in the fact that each of his innovations could be directly imitated, loosely adapted, or varied in nearly endless permutations and combinations. It was not a hindrance that these structures were residential; the geometric purity of their spatial designs could be adapted for any dignified building type. Another advantage was that Palladio's contribution happened to occur at a moment when European culture was experiencing a sea change, and innovations were very likely to have profound consequences. That Palladio's work exerted such broad and far-reaching influence is somewhat ironic in view of the circumstance that it had been carried out within a narrow context. His buildings were mostly constructed in the countryside around a minor city for an exclusive group of patrons, whose highly cultivated interests were focused on arcane lore from a distant past. But this limited scope also just happened to encompass universality.

Classical architecture fed off the ideal forms introduced by Alberti and Palladio for the next three centuries. Indeed, except for the brief and limited predilection for pure geometric shapes—such as the sphere, the cylinder, the cube, and the pyramid—in the late eighteenth century, no other ideal images were introduced to supplant them.

Underlying all these forms was the ideal of bilateral symmetry, which Alberti had introduced. But in the nineteenth century both bilateral symmetry and the formal ideals fell into disfavor. As Viollet-le-Duc explained at length in the second volume of the *Discourses,* its retention in architectural design was a sure sign that the internal spaces had been compromised in the interests of the exterior. Together with Ruskin's advocacy of a more general balance of parts across the central axis to replace the mirror images, this rejection of bilateral symmetry brought its status as high dogma in architecture to an end, at least as far as theory is concerned.

When the Gothic cathedral displaced the classical temple as the ideal, a major shift in the role of the ideal occurred, for the appeal of the cathedral was less that of an image than a source of conceptual inspiration. Admired for the rational composition of its structure, skeletal in character and economical of means, its form was adapted to other building types only in highly limited circumstances. The Gothic cathedral never served, then, as an ideal in the modern world in the same sense that classical archetypes had done in the preceding three and a half centuries.

CLASSICAL DESIGN METHOD

If Vitruvius's accounts may be taken as an accurate indicator, classical design method comprised a variety of approaches. As already mentioned, geometrical schematization was employed to plot the location of the formulaic features of an amphitheater. By contrast, the proper juxtaposition of functions was the rationale for devising the spatial scheme of a house. And the formulation of a peripteral temple was based on an aesthetic code. Vitruvius did not cite design method as an explicit issue, but it lay at the heart of his instructions for these various building types, all three of which have conventional formats. Among the three, the one that remained relevant for the broader theory of architecture was that employed to design the peripteral temple.

For that purpose Vitruvius was preoccupied by the peristyle, the design of which emanated from the thickness of the column shaft at its base, taken to represent either a single or a double module. This module was employed in the spacing of the columns, determined by formulaic variations. The dimensions for the platform resulted from the total number of modules in the columns and intercolumniations. (Paradoxically, the configuration of the naos—the enclosed portion of the building that served the cult function of the temple—and its siting within the peristyle did not occupy his attention.) The module also determined the height of the columns and, in turn, influenced the height of the entablature. The total height of the order was coordinated with the total width of the temple and that, in turn, with the length. So the choice of a particular dimension for the module had ramifications for the entire design process. Although Vitruvius never discussed the rationale of the temple plan as a whole, an ideal image—a pedimented temple front—governed the design.

Once the basic composition had been determined, a whole series of refinements needed to be incorporated in order to ensure correction of optical distortions imposed by distance or restricted viewing conditions. Sometimes both the platform and the entablature were to be curved slightly upward in the middle of each of the four sides of a temple to avoid the illusion of sagging. If a column was unusually tall its taper needed to be curtailed to compensate for the impression of greater diminution over distance. So, likewise, the spread of the capital and the thickness of the architrave had to be proportionately increased. Columns set behind other columns needed to be thinner, but they ought to have more numerous flutes for the sake of suggesting greater thickness than they actually possessed. Tall columns on the long side of a temple must lean inward slightly on their outer face, but needed to be perpendicular to the platform on their inner face in order to make them appear straight. And finally, any proportions were to be adjusted according to the judgment of the eye when conditions of viewing imposed apparent distortions. (*De architectura* III.iii.11–13, III.iv.5, III.v.4, 8–9, IV.iv.2–3, VI.ii.4.)

The upshot of such a design method was that for any building based, however loosely, on the peripteral temple, the requirements of the columnar feature and its coordination with the main block dominated the procedure. However carefully the spaces of that block may have been composed in order to serve their respective purposes, their arrangement within the block and their dimensions would be affected by the limits imposed by the columnar order and the requirements of spatial proportion. Consequently, if the design of a building was rooted in the classical tradition, it was necessarily conditioned by an ideal image, one largely formulated from the outside in.

The Orders: Evolving Rules for Formal Beauty

For the centuries prior to Vitruvius, the absence of any surviving theoretical treatises leaves the evocative ruins of ancient temples as the sole evidence of their creators' aesthetic intentions. Hence the ideas that shaped the buildings may be discerned only by analyzing the evidence visible in the stones. Although a modern formal analysis may not fully represent Greek and Roman intentions, such an interpretation is based on incontrovertible data, which affect both the elements of the orders and their role in the overall composition. Such an analysis is worth making because it permits a meaningful distinction between Greek and Roman usage.

As the central concern of theory based on conventions, the lore of the orders is of the highest importance. Although at any given moment their formulation was subject to precise stipulations, the aesthetic concept governing the rules was continually evolving. For that reason, it is necessary to follow the course of that evolution, examining the key moments of its development.

THE DORIC ORDER

According to Vitruvius, the orders were first formulated in wood and then translated into stone. Each of the component parts is held to represent a structural member. In the wooden prototype (fig. 5-1) of the Doric order the columns are posts, presumably set into the platform. The columns are capped with members that provide a transition to the superstructure. This upper structure consists first of a horizontal architrave, which connects the posts. Above it the triglyphs of the frieze are taken to represent the ends of beams connecting the colonnade of one long side of the building to that on the other. The guttae beneath the triglyphs connect the frieze to the architrave. The intervals between the triglyphs are filled with nonstructural blocks, or metopes. Above this frieze of triglyphs and metopes the mutules project in a downward slant, supposedly representing the ends of the rafters. And immediately above the mutules is the molded cornice. Hence the Doric order ostensibly represents a rationally composed structural system.

Unaccounted for in this explanation are several awkward contradictions. To begin, the triglyphs representing beam ends are to be seen on all four sides of the building (figs. 4-1, 5-2), despite the fact that beams would have been set over the narrow span but not over the longer one. Equally contradictory is the location of a triglyph on both faces of each corner, purporting to signify beams coming from two different directions to occupy the same space. Also unaccounted for is the fact that the entire entablature, as it rests on the peripteral columns, necessarily sits below the top of the cella walls on which any structural beams would actually lie. The formulation of the Doric order as seen in stone, then, is at most an analogue of structure rather than a literal representation. But as an analogue it is a singularly effective expression of structure.

The aesthetic expressiveness of the Doric order as built by the Greeks (figs. 5-3, 5-4) is extraordinary in all architecture for its illusory quality of organic vitality. The illusion begins with the way the columns stand upon the stepped platform, with no plinth or base intervening, as if

Figure 5-1
Sir William Chambers's imagined wooden prototype of the Doric
order, shown evolving in two stages (Chambers, *A Treatise on
the Decorative Part of Civil Architecture*, London, 1791; reprint,
New York, 1965).

growing directly out of the platform surface. It continues
with the way the column shaft is modulated. Taper toward
the top suggests upward trajectory in the column and with
it a certain dynamic quality. The swelling entasis of the
shaft represents the strain of the column under the great
weight of the entablature and roof, conferring on the colonnade the quality of muscular exertion. Vertical channels, or

THE ORDERS: EVOLVING RULES FOR FORMAL BEAUTY

Figure 5-2
Doric entablature showing the "corner problem": Parthenon, Athens (FH).

flutes, gouged into the surface of the shaft, mask the breaks between the drums and visually unify the stones as if they constituted a single entity. Flutes also cast shadows along the vertical edges of the column, thereby emphasizing its roundness by contrasting with the highlights in the middle. Carved as shallow channels meeting at each boundary in a sharp arris, flutes enliven the inert quality of an unarticulated shaft. In the capital, the height, the spread, and the degree of curvature of the echinus all express the interchange between weight and support, endowing the building as a whole with an organic character parallel to the swelling musculature of Greek figural sculpture. The flat, square abacus places a lid on this sequence of expressions and provides a transition to the more abstract quality of the architrave, the adjacent member of the entablature.

Above the architrave the Doric frieze addresses the colonnade through its rhythm of triglyphs, with the aim to place one above each column and another above each

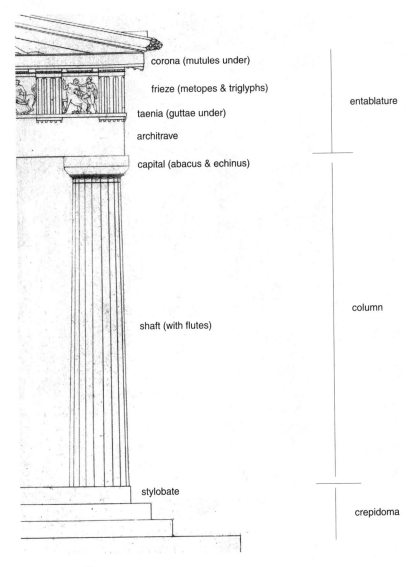

corona (mutules under)

frieze (metopes & triglyphs)

taenia (guttae under)

architrave

capital (abacus & echinus)

entablature

shaft (with flutes)

column

stylobate

crepidoma

Figure 5-3
Diagram of the Doric order (Stuart and Revett, *Antiquities of
Athens,* London, 1858).

Figure 5-4
The late archaic version of the Doric order: Temple of Athena, Paestum (FH).

intercolumniation (fig. 5-2). A dilemma ensues due to the insistence of the Greeks upon placing a triglyph at each corner of the entablature while aspiring at the same time to situate one over the axis of each column. Because the stone columns at the corners are too thick to allow both goals to be achieved, one desideratum or the other has to be sacrificed. Preference is given to the corner placement, resulting in an awkwardly wide interval between the corner triglyph and the next, which is supposed to be centered over the intercolumniation. This wider interval, or metope, sharply contrasts with the one on the other side of the intercolumnar triglyph, calling for some sort of adjustment. If the triglyph over the intercolumniation is moved closer to the corner, neither it nor the triglyph at the corner will stand respectively over the axis of the intercolumniation or that of the column. At the same time, though now nearly equal, these metopes flanking the penultimate triglyph will still be noticeably wider than those in the inner range of the frieze. This distortion can be partially alleviated if the corner intercolumniation is narrowed, allowing the two end metopes to be equal to all the others. But this compensation could potentially distort the rhythm of the colonnade. The "corner problem," then, involves contradictions that cannot be resolved in a straightforward manner.

The resolution of this dilemma can be aided by subtle adjustments in the intercolumniations of the colonnade on the narrow, or entrance, end of a peripteral temple (fig. 5-2). Because the corner intercolumniation is viewed against open space rather than the cella, its width seems somewhat greater than that between the columns that are seen against structure. For this reason it is expedient to make the end intercolumniation a bit narrower than the others. Meanwhile, the location of the entrance to the temple cella, which reveals the image of the god presumed to reside there, determines that the intercolumniation in the middle needs to be slightly wider than the other intervals. Hence in a hexastyle (six-columned) front, only the intercolumniations between the central and corner ones are to be the "normal" width. Such variations of spacing either interfere with the normal location of the triglyphs over columns and intercolumniations or they make the metope widths unequal. The solution to this apparent conundrum is to place the triglyphs slightly off the axes of both the columns and the intercolumniations, so that the metopes can be virtually equal. Once the problem of the frieze has been dispatched the rest of the entablature can be determined. The rhythm of the frieze extends both into the architrave below and the corona above due to coordination of the triglyphs with the guttae and mutules, respectively. In consequence, the three zones of the entablature are unified. Overall the effect of the modest axial displacement is a slight visual tension between the entablature and the colonnade. Seen in association with the taper and entasis of the columns, this tension conveys the effect of a muscular exertion. Altogether, these adjustments are so minor and their effect is so subtle that they may be only subliminally perceived, but they infuse the entire elevation with the illusory quality of inner vitality.

This complex and subtle system of adjustments was developed only over the course of centuries. As it evolved, all the devices expressive of organic quality were refined, transforming what had been an assertively robust formulation (fig. 5-4) into a composition serenely balanced (fig. 5-5), then graceful (fig. 5-6), and finally delicate. In the end, the thickness of the columns and the heaviness of the entablature were diminished to the point that the order's virile expressiveness was virtually neutralized. At the same time, the taper and entasis of the columns were gradually reduced until the shafts no longer seemed to strain under the weight of the entablature. Likewise, the spread and curvature of the echinus and the width and thickness of the abacus were so curtailed that the capital scarcely responded to its load. Indeed, the Greek version of the Doric order ended by becoming elegant and brittle, although it never lost its sublime coherence.

What Vitruvius specified for the Doric order transformed its very nature (fig. 5-7). Pointing out that it is difficult to use, he opined that it may not be worth the trouble it entails. For him the key issue lay in the portion of the order that stands above the colonnade. Indeed, he so concentrated upon this aspect of the composition that he neglected to deal with the juncture of platform and column. This

Figure 5-5
The classical version of the Doric order: Temple of Hera II, Paestum (FH).

Figure 5-6
The late classical version of the Doric order: Parthenon, Athens (FH).

THE ORDERS: EVOLVING RULES FOR FORMAL BEAUTY

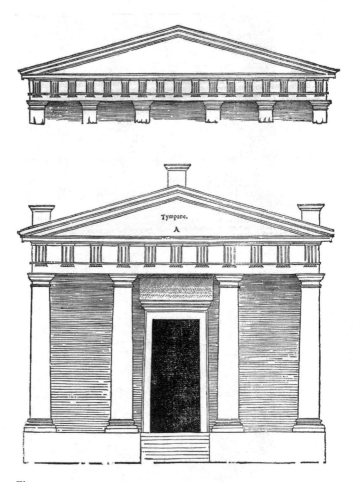

Figure 5-7
Vitruvius's version of the Roman Doric order, as envisioned by
Serlio.

omission is usually interpreted as indicating that his Doric order, like the Greek, was to have no column bases. Actual Roman use of the Doric order was so rare that this matter has never been definitively settled, but Renaissance theorists looking back to ancient Rome assumed the normality of a molded base. The Vitruvian characteristics that are indisputable, however, make the Roman order quite different. They include slenderer shafts more widely spaced than in any Greek norm, with a ratio of shaft thickness to column height of 1:7 compared to a Greek classical norm of about 1:4.5. More striking still is his alteration of the frieze, in which two or more triglyphs are interspersed in each intercolumniation, making light and airy a previously heavy and ponderous order. Although theoretically taper and entasis were retained in the column shafts, Vitruvius substituted a molded capital set off from the shaft by an astragal. Such a capital, like his slender shaft, no longer expressed the strain of supporting the entablature.

Equally drastic was his obliteration of the age-old corner problem by simply moving the corner triglyph inward to the columnar axis, relegating to the corner itself a fraction of a metope. This change purged the entablature of the inner tension normally arising from its conflict with the supporting colonnade. The theoretical significance of these modifications is that Vitruvius virtually obliterated the key elements of organic expression. In the process he transformed a structural system charged with the illusion of inner life into an architectural motif inert in expression and bereft of vitality, reducing to a decorative formula one of the most sublime of human creations. The transformation was not all loss, however, because the almost intractably rigorous system of the Greek Doric order was thereby opened up to highly flexible and imaginative application. Vitruvius, and even the later Romans, would gain little from the modification because they never favored the adoption of the Doric order in the first place, but subsequent theorists would treat the Roman version of this order as a treasure.

Because the unrecorded theory behind the changing versions of the Greek order was necessarily subject to continual revision, no single canonical formula for the orders could apply to their entire history. Hence it is a paradox of history that Vitruvius's account of what was actually an ephemeral moment in the development of the orders ended up seeming like a fixed code of rules. To readers after his lifetime for whom the classical tradition still remained alive, his account would probably have been regarded as old-fashioned, to be taken with a grain of salt. But to those following his treatise after that tradition was dead, readers who had at hand no currently evolving standard of comparison, his unequivocal specifications could scarcely have been regarded as anything other than unalterable. Accordingly, the Renaissance interpretations of Vitruvius ended up making of the Doric order something both more fixed and more broadly applicable than it had been throughout most of antiquity, thereby ensuring its continuation as a convention.

The Renaisssance theorists, having looked at Roman architecture for themselves, were keenly aware of the discrepancies between Vitruvian specifications and actual Roman usage. Whatever their attitude toward Vitruvius regarding these differences, they tended to adopt the practices they admired. So it was that they preferred to employ an Attic base with their Doric order (fig. 5-7), even though Palladio acknowledged in his treatise the literal Vitruvian version without bases (fig. 5-8). Moreover, they dutifully showed flutes on the shafts in their explanations of the orders, but in applications of their own devising the Doric order normally assumes an unfluted monolithic shaft. They also decorated the interval on the capital between the as-

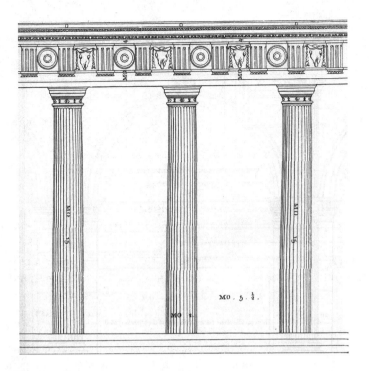

Figure 5-8
The Renaissance version of the Roman Doric order: Palladio.

tragal and the molded echinus with regularly spaced ro-
settes, thereby emphasizing the decorative, structurally in-
expressive character of the capital. In the entablature, the
architrave is usually shown with two fascias, borrowed
from the Ionic order, and the frieze almost always has metopes decorated with alternating roundels and ox skulls.
The corona usually substitutes elements from the Ionic corona for the mutules. On the other hand, the theorists seem
to have taken seriously the Vitruvian association of the
Doric order with the male gender and for that reason applied it in many more instances and circumstances than the
Romans ever did.

The Ionic order developed in geographical and chronological parallel to the Doric, but as the primary order of a different ethnic division of Greeks and hence not as a stylistic alternative to the Doric. Like the Doric, Vitruvius regarded the Ionic as the translation into stone of a structural system originally devised in wood. In it he saw the dentil frieze as representing horizontal members holding up the roof, much like the triglyph "beam ends" of the Doric. Associating the Ionic order with the feminine gender, he regarded it from the beginning as more graceful (and, implicitly, more restrained in organic expression) than the Doric. Indeed, historically the formal evolution of its component parts produced less differentiation. On the other hand, the formats in which it could be employed were not so narrowly circumscribed as for the Doric, because its entablature imposed no special demands.

Like the Doric order, the Ionic comprises a platform, colonnade, and entablature, each subdivided into three parts (fig. 5-9). An important difference, though, lies in the fact that the columns standing on the three-step platform have a round molded base set upon a square plinth, the effect of which is to abstract the colonnade from its supporting surface. Although the shaft is tapered and swells with entasis, both modulations are so subtle as to be barely perceptible. The flutes are at once deeper and narrower than Doric flutes. Moreover, they are also separated by flat strips, or fillets, that denote the original surface of the cylindrical shaft. The effect is one of artifice, only remotely evocative of organic nature. The capital, with its large drooping volutes, is in expression an exact parallel of the shaft—faintly evocative of feminine curls but abstractly decorative all the same. There is no pretense that it is

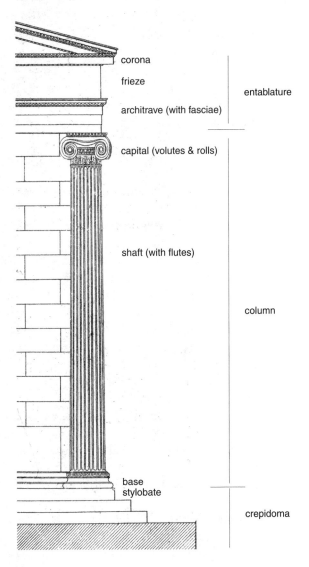

corona

frieze

architrave (with fasciae)

entablature

capital (volutes & rolls)

shaft (with flutes)

column

base
stylobate

crepidoma

Figure 5-9
Diagram of the Ionic order (Stuart and Revett, *Antiquities of Athens*, London, 1858).

responding to the weight of the entablature. Rather, it serves more as a decorative articulation of the transition between weight and support.

The entablature purports to be simple, but it offers the opportunity to include all manner of refined ornaments. The architrave is subdivided into three overlapping horizontal strips, or fascias, topped by a projecting stringcourse, or cymatium, frequently embellished with an egg-and-dart motif. Then comes the frieze, which can be left plain or decorated with a continuous motif carved in relief. The top zone, the corona, includes a dentil frieze and molded cornice. Anywhere along the way the subparts may be underlined with a string of bead-and-reel ornament. Taken as a whole, the entablature provides an unbroken horizontal crown of three horizontal layers for an evenly spaced file of vertical supports, a play of contrasting forms evenly and elegantly detailed from bottom to top.

The only complication in the order is introduced by the capital. Seen from the front, it presents two scrolled ends hanging down from a sheet laid across a thin cushion. Seen from either side, it presents the cylindrical form implied by the scrolled ends. For as long as a row of columns continues in one direction there is no problem, but when the file of columns turns a corner the end column incongruously shows a side of the capital rather than its front. There were two ways to deal with this problem. The first was to carve volutes on both the front and the outer side and rolls on the back and inner side. On the outer corner of the capital, then, the two intersecting volutes would collide unless they were canted 45 degrees. The same solution was needed on the opposite corner, where two rolls met—a less satisfactory expedient. So long as the volutes on the front faced directly outward this solution to the problem could not be avoided. But it was possible to forgo the roll sides altogether, making pairs of volutes meet at 45-degree angles on each of the corners. This version of the capital was developed in the Hellenistic era and was available thereafter, but seldom adopted prior to the seventeenth century. (Roland Fréart de Chambray credited Vincenzo Scamozzi with its invention, prior to publication of the latter's treatise in 1615. This attribution has generally stuck, even though both solutions were actually used from the second century B.C.E.).

The Ionic order is perhaps most distinguished from the Doric by its versatility. In special circumstances, where the adherence to canonical proportions for the Doric order prevented its consistent use throughout a building, the Ionic order could be substituted to solve the problem. Although the Doric order was versatile to the point of accommodating the substitution, only the Ionic could be flexible enough in its proportions to provide solutions to intractable problems. For that reason, the Ionic order spread beyond its native territory to become a feature of three of the most prominent Doric monuments of the classical era. They were the treasury (or rear chamber) of the Parthenon, the interior passageway of the Propylea to the Athenian Acropolis, and the interior of the Doric temple of Apollo at Bassae. In unmixed application it also served the most unorthodox plan among ancient temples, the Athenian Erechtheum (fig. 5-10).

Through the course of its evolution the Ionic order changed only in certain details. The column base, originally composed of a convex torus above two successive concave hollows, was revised to have a sloping profile, comprised of a thin torus above and a thick torus below, separated by a hollow. The latter type, known as the Attic base, was adopted in Greek Doric territory and was the preferred form in ancient Rome. The second change occurred in the capital, in which flat, frontal volutes acquired a deep spiral channel and curved flare while the roll on the sides tightened toward the middle. The third change was in the corona, where

Figure 5-10
Use of the Ionic order for an irregular plan: Erechtheum, Athens
(courtesy Ann Thomas Wilkins).

additional rows of egg-and-dart or bead-and-reel ornament
were added under or over the various standard features. Altogether the evolution was toward a more supple grace and
sumptuous richness.

Vitruvius ostensibly regarded the Ionic as the standard
order, using it as the exemplar for his only full explication
of an order. The Doric, as already noted, was treated only
in part because he regarded it as too much trouble, and the
Corinthian he regarded as simply a variant of the Ionic. The
Ionic order as he presented it was much closer to the actual
Greek version than was his Doric. Indeed, it is from Vitruvius that we have a documentary account of the various optical corrections of the Greeks, cited in his explication of
the Ionic order. His version of the Ionic order, then, has very
nearly the same structural intent as that of the Greeks, except that he neglected to deal with the corner problem
posed by the capital. Implicit in that omission is his apprehension of the order as a motif rather than as a structural
system, similar in character to his treatment of the Doric.

The Corinthian order has always been regarded as simply a variant of the Ionic, originally identical in every feature except the capital (fig. 5-11) and gradually acquiring only a few other differences in the corona (fig. 5-12). After centuries of use restricted to exceptional circumstances, it became a functionally independent order only in the Hellenistic era; its frequent adoption occurred only after the time of Vitruvius. But it always offered more freedom of composition for a building and more flexibility of scale, ranging from the gigantic to the miniature, than either of the two earlier orders could accommodate. This was in part because neither the capital, with its uniform design on all four sides, nor the entablature posed a corner problem. It was also because the taller capital increased its capacity for both relative height and absolute size within the limits imposed by the proportional system of all the orders. Finally, the order carried within itself, due to the circumstances of its creation and more than two centuries of use in exceptional situations, a special aptness for unorthodox designs. Exactly what these qualifications mean needs to be explained.

In contradistinction to the remote origins of the Doric and Ionic orders, both modern archaeology and Vitruvius assign the genesis of the Corinthian to a specific moment and a specific individual, although each authority ascribes it to a different set of circumstances. For archaeology the invention occurred in the temple of Apollo at Bassae (fig. 5-13), on the Peloponnesus, about 430 B.C.E., at the instance of Ictinus, the putative architect of the Parthenon. For Vitruvius it occurred near Corinth, at an unspecified date, at the instance of a sculptor named Callimachus, for use on a colonnade in Corinth. On the interior of the Doric temple at Bassae, attached Ionic half-columns had been adopted in order to prevent propor-

Figure 5-11
Earliest surviving Corinthian capital: Aesklepion, Epidaurus (FH).

tional violations. An exceptional situation was presented by the need for a freestanding column on the main axis, in order to accommodate a side entrance and passageway behind the statue chamber. In order to avoid an inconsistency with the Ionic half-columns, it was deemed preferable to invent a new type rather than use different formats for the same order. By contrast, Vitruvius relates that the sculptor-inventor Callimachus copied a striking ensemble he happened to see on the grave of a young maiden. This ensemble consisted of a votive offering of a basket (filled with personal objects belonging to the deceased) covered by a tile, around which an acanthus plant had grown. In both instances, it should be noted, this order, which was taken to be a variant of the Ionic, was actually invented in Doric territory and not for an Ionic building. Such a paradox helps to underline the thoroughgoing exceptionality of the Corinthian order.

Figure 5-12
Diagram of the Corinthian capital and entablature (Stuart and Revett, *Antiquities of Athens,* London, 1858).

Figure 5-13
Origin of the Corinthian capital: reconstitution detail, Ionic-Corinthian interior of the Doric temple at Bassae (F. Krischen, *Der griechische Stadt*, Berlin, 1938).

The height of the capital—with its acanthus leaves and tendrils hugging an inverted-bell-shaped core in a standardized design, articulated with four faces and four diagonals—is the key to the flexibility of scale which occasioned several differences between the Ionic and the Corinthian orders (fig. 5-11). First, consider the matter of scale. The additional height of the capital makes possible both a slightly taller and proportionately slenderer column, even if the two orders use shafts of the same thickness and height. But it also aids the creation of very tall columns, simultaneously providing an emphatic enough capital and retaining a slim enough shaft to be graceful at gigantic scale. The same combination serves a need for delicacy at miniature scale. This means that the entablature taken over from the Ionic order needs enhancement to be in scale with a huge Corinthian colonnade. Accordingly, the corona is projected further outward from the plane of the fascias and frieze. Support for this projection is provided by S-scrolled modillions, a Roman addition to the order. Modillions also visually integrate the jutting corona with the two lower zones of the entablature.

Flexibility of composition has a great deal to do with the fact that the Greeks used the Corinthian order only in exceptional circumstances until the second century B.C.E. At first it was employed solely in interiors of Doric temples where the space was too limited to accommodate an interior Doric colonnade. Its initial exterior appearance was as a decorative order on a monument of unprecedented format. The order was finally adopted for regular exterior use in peripteral temples, one instance being a temple of Doric format in Ionic territory (Zeus Olbius at Uzuncaburç, in south-central Turkey), and the other a temple of Ionic format in Doric territory (Olympian Zeus at Athens, fig. 5-14). And when it entered the repertory of Roman architecture it was usually on a temple of Tuscan format (as on the so-called Maison Carrée at Nîmes). Otherwise, this order was adopted early on by the Romans for highly imaginative architectural forms in fresco paintings (of which more in the next chapter). So it is clear in actual architectural use that the Corinthian order was created and maintained for centuries as a means to serve unusual circumstances.

Vitruvius understood that the Corinthian was to be regarded as a full-fledged order, but in passing he made

Figure 5-14
The Corinthian order used as a regular order: Temple of Olympian Zeus, Athens (© Alinari/Art Resource, NY).

oblique statements implying ways in which he regarded it as singular and peculiar among the orders. When he associated it with the qualities of young maidens, he observed that maidens—and, by implication, the order—"admit of prettier effects in the way of adornment" (IV.i.8). In other words, structures built in the Corinthian mode may be more freely elaborated and less rigorously configured than those employing the other orders. Such a principle was abundantly demonstrated after his lifetime, in architecture that employed the Corinthian order or variants based on it.

Another way in which Vitruvius allowed for variations is in the design of the capital itself, either modifying its format or substituting other compositions made up for the immediate purpose (IV.i.12). A conspicuous example, left unnamed in his treatise, is the composite capital, in which Ionic volutes are superimposed upon the acanthus-covered Corinthian basket. Although it was not singled out as a distinct order until the Renaissance, when Sebastiano Serlio gave it a name, this variant order already existed as an option. In Roman architecture after the time of Vitruvius, Corinthian capitals show a substitution of animal or other forms for some of the plant motifs, witness the outward-facing horses replacing the corner tendrils in a capital from the Temple of Mars Ultor. Similarly, human figures could be superimposed or substituted, as in the composite capital surviving from the Baths of Caracalla. Indeed, modification and substitution became a staple of the Corinthian order in medieval Christian architecture, most notably in the Romanesque era, when the substitution became complete (fig. 5-15).

Finally, the Corinthian order admitted greater freedom in the choice of entablature. Vitruvius noted (IV.i.2) that instead of the Ionic entablature it was permissible to apply respectively the mutules and guttae of the Doric triglyph system to the corona and the architrave. The implicit mixing of Corinthian colonnades and other entablatures actually did become an option, as demonstrated at Paestum in the Doric-Corinthian temple. The Corinthian order, then, could be used as a pure variant of the Ionic or as a decoratively freewheeling option when an architect wanted to be released from the constraints imposed by the more traditional orders. Vitruvius only hinted at that freedom in his discussion of the orders, but later in his treatise he unwittingly provided a much deeper insight into that possibility (discussed in the next chapter).

After Vitruvius's lifetime the Romans came to rely upon the Corinthian order as their favorite. One reason may be that as they increasingly varied the formats of their buildings

Figure 5-15
Romanesque Corinthian capital transmogrified with beasts: St. Benoît-sur-Loire (FH).

the Corinthian decor posed no impediments. Another is that they often favored gigantic size, even in orthodox formats. Still another is that their architecture, which developed interior space beyond anything ever attempted by the Greeks, relied a great deal on plastically conceived decor, and the Corinthian order could provide the requisite richness.

It was this legacy of post-Vitruvian Roman architecture that the Renaissance theorists had all viewed and measured and to which they tried to apply the strictures of Vitruvius. For them the Corinthian order was manifestly a distinct and normal order in a way it never was to either the Greeks or Vitruvius. Accordingly, they treated it as equal in every way to the Doric and Ionic orders, and they readily adopted it for their own architecture.

To the repertory of Greek orders Vitruvius added the Tuscan (IV.vii.1–5). According to his description, ostensibly based on ancient Etruscan precedents, this order was not envisioned for a peripteral temple but for a three-chambered sanctuary fronted by a deep portico with two rows of four very widely spaced columns (fig. 5-16). Indeed, this format of a chamber or chambers on a raised platform, approached by a front stair leading to the portico, was in fact to dominate Roman temple architecture. But little surviving evidence suggests that the Tuscan order itself was a still living tradition in his time. Indeed, given the paucity of archaeological evidence for actual use of the order, Vitruvius's account may have been prompted less by the desire to introduce a fourth order than to present the format associated with it. His description implicitly justified the difference between the Roman and Greek temple formats, despite the Roman preference for the three Greek orders over the Tuscan.

The Tuscan order has value because it is simpler in several respects than the Doric (fig. 5-17). It eschews flutes on the column shafts and sometimes entasis as well. It affects a simpler capital and an entablature so simple as not to require any special formula. Like the Roman Doric, the Tuscan column was assigned proportions of 1:7. According to Vitruvius the shaft stands on a base of rounded profile and that, in turn, on a circular plinth. The capital is similar to the Roman Doric except that above the astragal at the top of the shaft the molded echinus includes no annulets; as with the Doric, the abacus is a simple square. The entablature consists of two layers of beams, separated by dowels that leave an air space "two fingers in breadth," and projects mutules beneath the pediment and roof. The account of the order is so quaintly archaic and sketchily described

Figure 5-16
Model of the Tuscan order according to Vitruvius (courtesy of
Museo dell'Istituto di Etruscologia e Antichità Italiche, University
of Rome).

that it seems Vitruvius had no reason to think it was going
to be used in actual practice. Indeed, during the succeeding
centuries of Roman architecture the Tuscan order was ignored and remained little more than a potential option. It
had to wait for architects of the Renaissance to discover in
its format the virtue of something simpler than the Roman
Doric and peculiarly appropriate to rustic circumstances.

ALBERTI'S ADJUSTMENTS TO THE ORDERS

Concerning the design of buildings, Alberti found himself
in something of a quandary. Although his undertaking of
a treatise was founded on the premise that architecture

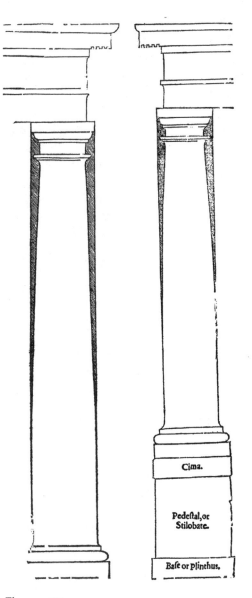

Cima.

Pedeſtal, or
Stilobate.

Baſe or plinthus.

Figure 5-17
The Tuscan order according to Serlio.

THE ORDERS: EVOLVING RULES FOR FORMAL BEAUTY

should employ the classical orders, he could not be faithful to the needs of his own culture without substantially altering the form or function of most of the building types Vitruvius discussed. As nearly as he could, Alberti observed the conventions inherent in Vitruvius's building types, but it was eventually evident that the formats could not remain the same. Even so, he wanted to give the appearance of subscribing to classical norms. Like Vitruvius, he presented the orders in a straightforward way, albeit in even greater detail and with the benefit of divergent data he had gleaned elsewhere. As far as he was concerned, he had not altered classical practice in any serious respect. Yet he took for granted certain Roman usages that had been adopted after Vitruvius's lifetime, usages that violated both the letter and the spirit of the orders as Vitruvius defined them. So it transpired that Alberti's treatise contains the first instance in written theory recommending the application of the orders as surface ornament and the use of the orders in conjunction with arches. The former violates the structural nature of the orders whereas the latter violates their structural function, confounding the rules of proportion as well, but both were taken from good Roman examples built after the time of Vitruvius.

Applied orders occur when columns or half-columns are attached to a wall or when pilasters—by their very nature, attached—are employed. In these situations the entablature, along with the column, is transformed from a structural ensemble into surface articulation. Strictly speaking, such a usage should fall into Vitruvius's category of licentious deformities. Yet Alberti, examining buildings and ruins in Rome with Vitruvius in mind, would have encountered an applied Ionic order on the Temple of Fortuna Virilis and orders used in conjunction with arches on the Theater of Marcellus and the Colosseum (fig. 4-2), to name only three obvious examples. Because they were applied in sober formulations, he probably assumed that they had always been permissible. He could feel equally free to prescribe them in miniature form, as seen in the Pantheon (fig. 3-4), as ornament for niches, doors, and windows, both real and false, and also as articulation of interior elevations in basilicas (*De re aedificatoria* VI.12 and VII.12). He thus gave authority to the version of the orders that was most useful to Renaissance architects. Given the building types they worked with the most, the basilican church and the urban palace, the opportunities to incorporate the freestanding orders were rare. Hence applied orders came to constitute Alberti's principal means of embracing classicism.

SERLIO'S ADJUSTMENTS TO THE ORDERS

Serlio was the first theorist to canonize the composite order with a name and to place it on an equal footing with the other four orders. He was also the first to give the Tuscan order a visual reality and a practical adaptability. He brought it into standard usage by substituting an Attic base and square plinth and an entablature consisting of a plain architrave and frieze, separated by a curved taenia and surmounted by a simple corona (fig. 5-17). Moreover, he was the first to create a standardized representation of all five orders, set out in the sequence of plain to elaborate (fig. 5-18). In his initial image he represented the five as columns of varied heights and thickness, all standing on pedestals. The proportions of the orders were systematized by the inscription of a Roman numeral on each indicating the number of shaft thicknesses appropriate to the height of the column.

Serlio was also the first theorist to provide a multitude of different applications for the orders, almost all of his own devising, in designs for a variety of hypothetical situations, including gates, walls, fireplaces, doorways, triumphal

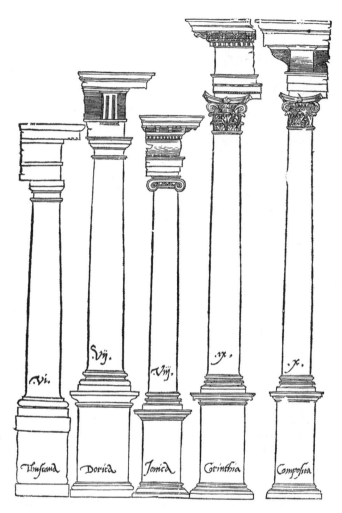

Figure 5-18
The five orders, as schematized by Serlio.

arches, and facades of urban palaces. As a matter of decorum, he reserved all the applications outside the sphere of dignified urban circumstances to the Tuscan and Doric orders, which were accorded many more variations than the others. Hence, aside from those devoted to the parts of the orders themselves (and to some technical details or plans corresponding to elevations), 19 illustrations represent Tuscan examples, 16 Doric, 8 Ionic, 13 Corinthian, and 3 composite.

PHILIBERT DE L'ORME'S ADJUSTMENTS TO THE ORDERS

As a follower of Serlio and as the first non-Italian to publish a theory of architecture, de l'Orme embroidered all that Serlio had collected on the orders. His main contribution was the invention of a "French" order (fig. 5-19), which added decorative bands to the shafts of columns, introduced convex curvatures to flutes in addition to—and in combination with—concave curvatures, and varied and embellished the canonical capitals and entablatures. This "order" was never widely or permanently adopted, but it created a powerful precedent for the freedom to continue developing and enlarging the repertory of orders.

PALLADIO'S ADJUSTMENTS TO THE ORDERS

As with Serlio's, Palladio's orders were represented in their freestanding formats (fig. 5-20), in their decorative applied formats with arches (fig. 5-21), and in detail, showing the base, capital, and entablature. More important, however, is that he devised a way to adapt the freestanding orders to the architectural types of his own time

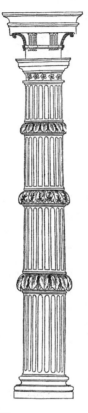

Figure 5-19
The "French" order, devised by Philibert de l'Orme.

and thereby bring back into currency a nearly authentic
version of antique architecture. Although Alberti had
tried to convey the impression that he was prescribing the
use of freestanding orders, the most he could do was to
promote the fiction of columnar porches on churches
and to pretend that the main arcade of a church was actually a colonnade. But by adopting the temple front as a
portico for houses, Palladio devised a way to employ the

Figure 5-20
The freestanding version of the order: Palladio.

Figure 5-21
The applied order used in conjunction with arches: Palladio.

freestanding orders as a standard feature. Moreover, he enlarged their use by employing stoa-like colonnades in the loggias that connect the residence with the outbuildings of his rural complexes. Although he also freely and frequently employed the applied orders on facades and courtyard elevations, especially of urban houses, he greatly increased the opportunities for adopting the freestanding orders.

Within the context of straightforward orders, Palladio pioneered the adoption of Michelangelo's colossal order for the embellishment of houses. From the time of Alberti the applied orders had been employed on single stories. This might be done by combining a rusticated ground story with a columned upper story. Or, as in Alberti's Palazzo Rucellai or in Serlio's hypothetical examples, half-columns or pilasters might be stacked in two or three layers, according to the number of stories. But Palladio achieved an unprecedented grandeur by applying a single order to two-story elevations, with subordinate articulations for the separate stories. This he did with both half-columns applied to street elevations and structural columns placed around courtyards. By contrast, he also pioneered the use of stacked freestanding orders, both for the stoa-like loggias of the Palazzo Chiericati in Vicenza and for the porticoes of several of his country villas. This usage promoted a refined elegance in buildings of monumental proportions, a restraint that helped to distinguish their private character from the imposing solemnity more appropriate to public buildings. These two treatments, taken together, represent both an expansion and a contraction of the scale normally accorded to a portico or colonnade. In his designs Palladio employed the classical orders on all exterior elevations, in courtyards where relevant, and for the decoration of interiors as well.

Figure 5-22
The neoclassical order: Barrière Monceau, Paris, by Ledoux (FH).

Laugier's call for a restoration of the structural purity of the orders coincided with the first generation of archaeological investigation, beginning around 1750. Prompted in part by discovery of the ruins of Pompeii and the exploration of ancient Greek sites, this direct contact resulted in the rediscovery by Western culture of the Greek version of the orders. That, in turn, had the effect of ushering in the neoclassical style and an emphasis upon the freestanding orders employed for their original structural purposes. A corollary result was the rejection of applied orders, particularly of their manipulated versions. Despite considerable freedom of design composition, like that practiced by such neoclassical exponents as Étienne Boullée and Jean-Nicolas-Louis Ledoux (fig. 5-22), the renascent structural use of the orders guaranteed that they were employed in a fundamentally correct manner. Indeed, as archaeological awareness of antique usage increased in the early nineteenth century, so also did purity of the orders in architectural practice. The return to authenticity was accompanied by a dismissal of earlier transcendental and symbolic associations of the orders and the classical tradition in general.

The widespread acceptance of an architectural aesthetic based on the rules of the classical orders and the serene harmony they produced somehow prompted a contrary reaction. This reaction generated a rival aesthetic founded on the concept of violating the rules. Perhaps such a development could occur because the canonic use of the orders, fraught with conflicts and complications, invited perverse solutions to design problems. Whatever the initial motivation, an alternative aesthetic did evolve, so that the resulting two versions of the classical tradition ended up constituting a stylistic duality. The importance of this duality transcends use of the orders themselves; it has continued in Western culture as one of the fundamental options of artistic expression.

VITRUVIUS

Buried deep within Vitruvius's seventh book, dealing with the interior decoration of houses, is a passage singular for both its literary tone and content, the chapter on "the decadence of fresco painting." Taken at face value, this chapter is devoted to the embellishment of elaborate domestic rooms that are not vulnerable to being spoiled by the smoke of fires and torches. Of particular concern are the kinds of scenes that may properly be painted upon (freshly) plastered walls. The discussion breaks down, however, into a vehement polemic against one particular style of painting, outstripping in significance the subject at hand; indeed, it constitutes the most important aesthetic statement in the entire treatise. In order to explore its meaning, Vitruvius's colorful characterization of the issue must be savored in his own words.

The ancients required realistic pictures of real things. A picture is, in fact, a representation of a thing which really exists or which can exist; for example, a man, a house, a ship, or anything else from whose definite and actual structure copies resembling it can be taken. Consequently the ancients who introduced polished finishings began by representing different kinds of marble slabs in different positions, and then cornices and blocks of yellow ochre in various ways.

Afterwards they made such progress as to represent the forms of buildings, and of columns, and projecting and overhanging pediments; in their open rooms, such as exedrae, on account of the size, they depicted the facades of scenes in the tragic, comic, and satyric style; and their walks, on account of the great length, they decorated with a variety of landscapes, copying the characteristics of definite spots. In these paintings there are harbors, promontories, seashores, rivers, fountains, straits, fanes, groves, mountains, flocks, shepherds; in some places there are also pictures designed in the grand style, with figures of the gods or detailed mythological episodes, or the battles of Troy, or the wanderings of Ulysses, with landscape backgrounds, and other subjects reproduced on similar grounds from real life.

But those subjects which were copied from actual realities are scorned in these days of bad taste. We now have fresco paintings of monstrosities, rather than truthful representations of definite things. For instance, reeds are put in the place of columns, fluted appendages with curly leaves and volutes, instead of pediments, candelabra supporting representations of shrines, and on top of their pediments numerous tender stalks and volutes growing up from the roots and having only half-length figures, some with human heads, others with heads of animals.

Such things do not exist and cannot exist and never have existed. Hence, it is the new taste that has caused bad judges of poor art to prevail over true artistic excellence. For how is it possible that a reed should really support a roof, or a candelabrum a pediment with its ornaments, or that such a slender, flexible thing as a stalk should support a figure perched upon it, or that roots and stalks should produce flowers and now half-figures? Yet when people see these frauds, they find no fault with them but on the contrary are delighted, and do not care whether any of them can exist or not. Their understanding is darkened by decadent critical principles, so that it is not capable of giving its approval authoritatively and on the principle of propriety to that which really can exist. The fact is that pictures which are unlike reality ought not to be approved, and even if they are technically fine, this is no reason why they should offhand be judged to be correct, if their subject is lacking in the principles of reality carried out with no violations. (VII.v.1–5, translation of Morris Hickey Morgan)

Vitruvius expressed here a preference for painting that is realistic in style, depicting subject matter in a fashion that is sober and straightforward. These remarks about representation, applicable to architectural images as much as to natural scenes, can be extended to architecture itself, denoting a preference for design that honors all the rules. Nothing else could reasonably be expected of the author of strict formulas for the orders. Indeed, his position on aesthetics was undoubtedly prevalent in the Rome of his time.

One of the leading artistic authorities of the day, and Vitruvius's contemporary, Quintus Horatius Flaccus—known to the English-speaking world as Horace—had expressed a similar sentiment in the opening passage of his important treatise on poetics, *Ars poetica*. Written in verse, but quoted here from a prose translation (by H. Rushton Fairclough) for the sake of clarity, he opines:

If a painter chose to join a human head to the neck of a horse, and to spread feathers of many a hue over limbs picked up now here now there, so that what at the top is a lovely woman ends below in a black and ugly fish, could you, my friends, if favored with a private view, refrain from laughing? Believe me, dear Pisos, quite like such pictures would be a book, whose idle fancies shall be shaped like a sick man's dreams, so that neither head nor foot can be assigned to a single shape. "Painters and poets," you say, "have always had an equal right in hazarding anything." We know it: this licence we poets claim and in our turn we grant the like; but not so far that savage should mate with tame, or serpents couple with birds, lambs with tigers.

Horace was concerned with defining the difference between poetic license and unbridled licentiousness. His concept of poetic license permits imagining things of long ago, far away, or fanciful occurrence, but they must be represented in terms of the real world as confirmed by the senses. He expressly excluded the surreal, the phantasmagoric, or the frivolous reconfiguration of the real world for the sake of shock or titillation. The distinction he drew is parallel to Vitruvius's for fresco paintings. These two authorities both expressed what would generally be regarded as a common-sense view of the arts. The licentious practice, for Horace, was only hypothetical—*what if* one expressed oneself with chimeric images. Vitruvius, on the other hand, wrote about specific examples as if he had seen them on actual walls. What he did not tell us is that if such images were desirable enough for someone to commission them, they presumably represented an aesthetic option that had been defined by others in positive terms.

Such an alternative was one that delighted in violating normal visual expectations. It reasoned that if the delectation of an aesthetic based on rules—rules like those controlling the orders—is satisfied by recognizing how the rules have been followed, then an aesthetic based on violation of the rules raises knowledgeable delectation to a more rarefied plane. The viewer attuned to such a work enjoys simultaneously both a knowledge of the rules and an awareness of how they have been broken, a more sophisticated kind of cognition than the straightforward appreciation of regularity. Thus the myriad ways in which rules can be broken became the basis of ingenious creation. What Vitruvius and Horace unwittingly revealed was a glimpse into an artistic sensibility that existed in classical antiquity but was never overtly voiced, at least not in a surviving antique treatise.

In actual Roman frescoes (fig. 6-1) and in Roman architecture after Vitruvius, there are numerous ways in which the orders were perversely manipulated, and instances can be cited for each member. For instance, the drums of a column shaft can alternate between bulging rusticated and smoothly rounded ones. Columns can be arranged with varied intercolumniations so as to introduce visual rhythm into a colonnade (fig. 6-2). This can be accomplished either by creating pairs or groups of columns or by arranging them with incremental intervals. Moreover, the rhythm of a colonnade can be introduced in the third dimension by projecting some of the columns forward of the plane of reference. Correspondingly, the entablature can be rhythmically broken to correlate with groupings of columns. A pediment can be broken in conjunction with variations in the colonnade and entablature. Or it can be interrupted either to introduce a dramatic interval or to permit the intervention of some other kind of feature. The placement of entablatures or pediments over pairs of columns, separated by breaks in the entablature, can transform a colonnade into a row of miniature structures (fig. 6-3). The superimposition of three stories of these miniatures can be alternated so that the sequence of the little structures is syncopated. The entablature between the columns framing

Figure 6-1
The Corinthian order manipulated: Roman fresco from Hercula-
neum, Naples Archaeological Museum (© Alinari/Art Resource,
NY).

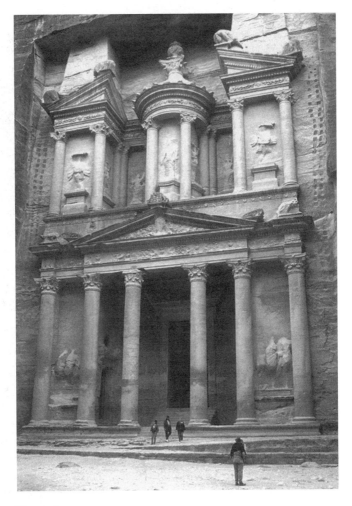

Figure 6-2
The Corinthian order manipulated: the Khazne at Petra (courtesy Jordan Tourism Board North America).

THE ALTERNATIVE AESTHETIC: BREAKING THE RULES

Figure 6-3
The Corinthian order manipulated: the library of Celsus, Ephesus
(courtesy Jana Hearn).

an axis can be curved upward into an arch (fig. 6-4). An arch
can protrude into a pediment. The keystone of an arch can
appear to have dropped a few inches. The voussoirs of an
arch can be exaggerated in length and can protrude through
an entablature or into a pediment. A pediment can be formed
with an arch instead of a gable. These are just some of the options exercised by the Romans; in later times the possibilities
proved to be virtually unlimited (see Lyttelton 1974).

In sum every regulation of the orders can be violated
and every aspect inventively varied. From Vitruvius's point

Figure 6-4
The Corinthian order manipulated: Hadrian's temple, Ephesus
(FH).

THE ALTERNATIVE AESTHETIC: BREAKING THE RULES

of view all this kind of deformation is reprehensible. In reality, not much of it was actually practiced in architectural design until after his lifetime, but the possibility was already acknowledged in his diatribe on the decadence of fresco painting. Without his intending it, Vitruvius's aesthetic legacy to the theory of architecture was an awareness of this duality, embracing a canon of classical (or straightforward) beauty and anticipating a canon of mannered (or distorted) beauty. The latter could not exist without the former, but, lacking mannerism to provide a foil, classicism would not have acquired its aura of purity. Such a level of aesthetic consciousness is not inherent in Vitruvius's text, but when read in light of later architecture this passage took on a life of its own and ever afterward became the plaything of his readers. In the long course of Western architecture the freedom to experiment with the orders in creative variation has sustained their vitality and thereby prolonged their use. Thus this passage in Vitruvius, which appears at face value to have little relevance to architecture, represents the germ of a principle that acquired great significance.

THE RENAISSANCE TRADITION: SERLIO AND MICHELANGELO

In architectural theory this inverted aesthetic did not appear full-blown until the sixteenth century, appearing only by implication in the first treatise conceived primarily in terms of images, that of Sebastiano Serlio. Whereas Serlio's illustrations constitute a tacit manifesto of the mannerist aesthetic, one would scarcely know it from reading the text, except for a few phrases that seem to imply extraction from an articulated theory of breaking the rules. He repeatedly refers to license or licentiousness in design (e.g., IV.99v; see

Payne 1999, 116–122). For instance, in Book V.20r, he cites the "harmonious discord"—tantamount to a "becoming awkwardness" or, to put it more strongly, a "beautiful ugliness" (Summers 1981; cf. Hearn 1981)—in the unevenly graduated proportions of stories marked on a church tower. Also, in his book on doors as well as in the main treatise, he frequently appeals to license as the warrant for inverting the formal rules of the orders.

This inversion draws upon the aesthetic value of both the grotesque and artistic license, and those departures from established norms, in turn, signify an apprehension of the anticlassical aesthetic decried by Vitruvius. The understanding and appreciation of such an inversion was introduced into Renaissance art by two different means, the first being visual contact with recently discovered Roman architectural ornament, the second a philosophical speculation on the negative passage in Vitruvius.

The former, the visual experience of this aesthetic inversion, was afforded by the discovery, around 1480, of the ruins of the Golden House of Nero underneath the ruins of the Baths of Trajan. Sequestered in chambers still buried underground (hence "grottoes"), chimeric figures and fanciful ornaments in the painted and stuccoed decorations soon became famous in the city, attracting the curious, especially young artists, who named them *grotteschi*. The chief point of their entry into Rome's artistic circles was at the pinnacle of practice, namely, the workshop of Raphael (see Dacos 1969). It is ironic that this paragon of classical purity was attracted to the strange aesthetic and, together with assistants such as Giulio Romano, Giovanni da Udine, and Perino del Vaga, absorbed it into some of the projects then being carried out by his workshop.

From there, this aesthetic entered the architectural work of Giulio Romano, soon to depart in 1524 to carry out commissions for the Gonzaga family in Mantua, and of

Baldassare Peruzzi, one of the succession of architects in charge of St. Peter's and the architect of the Palazzo Massimi. Serlio knew and admired them both, having included drawings by Peruzzi in his Book III, on antiquity, and having cited Giulio's paradigmatic mannerist design of the Palazzo del Te (fig. 6-5), outside Mantua, as "a true exemplar of architecture and painting for our times" (IV.133v). The latter encomium was issued in the context of illustrating a highly inventive rusticated door, which Serlio attributed to Giulio. The principal courtyard facades of this palace, with their "dropped" triglyphs in the frieze and their straight arches composed of outsized voussoirs, to name only two of the many imaginative ornaments, were not included in the treatise.

The second pathway of the alternative aesthetic into Renaissance architecture was a combination of the putative theory and actual buildings devised by Michelangelo. Although never written down by Michelangelo himself, the theory was attributed to him in the biographies compiled by Francisco de Hollanda, Giorgio Vasari, and Ascanio Condivi, as well as in a treatise on proportions by Vincenzo Danti. This theory was enunciated with the conscious knowledge that Vitruvius's diatribe was being inverted, as was also the still more famous opening passage of Horace's *Ars poetica* in which the license of poets and painters is at once both celebrated and circumscribed. Vitruvius had written in terms of structural fantasies, Horace in terms of chimeric figures. But both were describing inventions that conformed to the concept of the grotesque as it was newly defined in the Renaissance. Asserting the right to enjoy the creative freedom inherent in artistic license, Michelangelo fixed upon the grotesque as a metaphor for invention. Cognizant of a difference between elegant and vulgar inventions, he sought to adhere to Horace's circumscription of

Figure 6-5
Breaking the rules of the orders: Palazzo del Te, Mantua, by Giulio
Romano (© Scala/Art Resource, NY).

license by the exercise of judgment, namely the judgment of
the eye (see Summers 1972).

The intersection of this germ of an aesthetic theory
and actual architecture was realized in terms of the composite order, or, more precisely, of the composite order
taken as a point of departure. As a combination of the
Ionic and Corinthian orders, the composite could be regarded as equivalent to a figurative chimera, insofar as
both are composed of parts of two disparate things. Accordingly, much more than the three Greek orders and
the Italic, Tuscan order, the composite was designated the
ideal medium for inventive license in architectural design.
As is well known, Michelangelo reshaped and rearranged
the elements of the column and entablature, inverting and
reassigning their apparent functions. Moreover, he created

all sorts of new configurations for standard features, such as moldings or frames for niches and doors. Tightening intervals within compositions, emphasizing subordinate elements, and effacing the accustomed role of dominant elements, he invested architectural decor with the visual equivalent of emotional expression. In sacred or culturally elevated settings like the Medici Chapel or the Laurentian Library (fig. 6-6) in the church complex of San Lorenzo in Florence, this expression could even be imputed to spiritual struggle. In such a context his bold inventions, more distinctive than anything known within the entire classical tradition, assumed the quality of an analogue to the creative power of divinity. Indeed, architectural invention, by its very abstractness, put the art of buildings on a higher plane than invention in the figurative arts because there were fewer limits on the creativity that could be achieved with it (see Summers 1972).

This level of interpretation of Michelangelo's architecture was probably shared by only a privileged few, the cultural elite and some fellow artists. But aspects of it undoubtedly filtered down far enough into Renaissance society to become part of the general theoretical understanding of art. Whether or not Serlio knew the works of Michelangelo or these theoretical ideas is not known; at any rate nothing by the man or of his precepts is included in the treatise. Yet both the work and the theory played a conspicuous role in the artistic movement of mannerism. That Michelangelo's architecture was difficult to imitate means that, for all the admiration it evoked, it did not make as pervasive or lasting an impact as the simpler mannerism of Giulio Romano, in which inventiveness was addressed to the arrangement of the orders as they already existed.

Both versions of the manipulative aesthetic—that which invented anew and that which merely violated

Figure 6-6
Recreating the orders: Laurentian Library, Florence, by Michelangelo (© Scala/Art Resource, NY).

norms—depended upon an audience familiar with the norms and with the rules that controlled the norms. Deviations from the norm appealed to a high level of cultivation as expressions of intellectual play. According to the circumstances in which they appeared, they could be interpreted as witty, ironic, allusive, or even allegorical, and always as poetic. Renaissance architects thus employed the orders not so much as a message in themselves, which was the way Vitruvius had contemplated them, but as a vocabulary for composing messages. Unwittingly, Vitruvius had already begun that process when he altered the Greek orders, thereby converting them from structural systems into motifs. By the time Alberti prescribed their use as decorative articulation with applied orders, the change was nearly accomplished. Acceptance of the principle of manipulation in the early sixteenth century completed the transformation. Once it had occurred it no longer needed to be commented upon. This would largely account for the circumstance that Serlio could illustrate in his treatise so many examples of the manipulated orders, alongside others that are straightforward, without explaining them as such. Indeed, by the time he published his Book IV in 1537, the principle of breaking the rules had been absorbed into the concept of classicism itself.

Illustrating the orders in Book IV, Serlio presented a variety of formats for the straightforward use of the orders. But he also provided other formats in which he was at pains to demonstrate a high degree of manipulation—namely, elaborate doorways and facades of hypothetical urban houses. Common to nearly all of them is a motif he introduced to the theory of architecture: a sequence of four columns in which each outer intercolumniation is spanned by a horizontal entablature and the central one is crowned by an arch (fig. 6-7). Although it had been employed in antiquity in the Villa of Hadrian at Tivoli, which he probably knew, as well as the Temple of Hadrian at Ephesus (fig. 6-4), it was Serlio who introduced this device into a theoretical context. Long identified as the "Palladian motif," because of its prevalence in Palladio's architecture, this composition is now more properly known by its propagator's name, as the serliana.

In one of his ornamented doors (IV.23v) the flanking Doric half-columns are composed of alternating short and tall drums, which continue the layered blocks of the door

Figure 6-7
Hypothetical facade with superimposed manipulated orders:
Serlio.

THE ALTERNATIVE AESTHETIC: BREAKING THE RULES

jambs (fig. 6-8). The tall drums are shown rusticated, thus making of the half-columns an enigmatic combination of the primitive and the refined. The capitals and the entablature above them purport to be straightforward Roman Doric, except that the entablature is interrupted by a splay of giant voussoirs which form a straight arch, supported underneath by a lintel over the doorway. These voussoirs project above the area of the entablature, filling out the entire tympanum area beneath the crowning pediment. There is, then, in both the vertical and the horizontal elements of the door, the irony of formal composition contradicting structural function. To superimpose a blank escutcheon over the central voussoirs is to underline the artificiality of function of the straight arch. The whole constitutes an exercise in the uncanny.

A two-story facade (IV.27r), shown as a segment from a whole of indeterminate length, has an arcaded loggia at ground level, composed of a continuous sequence of serlianas (fig. 6-7). Each arch frames a door or window in the inner wall, and each is surmounted by an oculus opening. Each pair of columns connected by an entablature frames a blind, round-headed niche and supports a square panel tangent to the adjacent framing arches. The whole lower story, topped by an elaborately molded stringcourse, creates a rich counterpoint of various geometric figures and also of solid and void. The upper-story windows, aligned with those in the story below, are underlined by a stringcourse at sill level, which simultaneously serves as the pedestal for an order of paired pilasters between each window. Each pair of pilasters is integrated as a single visual unit by two devices, the insertion of a round-headed niche between the pilasters to fill the intervening area and the forward projection of the unit to produce a rhythmic articulation of the upper story. The windows are crowned with pediments, alternating between arched and gabled

Figure 6-8
Hypothetical doorway with manipulated order: Serlio.

THE ALTERNATIVE AESTHETIC: BREAKING THE RULES

versions. The story as a whole is surmounted by a regular Roman Doric entablature. The combination of the two stories, different but complementary, presents a rich variety of articulations, rhythms, motifs, and textures. The violations of the Doric rules, more pronounced regarding arrangement and function than form and proportion, are discreetly balanced with the observances of the rules. Other than structurally supporting a loggia, all this array of putatively structural forms has been deployed toward a purely decorative end. Except for the arcade itself, the architecture is all on the surface and serves no supportive purpose, but it creates an animated and highly expressive facade.

The significance of Serlio's manipulated orders is far greater than just the confirmation of an alternative aesthetic within the framework of the classical orders. By their very nature they are to be primarily used as applied rather than as freestanding orders, but that means that they can be employed on any vertical architectural surface whatever, interior as well as exterior. Indeed, their flexibility of composition makes the applied orders a universal design medium, in which formal combinations are unlimited. They can be made wantonly elaborate or chastely simple, elegantly delicate or dramatically forceful. Moreover, comprising mostly applied ornament in which the degree of relief can be minimal, they can be fabricated out of inexpensive materials, such as stucco on brick, rather than of laboriously worked stone. In a phrase, everything necessary to create the design of a dignified building—ranging from a palace to a town house, a cathedral to a chapel, a city hall to a guild house—was embraced by the concept of the manipulated orders. And, indeed, it came to pass that the manipulated orders, in combination with the straightforward, sufficed to create virtually all European high-art architecture for the next two centuries, and a great deal more besides during the two centuries of the modern era.

THE MANIPULATED ORDERS IN THE BAROQUE ERA
AND LATER

It is a curious anomaly that although Renaissance architecture may largely be explained in terms of Renaissance theories of architecture, the same cannot be said for baroque architecture and the treatises of its time. Many pages of theory were written in the era of baroque architecture, but nothing in them explicitly explains or justifies the expressive use of the orders in contemporaneous architecture. Baroque interpretation of the orders served a very different context from that of the Renaissance. Sixteenth-century mannerism was largely employed to express intellectual concepts, even when they related to religion, whereas the seventeenth- and early eighteenth-century baroque aesthetic was propagandistic in intent. The former was cerebral in expression, the latter emotional.

There was one notion briefly discussed in the treatise of Vincenzo Scamozzi, a pupil of Palladio, that might be enlarged upon to establish a general convention behind baroque design. Book VI of his *L'idea della architettura universale,* published in Venice in 1615, attributed to the orders not only the quality of formal perfection but also a provenance in divine ordainment (see Kruft 1994, 100, and the reprint of Scamozzi, vol. 2, p. 2). The notion that they came from the Creator held the profoundest of implications for any architecture based on the orders, especially an architecture designed subsequent to the theoretical liberation inherent in the mannerist aesthetic.

To wit, once the orders could be regarded as subject to manipulation for purposes of stylistic expressiveness, it would be a small step to regard divinely ordained orders as a formal repertory peculiarly appropriate for creatively expressing the sacred. Moreover, if the sacredness of the

Figure 6-9
Baroque use of the orders: St. Nicholas, Prague (FH).

church could be expressed with the orders, then the sacredness attached to divinely appointed kingship could be similarly expressed. Conceived to serve the aims of an absolutist church by creating an environment expressive of the miraculous with heavenly splendor, the baroque style was also engaged to serve absolutist monarchy by creating an environment expressing unlimited power with overwhelming grandeur. Proper manifestation of the majesty of both church and ruler in architecture could be realized by employing divinely endowed orders that are manipulated within dramatic compositions.

Manipulation of the orders by a baroque architect could be manifested in rhythmic arrangements and pairings of columns, often on a gigantic scale, as well as projections and groupings of columns. Columns could overlap with pilasters and pilasters with one another, with broken entablatures enhancing the effect (fig. 6-9). Manipulation could also include undulation of orders and even whole facades, and the undulations of superimposed stories could be played against one another. For as long as a transcendent association with the orders prevailed, anything that could be expressed with grand rhetoric could find equivalent expression through the orders.

Scamozzi's notion of the divine origin of the orders still thrived in the late seventeenth century, in François Blondel's *Cours d'architecture,* and as an encompassing generality it seems to have been germane to the reality of all baroque architecture. The break from this association, initiated by Claude Perrault in the late seventeenth century in his *Ordonnance des cinq espèces de colonnes* (Paris, 1683), culminated in its general rejection by neoclassicists in the late eighteenth century, although to Laugier divine origin still seemed plausible. By the nineteenth century, however, such a metaphysical association was defunct, and manipulation of the orders had become a purely formal, academic exercise, albeit one fostered by the academies and still frequently employed.

Proportion: The Orders and Architectural Spaces

If to Vitruvius the orders are necessarily the means for making beautiful architecture, it is due regard for proportion that makes the orders—and architecture in general—beautiful. Harmony is achieved only when correct proportions are employed throughout. Indeed, he regarded them as ordained by nature:

Since nature has designed the human body so that its members are duly proportioned to the frame as a whole, it appears that the ancients had good reason for their rule, that in perfect buildings the different members must be in exact symmetrical relations to the whole general scheme. Hence, while transmitting to us the proper arrangements for buildings of all kinds, they were particularly careful to do so in the case of temples of the gods, buildings in which merits and faults usually last forever. (III.i.4)

When Vitruvius dealt with the process of design, the most painstaking aspect of his labors was the incorporation of appropriate proportions. The most detailed accounts of these efforts involve the achievement of eurythmy, and among them none are more detailed than his specifications for the individual parts of the Ionic order (III.v.1–13). Each component of the column and entablature is assigned a number proportionate to the fundamental dimension, the thickness of the column shaft at its bottom. But each set of ratios—for the components of the base, the capital, and the entablature—is different, so no predictable standardization occurs within the order as a whole. Moreover, the ratio of height to width of the column can also vary according to the category of intercolumniation. Manifestly, in order to determine such a body of proportions for an entire building, a concentrated intellectual effort was required. But once mastered, this proportional formula could be employed indefinitely.

Given the way the ratios for the Ionic order were set out, proceeding upward part by part from the plinth of the base to the cornice of the entablature, Vitruvius provided no hint of the overall governing concept. He simply attributed their prescription to Hermogenes, as if that were authority enough. In his prescription each feature has an explicit rule for its proportions, and no aspect is too minor for consideration. For instance, the formula even includes the ratio of depth to width for the channels articulating the capital volutes. Such minute detail of proportional specifications may have been ambrosial to any ardent classical architect, because it could guide him step by step in making an unassailable rendition of the order. But in our own time, when the rules of the classical orders are no longer of primary concern to architects, Vitruvius's proportional specifications lose their urgency. For this reason we may pass over his exact prescriptions, acknowledging as a generality that their use was intended to produce harmony in the design of the temple as a whole.

For Vitruvius, eurythmy is magnified into symmetry when adherence to due proportion extends beyond the individual column to the intercolumniation and thereby to the full colonnade and the entire building. The classification of intercolumniations is determined by the number of column widths across the interval (III.iii.1–6): pycnostyle is one and a half column widths (fig. 7-1), systyle is

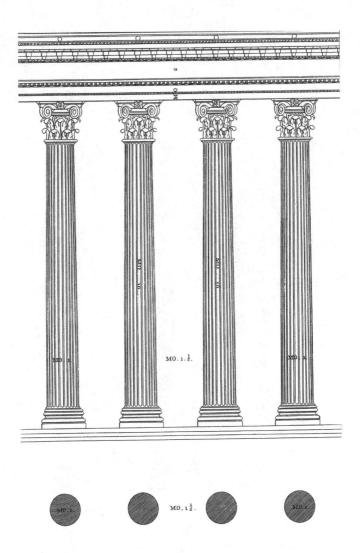

Figure 7-1
Pycnostyle, first of the five columnar intervals for the orders:
Palladio.

PROPORTION: THE ORDERS AND ARCHITECTURAL SPACES

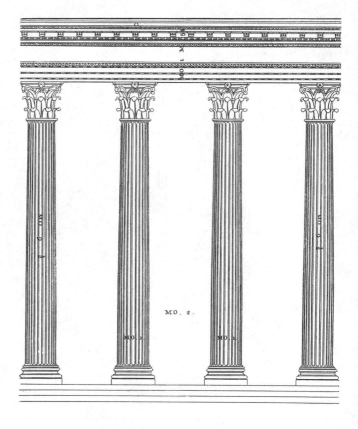

Figure 7-2
Systyle columnar interval: Palladio.

two (fig. 7-2), eustyle is two and a quarter (fig. 7-3), diastyle is three (fig. 7-4), and aereostyle is much more (fig. 7-5), so much that wooden beams rather than stone architraves must be used to span the columns. Of the five intervals the median (eustyle) is the ideal for (Greek) temples, but the diastyle is acceptable (especially for Roman). As we learn later in his treatise, the aereostyle is really only for functional contexts, such as the enclosure of a forum or the courtyard of a house (V.i.2, VI.iii.7). Each of the standard intercolumniations calls for a different proportion of columnar thickness to height, with shaft girth increasing along with the width of the interval. This system of specifications implies that constructed temples employed the full gamut of categories, but in practice the median types dominated.

Regarding symmetry, Vitruvius's prescriptions for the temple as a whole are less complicated. Those rules that are relevant to the orders concern the determination of the number of modules in a temple front (from which the sides can be calculated). The number of modules adopted varies according to the number of columns—four, six, eight, etc.—and the desired intercolumniation. The length of the module is determined by the thickness of the column shaft, which would govern thereby all the eurythmic proportions. Hence in a Doric facade, for instance, the column shaft thickness may be two modules, and all the other dimensions are determined according to a specified multiple or fraction of the module (IV.iii.4–7). The important matter is that nothing about the dimensions of a temple composition is arbitrary; all the dimensions are interrelated. A graceful composition is dependent upon the achievement of that integrated relationship.

Simpler but more pervasive in influence are the prescriptions for the proportions of architectural spaces. Vitruvius addressed this matter primarily to interior spaces, with concern for the relationship of width to length and

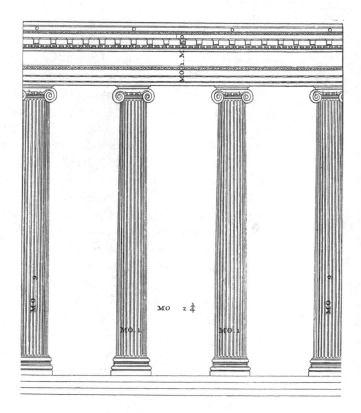

Figure 7-3
Eustyle columnar interval: Palladio.

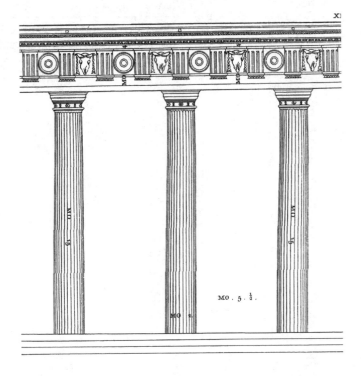

 MO . 5 . ½ . MO . 5 . ¾ .

Figure 7-4
Diastyle columnar interval: Palladio.

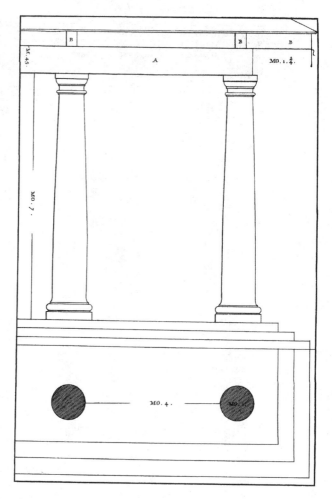

Figure 7-5
Aereostyle columnar interval: Palladio.

also to height. In aisled buildings, such as basilicas, the formula is more complex, because the width of the subsidiary spaces is usually related to the height of the columns supporting the high vessel (V.i.2–3). His most thorough specifications, though, were for the private villa (VI.iii.3–9). Widths and lengths were for the most part specified in whole numbers—such as three to five or two to three. Occasionally he employed geometric derivatives, such as the ratio of one side to the diagonal of its square. Heights, on the other hand, are often specified as arithmetic derivatives of other dimensions. In the case of a dining room—to cite a much imitated example—the length should be twice the width, and the height one half the total of those two dimensions. Such specifications assumed considerable importance when, in later centuries, Vitruvius was held to be the preeminent authority. In that connection also, his prescription of a ratio for the width to length of a forum became an important consideration in determining the proportions of exterior spaces, such as civic squares.

PROPORTION IN THE RENAISSANCE

Alberti took over from Vitruvius the principle that proportion is essential to the beauty of architecture. Indeed, substituting the word beauty for symmetry in Vitruvius's definition of the latter term, he intensified the principle by making proportion identical with beauty. His reverence for number and proportion as the underlying order of the universe was so great that he might have subscribed to the orders expressly because they were ordained with proportions. Consequently, he willingly accepted the Vitruvian notion of a fixed internal proportional system of the orders, although his own experience measuring Roman architecture led him to doubt Vitruvius's formula. Nevertheless, like Vitruvius, he did not justify his system to the reader, so it, too, ends up seeming arbitrary. As regards Alberti's orders, the matter of proportion is left as a complexity that simply has to be dealt with following prescribed formulas.

As regards the proportions of spaces, however, Alberti subscribed to a more systematic understanding of the derivation of proportion than his ancient Roman predecessor. Whereas Vitruvius simply assigned whole-number formulas to certain types of spaces, such as an urban forum or a domestic "Egyptian hall," Alberti acknowledged three different modes of derivation, based on ratios inherent in musical intervals, in geometry, and in arithmetic means. Regardless of which one an architect might adopt, proportion was to be a concern not just for the orders but for all dimensions of a building.

Ultimately all three modes were derived from Vitruvius, but under Alberti they were developed far beyond his explanations and applied in ways Vitruvius almost certainly never contemplated. For instance, Vitruvius wrote knowledgeably about the proportions of musical intervals in the context of acoustics, but he never attached them to architectural dimensions. In his discussion of the amphitheater he described a system of bronze sounding vessels arranged in niches between the seats, which, he held, were traditionally supplied to enhance the acoustical properties of the seating area. How they were to be installed he did not report—to the everlasting consternation of his readers—but in the course of this exposition he did set out, without any attribution of significance, the system of whole-number ratios assigned to the harmonious musical intervals. Whether or not Alberti felt compelled to make positive use of this material only because it appeared in Vitruvius's text, he recognized its parallel source in the doctrines of the Pythagoreans and decided to make something of it. The reason this association mattered is that the observance of proportion in architecture could then be related to the laws of nature, with the implication that harmonious proportions in architecture partake of the harmony of the universe.

This interpretation rests upon the ancient discovery that the strings of a musical instrument produce different tones according to their varying lengths. Correspondingly, the strings producing tones separated by a harmonious interval will have lengths measuring in mathematical proportion to each other. For instance, the interval known as a fifth will be produced by strings whose respective lengths have the proportion of 3:2, because the string sounding the deeper tone will be half again as long as that producing the higher. This phenomenon gains significance from the coincidence that all the other harmonious intervals are also produced by strings whose lengths make whole-number proportions.

Alberti did not elaborate on the broader meaning of this correspondence, but, in the context of a Renaissance culture eager to Christianize the wisdom and learning of antiquity, the existence of a universal relationship between musical tones and numbers was profoundly moving. It was taken to imply that the whole universe is suffused with a rational order based on number, the consequence of which is that numbers are the unseen reality behind all appearances. The extent to which one discerns those numbers is the extent to which one perceives the hand of the Creator in the natural world. Hence to design a building with a system of numerical proportions is to endow it with the aura of divinity. Because the classical orders accompany this understanding of proportion, it is not difficult to see that classicizing architecture was taken to be more expressive of the sacred than any other. The Renaissance predilection for architecture based on the orders, then, was probably prompted less by a taste for columns than a reverent respect for the proportions they embodied.

The proportions of the musical intervals can be applied, according to Alberti (Book IX, chapters 5 and 6), to the dimensions of widths and lengths, for instance those of a temple platform or a city square. Besides the interval of the fifth, with its 3:2 proportion, there is the fourth, 4:3, the octave, 2:1, the twelfth, 3:1, and the fifteenth, 4:1. These ratios can be manipulated beyond the most straightforward adoption of musical intervals. A striking instance is the double fifth, in which the lesser number represents, as usual, the width, but the greater number, which is normally half more than the lesser, is increased by half its own quantity to establish the length. That is, beginning with a ratio of 4:6, the 6 is increased by half its quantity to produce 9, resulting in a proportion of 4:9. That this is, famously, the governing proportion adopted for the Parthenon Alberti probably could not have known.

The arithmetic ratios of these musical intervals are just one of the ways of determining proportions from quantities inherent in the natural world. Another resides in the fixed relationships of geometric figures, employing the proportional dimensions of their sides and often of their diagonals as well. In this system the dimensions are frequently not discoverable in terms of simple numbers, but instead must be derived from the proportional relationships of the parts of the figures expressed in roots and powers. These relationships involve finding the area of a face of a geometric solid, multiplying the length by the width; and the cubic power, multiplying the area by the height. The proportions to be derived from such a relationship are not, however, straightforward adoptions of dimensions based on the side, the area, and the cube. Rather, they consist of the original dimension of the side and the respective diagonals of the area and the cube, both expressed as square root quantities. This is one way of arriving at three dimensions that are geometrically proportional, adaptable to the three dimensions of a room. In such a case the width of the room is the smallest quantity, the side; the length is the greatest, the cube root; and the height is the intermediate quantity, the square root of the area.

A more convenient method for arriving at three proportional dimensions is to employ one of the three ways to determine means. The simplest is the arithmetic mean: add the quantities of two proportional dimensions and divide the sum in half to arrive at the third dimension. Most subtle is the geometric: multiply the quantities of two proportional dimensions and take the square root of the product. More laborious to determine but also more elegant is the musical mean, which is twice as far from the greater of two proportional dimensions as it is from the lesser. This mean is found by subtracting the lesser quantity from the greater, then dividing the remainder by the sum of the smallest proportional numbers contained in each of the two quantities and adding the quotient to the lesser quantity. All three types of means, Alberti averred, have produced excellent proportions in architecture.

The matter of proportion in architecture cannot be treated without considering its relevance to human proportions. Alberti took this relationship from Vitruvius as the determinant for the traditional proportions of columns in the three orders: 1:7 for Doric, 1:8 for Ionic, and 1:9 for Corinthian. These were arrived at through a series of arithmetic means, using two human dimensions in proportion to the height of the full male figure as the extremes. The lesser ratio, 1:6, was discovered by comparing the thickness of a man to his height; the greater, 1:10, by comparing the distance between the navel and kidneys to height. The Ionic is the mean between the two extremes, the Doric between the Ionic and the lower ratio, and the Corinthian between the Ionic and the greater ratio. This relationship between columnar proportions and proportions of human beings underlines the association of the use of proportions in architecture with the unassailable standard of nature. Nature provides both the authority and the justification for this concern of architectural design.

Alberti thus bequeathed to theorists of the mature Renaissance two different sets of proportional standards, the ratios representing the musical intervals and the width-to-height proportions prescribed for the columns of the orders. Ratios were to be applied to the various rooms set out in a plan and also the principal facade. Palladio did not discuss the theory of these ratios but directly demonstrated how he employed them by inscribing dimensions on his plans of villas. Although he varied the ratios from one plan to another, he had certain favorites. As Rudolf Wittkower observed (1962, 131–135), the dimensions of 12, 16, 18, 20, 24, and 30 show up frequently on his plans and are used in various combinations—for instance 18 × 30, or 12 × 20, for a ratio of 3:5, representing the musical interval of a major sixth. A simpler example, 12 × 24, for a ratio of 1:2, represents an octave; a more complex one, 16 × 27, read as 16:24:27, represents a fifth (2:3) plus a whole tone (8:9). The ideal use of proportion would also include a third dimension for the height, itself related in harmonic ratios to the length and width. However, it is not always possible to determine whether or not it was achieved, because Palladio often does not specify that dimension in the *Quattro libri*. Whether or not the proportions in Palladio's work represent a conscious association with musical intervals cannot be proved because only certain of his designs reveal such a correspondence. As Branko Mitrović has shown (1990), whereas some of Palladio's proportions can be related to harmonic ratios, he evidently employed some other methods of determining proportions as well, but none consistently enough to ascribe cultural associations to them.

Following Alberti's concern for the different proportions of the three main orders, Palladio applied the Vitruvian standard of graded intercolumniations respectively to the five orders. Hence the pycnostyle was assigned to the composite (fig. 7-1), the systyle to the Corinthian (fig. 7-2), the eustyle to the Ionic (fig. 7-3), the diastyle to the Doric (fig. 7-4), and the aereostyle to the Tuscan (fig. 7-5). Correspondingly, the piers of arches to which the applied orders can be attached must also vary in their proportions from one order to the next, relative to those assigned to the column. Even the pedestals for each order were given correspondingly different proportions. As an academic exercise it increased the systematic character of each individual order, but the assignment of these respective intercolumniations to the five orders can scarcely have been adopted as a firm rule of practice.

The discrepancies between the proportions prescribed by Vitruvius and those empirically observed in Roman architecture by all the Renaissance theorists was a continuing cause for consternation. They wondered if there really had been a fixed Roman proportional system. Concerned to reconcile the discrepancy, they did not deny that proportions were of the essence, but they sought a consistent basis for determining them. Alberti, Serlio, Vignola, and Palladio all set out independently to establish a clear and definite system, based on the Vitruvian module of half the thickness of the column shaft. Each of them faced the necessity of assigning fractions of a module to the various components of the base and the capital, as well as to those of the entablature. Vignola sought to demonstrate "a definite correspondence and continuous proportion of figures," like that in musical theory (Wittkower 1962, 123). But for as long as theorists adhered to the notion that the proportions of the orders were based on proportions of the human body, there was no apparent way to escape a system employing fractions of modules.

The Gordian knot was cut by Claude Perrault, in *Ordonnance des cinq espèces de colonnes* (Paris, 1683), when he disavowed any transcendent or symbolic association with proportions in the orders and dealt with them as purely numerical values. Shifting to a module based on one-third of the width of the column shaft, he was able to assign whole numbers to the parts of the orders. Proportion retained its value as an indispensable desideratum, but the use of abstract number—arbitrarily adopted—made proportions simpler to apply.

For as long as the classical orders were the basis for architectural design, the use of rational proportion was one of the architect's key obligations. However, after 1800, when the Greek peripteral temple had been replaced as the ideal by the Gothic cathedral, the cultic adherence to the convention of proportions came to an end.

Principles (Theory from 1800 to 1965)

Expression in terms of conceptual principles rather than of regulatory conventions is the distinction that divides architectural theory of the modern era from all that went before. The readiness to formulate theory differently was marked by the shift of ideal type from the classical temple to the Gothic cathedral, a shift that was less about form than about method. Whereas the temple imposed rules, the cathedral inspired concepts. The differences in response may have had to do with the fact that the classical temple had been passed down with the written regulations of Vitruvius, while the cathedral was accompanied by no such textual authority. The modern understanding of Gothic architecture, then, was made up of ideas projected upon it by external observers, ideas that belonged to the rationalism of the nineteenth century rather than to the scholasticism of the Middle Ages.

The observers saw it as an architecture formed in a spirit of problem solving rather than of adherence to tradition. The complex spatial composition of the Gothic cathedral was interpreted as a synthetic accommodation of multiple functions. A logical role in the stability of the building was imputed to every element of its structural assembly. The use of materials was regarded as having achieved an optimal level of economy. Some observers even assigned a practical purpose to each decorative feature. And theorists called for a modern architecture generated according to these principles. These Gothic-inspired concerns for planning spatial configuration, forming structure, using materials, and devising decoration came to comprise the core of the theory of designing according to principles.

Meanwhile, issues other then just the design and construction of individual buildings came into play. For the first time in Western civilization, an awareness of the desirability of preserving the legacy of architecture from a glorious past posed the urgency of adopting some guiding principles for restoration. These were developed in the course of the effort to preserve the Gothic cathedrals. At the same time the rapid growth of cities from the mid-eighteenth century brought home the need to think aesthetically about the design of cities. The requisite principles were initially drawn from observations of medieval and Renaissance precedents.

Until the modern era, writers of architectural theory assumed no responsibility for providing a methodical procedure for the creation of a design. For the orders, yes, but not for the building as a whole. A strategy to achieve rational designs was set out by Jean-Nicolas-Louis Durand, in his *Précis des leçons,* which began to appear in 1802. Although the steps of his procedure were couched in terms of formal development, Durand's method assumed that the process was driven by the requirements of a functional program, even though—compared to later theory—his notion of such a program was confined to the macro level. Accordingly, the simplicity or complexity of the program would determine whether the building would be contained by a single mass or would include dependencies in the form of wings or attached pavilions. It would also determine whether the masses of the composition would be open or closed, accessible to the public or sequestered behind walls; and whether the dependencies would all be alike (if all had the same function) or would be differentiated (if they had various functions). If such a complex is to have multiple functions, which are to be dominant and which subordinate? How are they to be differentiated in size and in location within the complex? Having worked out such a scheme, the designer must then test it by justifying every aspect of it with regard to the program and its formal requirements. However, practical matters such as site characteristics, structural means, and choice of materials—all factors of serious concern to Durand—did not have an integral place in his method of design development.

At least as important as Durand's strategy for working out a design was his method of laying it out on paper (fig. 8-1). The process must always begin with the plan, never with the elevation. The elevation must grow out of the plan, but its regularity is safeguarded by the requirement that the plan be simple, clear, and symmetrical. In neither the plan nor the elevation should anything be included that does not contribute to the usefulness or meaning of the building. To lay out the plan he began with a grid, which established from the outset a modular system. He specified that walls were to be laid out on the grid lines and columns were to be centered over their intersections. If columns play a prominent role, the width of their intercolumniations could determine the dimensions of the grid module. These simple restrictions automatically discipline the configuration of the design with a degree of regularity and increase the likelihood of achieving pleasing proportions.

The urge to impose rational simplicity and regularity of this sort was consistent with the earlier imposition by the regime of Napoleon Bonaparte of uniform weights and measures in the form of the metric system. It expressed a perceived need in architecture for an alliance of art with practicality, at least in regard to function if not to the process of construction itself. This method could be applied equally to the classical tradition or to any of the other historical styles. Given Durand's outlook of cultural inclusiveness, demonstrated earlier in his *Recueil et parallèle des édifices de tout genre* (Paris, 1800), design devices from all periods and cultures were fair game for appropriation. His main concern in that respect was that the artistic expres-

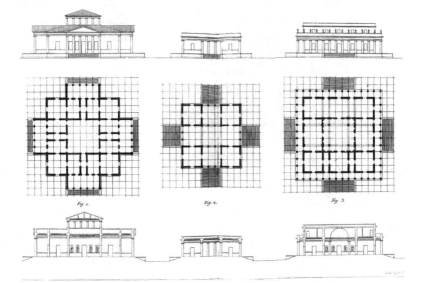

Figure 8-1
Design generated in plan and projected into the elevation and section: Durand (*Précis des leçons,* Paris, 1817).

siveness of a building be consistent with its function and the sociological hierarchy of building types. To the extent that it provided an orderly procedure, Durand's design method was broadly useful, especially at a time when changes in society were fostering a proliferation of building types. Accordingly, it was incorporated into French academic tradition, where it remained into the twentieth century.

VIOLLET-LE-DUC AND RATIONAL DESIGN METHOD

Viollet-le-Duc, with his penchant for rational analysis, was the first to articulate a comprehensive theory of design method. This method owes much to Durand and the subsequent development of Durand's system within the École des Beaux-Arts, an institution that Viollet-le-Duc loved to revile. Nevertheless, it was Viollet-le-Duc who put the method together in a coherent and attractive way, and in great detail. Indeed, his is very nearly the only such theory, for none has displaced it, and it remains largely intact even in current practice. To be sure, it has been adjusted and altered, and most practitioners who employ it in their daily work are unaware of its origin, but it remains one of Viollet-le-Duc's most important contributions to the theory of architecture. Set out in *Histoire d'une maison* (1873), his step-by-step method for developing a design provides the intellectual basis for organizing and activating the theoretical principles that he and others after him have enunciated.

The first premise of this design method is that the architect's scheme for a building is not just the free play of his own fancy but a response to the patron's needs. In other words, the design must be governed by the functional program, which, by and large, must be articulated in detail by the patron or agents of the patron. The program, through the imposition of limits, challenges the architect's imagination and channels the creative impulses. The second given factor is normally the choice of a site. Together, the program and the site make the patron a partner in the creation of the building. As architects acknowledge, the participation of an inspired patron inspires the designer. It is only after the patron's contribution has been made that the design method comes into play.

Engagement of the architect usually comes as the result of a fruitful discussion of the program, but it is unlikely that this initial step can be taken without an examination of the site as well. At that point it is up to the architect to make a thorough analysis of the site, most likely with the consultation of technical experts. A soils test must be made to determine the extent to which the site can support the proposed building(s). The factors involved include a determination of which parts of the site are so-called virgin soil—that is, never before disturbed—and which parts are so-called made ground—filled in or built up by human efforts; and of the kind of soil, such as clay or sand, and the location and depth of bedrock, because these factors delimit the weight and height of a feasible structure on the site. Closely related is the factor of drainage and whether or not it must be artificially contrived. Except on a standard urban site, the availability of fresh water and provision for waste drainage must also be considered. Within a city, especially, the architect must be aware of legal restrictions placed on building activity by the community. These include zoning for building types, height of construction, proximity to the street front, and density of occupancy.

Then, and only then, can the architect begin to study the site for optimal location and orientation of the new building. Factors impinging upon this decision are views from the site, the direction of light and prevailing winds, the direction of approach to the site, and the most feasible location of service areas and service access routes. After all these practical matters have been considered, it is possible to start thinking about artistic composition of the building or complex of buildings and exploitation of the site's natural features. Often the study of the site will have provided enough inspiration or limiting factors that the design is already beginning to take shape in the architect's mind.

Development of the plan (fig. 8-2) begins with a careful review of the program. The space for whatever activity can be regarded as most important must be located and desirably oriented on the site. The other activities associated with the program follow in hierarchical order. Those most closely related to the primary activity will be located adjacent to its space. Those housing honorific functions will be in prominent locations; those housing service functions will

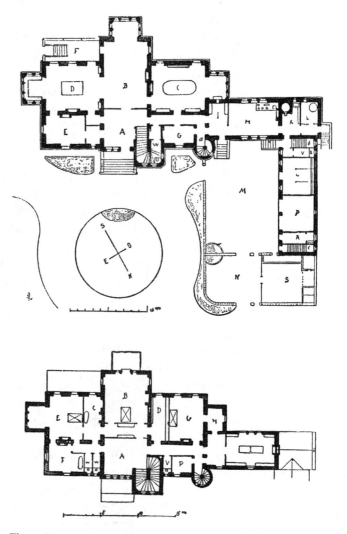

Figure 8-2
Hypothetical plan of a rationally designed house, ground floor
and first floor: Viollet-le-Duc (*How to Build a House*).

be in more obscure places. Functions of a very different nature will need to be separated from this group of spaces, but with clear and logical means of access. In other words, the plan begins as a series of adjacencies, which may be adjusted according to exterior exposure to views and light. Then it is clarified as a composition of definite shapes. A plausible scale must be imposed, with dimensions corresponding to feasible sizes and proportions to serve the various functions. Dimensions must take into consideration the thickness of walls and any other structural features. Circulation and access spaces must be introduced into the scheme before the composition can be adopted as a working plan. Entrances, interconnecting doors, and fenestration must be incorporated before the plan is complete.

Beginning with the plan means that the design is generated from the inside out and in terms of functions rather than of formal arrangements. Given this procedure, geometric regularity in overall shape or bilateral symmetry in the disposition of spaces are unlikely results, except when there must be frequent duplication of functions within the total scheme. The other aspects of the design, notably the structural framework and the elevations, are determined by and subordinate to the plan.

The second step in the design method is to devise a way to cover the plan with a roof (fig. 8-3). To do so presupposes the provision of adequate structural support, but it underlines the priority of the covering as the determinant of the structural framework. Viollet-le-Duc recommended making a section as a vertical projection of the plan. This representation would show the heights of the respective stories of the building, the number of which would also be a key factor in devising an appropriate structural framework. In conjunction with the plan, the section would also help the architect to visualize the covering of the spaces.

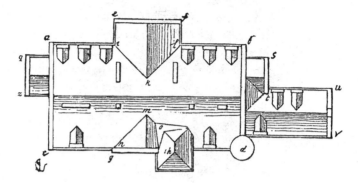

Figure 8-3
Roof scheme for a rationally designed house: Viollet-le-Duc (*How to Build a House*).

Given the marked differences between various types of structure available to modern architects—such as wooden balloon frame, load-bearing masonry, and steel cage frame—the scope and budget of the project will likely have predetermined the basic materials and the structural type they imply. For instance, it makes a great deal of difference whether the project is a private house or a multilevel commercial building. So in reality, devising the structural framework is largely a matter of determining specific details of an already prescribed structural type. For instance, the roof of a house with lots of projections may require a number of geometrically integrated pitches, carefully calculated to make all the valleys of the roof slope to exterior corners. Such a covering will dictate where supports are needed, thereby automatically configuring most of the structure. However, in a larger building, which frequently will have a more cohesive overall shape, the support for the roof is likelier to be determined by spatial spans.

Designing the elevations (figs. 8-4, 8-5) comes third in this method. Even though they constitute the most conspicuous—hence important—elements of the building seen by

Figure 8-4
Front elevation for a rationally designed house: Viollet-le-Duc
(*How to Build a House*).

Figure 8-5
Rear elevation for a rationally designed house: Viollet-le-Duc
(*How to Build a House*).

a passerby, they are meant to evolve from a combination of the plan and roof-supporting structure, even when they are load bearing. The openings are to be determined by the needs of the interior and not by any kind of pattern imposed for the sake of consistency on the exterior. The size, the location, and the shape of each window should conform only to functional convenience. Similarly, the entrances should be located where they best fit the plan, without deference to central axes. Viollet-le-Duc asserted that the asymmetry and variation in elevations that results from strict adherence to functional requirements will read as rational design and, as such, will be preferable to irrational formal consistency.

The way the elevations are designed will have virtually everything to do with the materials and structural type already adopted. In a metal-frame building, for instance, the elevation design may properly result from the articulation introduced by the supporting columns. However, on a masonry building with load-bearing walls, elevation articulation is more a matter of aesthetic preference than rational expression of structure. In that regard, Viollet-le-Duc warned that because nonstructural articulation with pilasters and half-columns does not express structure, it should be avoided as irrelevant to the needs of the building.

Decoration is appropriate to architecture, but it should emanate from the handling of the structure and not be tacked on as an afterthought. In many cases, an efficient solution to a structural problem can be incorporated in a decorative manner. For instance, the pieces composing a metal girder can be assembled in a pattern that is decorative as well as structurally efficient. The principle of inherence is reflected elsewhere in such examples as the patterns of the brick and terra-cotta cladding of Louis Sullivan's skyscrapers and the geometric patterns cast into concrete support piers of Frank Lloyd Wright's buildings. This principle of decoration promotes integration of all the ornamental treatments of a building, hence an appreciation for total design.

Ultimately, a design method prescribing an orderly series of steps was to give architects the means for creating architecture free of regulations from the past. It empowered them with the liberty implicit in a theory based on principles rather than conventions, and it served as the basis for generating the international movement comprehended under the names of Art Nouveau and then modernism. It made possible the synthesis of engineering and art that Viollet-le-Duc had advocated.

METAPHOR AS THE SPUR TO DESIGN IMAGINATION

If rational design method could free architects from both the regulations and the inhibiting models of the past, it could not arm them with a fresh artistic vision. Viollet-le-Duc was the first to admit that, although he had been permitted through his theory to gaze into the promised land of a new architecture, he could not go there himself; his imagination failed him. Even so, it was he who identified the means by which the journey could and, in time, would reach the goal, namely the liberating agency of metaphor. To think of anything in terms of something else has been the chief means by which humankind has entered into uncharted realms of imagination. But it was Viollet-le-Duc, in the *Discourses*, who recognized its value for architectural design. He named three such metaphors—the machine, the organism, and the crystal—one from human culture and two from nature, one organic and one inorganic.

The metaphor of the machine, of course, reflected his admiration for the creations of engineering and his concern for directness in the approach to design. Because machines, especially the steamship and the locomotive, had no precedents and therefore no models to emulate, they represented examples of unadulterated problem solving. Because they were designed to perform a particular function and nothing else, there was nothing either unnecessary or superfluous in their makeup. The form of each part was directly related to that of the next and to the whole. As technological creations, they also represented the present and the future, escaping any opprobrium that could be attached to the past. This metaphor is readily compatible with the use of manufactured materials.

The metaphor of the organism represented a generalized version of the appeal anciently made to the human form as an absolute standard of excellence for architectural design. Viollet-le-Duc did not limit the metaphor to the human form, however, and used quite other examples in his writings (see *Learning to Draw*). As a product of nature, the structural composition of an organism could not be faulted. Like the machine, its parts were shaped to fulfill a particular function; it had nothing extraneous and lacked nothing that was needed. (This is untrue, of course, but there is no evidence that Viollet-le-Duc was acquainted with the work of Darwin, in which he could have learned that not every organism has evolved with an ideal combination of features.) Even more than in the machine, the parts of an organism are joined together in such a way as to seem inextricably related and inevitable in their formulation. Indeed, in a manner superior to the machine, the composition is integrated in such a way that it is hard to say exactly where one part ends and the next starts. This metaphor suggests drawing upon the qualities of natural materials.

The crystal represents the quality of abstract structure in nature in a way that other forms of natural architecture—notably the anthill, the honeycomb, the bird nest, and the beaver lodge—do not. It is useful as a spur to the imagination because of the geometric structure its form suggests rather than the solid mass it actually embodies and also because of its translucency or transparency. The facets of its form imply polyhedral or domical structures markedly different from any examples provided by historical architecture. The crystal, then, is more valuable as a suggestive image than as a model for structural makeup. Its inorganic nature calls to mind the inorganic building materials that are industrially manufactured from natural resources, the ones most appropriate to realize its form.

The value of the metaphor as a tool for innovative design was much enhanced by the examples put forward by the polemical tract writers of the early twentieth century. Antonio Sant'Elia's futuristic images of buildings for his *Città nuova,* exhibited in Milan in 1914 in conjunction with the publication of his *Futurist Manifesto,* showed how the metaphor of the machine could produce a totally unprecedented image for high-rise towers and train terminals (fig. 3-10). Their streamlined formats did not so much display a mechanistic structure as imply that beneath such a sleek case there could only be machinelike inner works. Along the same lines, Paul Scheerbart's *Glasarchitektur,* also of 1914, promoted the concept of a crystal house representing transparent construction in general. Implicit in the novelty of seeing through a building was the potential of an entirely unprecedented geometry for its structural framework. And Frank Lloyd Wright's essays, "In the Cause of Architecture," of 1908, promoted the organic metaphor. These examples of architectural images inspired by metaphors launched a different sort of ideal from the temple and the cathedral. Imposing no formal prescriptions, they did establish a generalized approach to design that proved to be inspirational to successive generations of twentieth-century architects.

The plan became the generator of architectural design when the image of the classical ideal fell from grace as design instigator. The principles of plan formulation were developed as strategies for arriving at a design, which varied as successive theorists approached the task from different starting points. To recognize that the philosophical issue involved was a matter of developing design principles as opposed to employing design patterns required the clear thinking of a Viollet-le-Duc, whose rational outlook led him to define the formulation of a design as an act of problem-solving.

Theoretical concern for the generation of plans in the modern era, extending from the middle of the nineteenth century through the first third of the twentieth, focused on the designing of private dwellings. That this should have been the case was due in part to the rise of democracy and, with it, the importance of the private individual. Concomitant with that phenomenon was the increased technological sophistication of ordinary domestic existence and a considerable increase in general prosperity. Hence in the modern era the development of the private household has achieved unprecedented importance within society in general.

ANDREW JACKSON DOWNING AND THE
SOCIOLOGICALLY CONCEIVED PLAN

In *The Architecture of Country Houses* (1850) Downing introduced the concept of domesticity to architectural theory. He addressed three classes of houses—cottage, farmhouse, and villa—for an economic range of hypothetical patrons reaching from the most modest tradesman to the affluent landowner or professional, but not above the level of moderate wealth (figs. 9-1, 9-2, 9-3, 9-4, 9-5). Three main concerns dominated his discussion of a number of specific designs representing all three categories: appropriateness to the economic level and geographical situation, the commodity of the arrangement of rooms, and the efficacy of the materials and construction methods. He was acutely aware of the house as a building type, cautioning that the design should look and feel like a house and not some other kind of building. He also stressed that a house should give scope to domestic expression imposed upon the structure by the occupants, such as vines cultivated over a bay window or entrance arbor. It should be a place that enhances the lives of its occupants and causes them to regard it lovingly. His design method was based on a systematic provision of appropriate features for the given sociological circumstance.

For instance, Downing stipulated that at the lower end of the economic scale people do not need either a parlor or a separate room for dining. Impromptu guests simply join the family at table in the room where the food is prepared. As people achieve prosperity they need both a parlor and a dining room, separate from the kitchen, where guests can be received with greater ceremony. In a more detailed example, the house on a prosperous farm should show an intimate relation to the soil, expressing ampleness, solidity,

Fig. 5

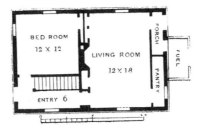

PRINCIPAL FLOOR

Figure 9-1
Small cottage design: Downing.

Fig. 37

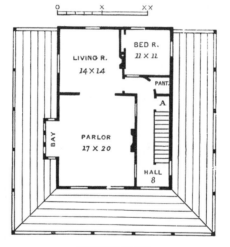

PRINCIPAL FLOOR

Figure 9-2
Larger cottage design: Downing.

Fig. 70

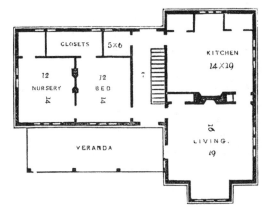

Figure 9-3
Farmhouse design: Downing.

Figure 9-4
Elevation of a suburban villa: Downing.

and comfort—a simple domestic feeling rather than elegance and grace. In keeping with the landscape, it should be more spread out than tall; indeed, tall interior spaces are aesthetically unsuitable to this kind of house. Chimneys should show prominently enough on the exterior to denote warm-hearted hospitality; the fireplace within should be expansive. A few large windows give more breadth and simplicity to the exterior than a number of small and narrow ones. Earth colors are to be encouraged, whereas white should be avoided altogether both inside and out. Interior wood should receive a natural finish of stain and oil, no paint. Ventilation is as important as good heating, and windows might well be double casement rather than sliding sash. (In the aggregate, the desiderata for this example are so similar to those enunciated a few decades later by Frank Lloyd Wright that it is difficult to imagine that he did not absorb them as a teenager in some Wisconsin library before

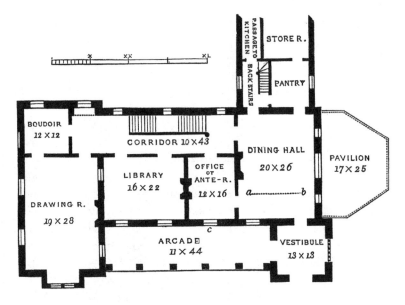

Figure 9-5
Plan of a suburban villa: Downing.

they were promulgated as his own.) Finally, for the suburban villa (figs. 9-4, 9-5), there is the presumption of carriages to bring family or guests to the porte cochere and of a genteel lifestyle, supported by servants, inside the house, which includes rooms for cultural pastimes.

VIOLLET-LE-DUC AND THE RATIONAL CONCEPTION OF A HOUSE

Viollet-le-Duc's greatest contribution to plan design was the conscious recognition that a plan should be generated from a program of functional requirements. This program necessarily begins with a list of the functions the prospective new building is expected to house, together with an understanding of how they are to be interrelated. It must also include practical and aesthetic desiderata, in order to provide healthful, safe, and pleasant accommodation for those functions. This understanding of the basis for planning was, to him, the great lesson to be learned from ancient Roman architecture, which he articulated in the *Entretiens sur l'architecture*. The way to get from the program to the plan and then to the total design was the rational method he had set out in *Histoire d'une maison*.

According to Viollet-le-Duc, a house plan must begin with the parlor, the space for the activity of central importance. Activities of secondary importance, such as dining, must then be either adjacent or nearby. Spaces for other secondary or tertiary activities may need to be arranged next to them, as dependencies, and so on. Intervening circulation space may separate some of these spaces from others, depending upon the nature of their relationships. Although he did not name this formulation, it is an organic approach to plan development. It encourages a refinement of the arrangement until all the functions conveniently relate to one another and to the whole, like the parts of a human body. It does not foster a bilaterally symmetric result, and indeed Viollet-le-Duc insisted that a symmetrical result should not be sought. Rather, he maintained, a rational, organically generated plan not only makes visual sense but is also far more likely to be beautiful than a plan stuffed into a preconceived box. Moreover, its window openings should be placed exactly where they are needed from the inside and should vary in size according to the needs of the interior. The variations, he asserted, will make sense on the outside in relation to the asymmetry of the plan and massing.

In the *Entretiens sur l'architecture,* a scheme for a hypothetical urban mansion presented a refined idea of zoning activities within the plan (fig. 9-6). The imaginary household for which the city house was designed included

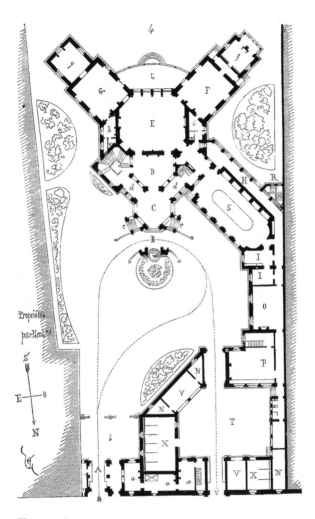

Figure 9-6
Functionally zoned plan: hypothetical mansion, by Viollet-le-Duc
(*Discourses*).

a great many functions, and the house accommodated not only the resident family but also a large staff of servants and a number of guests. Varying needs were to be met by segregating service areas from family areas, hospitality areas from the private ones, and in all cases quiet activities from the noisy. The residential portion of the household was placed at the back of the property, as far from the street as possible, and the courtyard was closed off from the street by extending the service area across the front. This zoning motive fostered the composition of the plan as a series of wings jutting out from a central reception core. Such an arrangement in turn facilitated provision of maximum exposure to light and air for all the residential rooms. The result was an uninhibited asymmetry of massing and a lively variety of window types and placements (fig. 9-7). Although the design had no particular visual distinction, the verbal explanation made it seem revolutionary to younger architects, and it exerted considerable influence upon the development of modern architecture.

The theories of domestic architecture enunciated by Downing and Viollet-le-Duc provided a foundation for the disparate conceptions of modern residential architecture devised by Wright and Le Corbusier. Their respective formulations of the organic house and the machine house have, in various permutations and combinations, provided the conceptual basis for most modern modes of residential design. Those formal strains that have countered modernity with "traditional" styles may equally be said to grow out of Downing's pioneering theory.

FRANK LLOYD WRIGHT AND THE ORGANIC PLAN

Frank Lloyd Wright was the most direct borrower from Viollet-le-Duc, a debt he graciously acknowledged on sev-

Figure 9-7
Asymmetrical, plan-generated elevation: hypothetical mansion, by Viollet-le-Duc (*Discourses*).

eral occasions. He also made the most of his loans. He frequently discussed the principles of his plan making, notably in a series of articles, "In the Cause of Architecture," published in *Architectural Record* in 1908 and 1927. A strong advocate of the organically conceived design, Wright sought to endow both the flow of the space and the composition of the structure with an organic character. He prided himself on the absence of complete separation between rooms, by which he really meant the hospitality rooms—entry, living, dining, and library, if any—although he had been far from the first to adopt that practice. Wright also sought another kind of unity, both stylistic and physical, by making as much of the furniture as possible integral with the building, therefore an aspect of the plan.

More distinctive as an aspect of organic planning was Wright's concern for the way buildings fit into their natural setting. The house should appear to belong to its site, in harmony with the land. Roofs should slope gently, with broad overhangs, and proportions should be low, emphasizing horizontal lines. Terraces and out-reaching walls should enclose private outdoor areas. He famously related houses to the topography of the site—Taliesin (1911) on the brow rather than the crown of its hill, La Miniatura (1924) standing in rather than avoiding its ravine, Fallingwater (1936) over rather than beside its waterfall—delighting in the challenge that difficult terrain posed for the resolution of the plan.

Inspired by the Zen Buddhist goal of the oneness of human beings with nature, an aspiration expressed in the Japanese architecture he so warmly appreciated, Wright was sensitive to the interrelationship of interior and exterior. He accomplished this in several ways, the most novel of which was to regard windows as transparent portions of walls rather than as holes cut into walls. He also opened rows of French doors onto terraces, themselves partitioned from the exterior world by unbroken balustrades, thereby making ambiguous the boundary between inside and outside. Upstairs rooms had terraces extending over a ground floor roof or even cantilevered as balconies. Windows wrapped around corners, sometimes with glass meeting glass. The more he designed, the more inventive he became in the interweaving of interior and exterior.

In laying out a plan, Wright employed various kinds of grids at different times in his life. During the early, Oak Park, period, he used a so-called tartan grid, with repeating patterns of diverse intervals (see Sergeant 1976). This method permitted the placement of features on grid lines and intersections while maintaining a rhythmic variation of modules. Later, in his Usonian period, he typically used square or rectangular grids (fig. 9-8). He was probably the first to experiment seriously with nonrectangular grids,

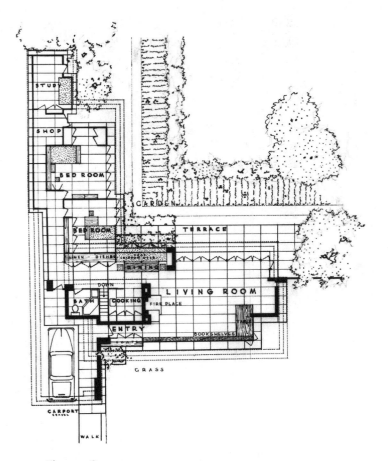

Figure 9-8
Rectangular grid plan, first Herbert Jacobs House: Wright (The
drawings of Frank Lloyd Wright are Copyright 2002 The Frank
Lloyd Wright Foundation, Scottsdale, AZ).

employing both hexagons (fig. 9-9) and parallelograms as plan units. The value of these shapes is that their forms consist of equilateral triangles, which leave no awkward intervals between grid units. Also, the hexagon could be justified as a grid taken from nature, as in the units of a honeycomb.

Working without a grid, Wright employed nonrectangular forms for basic structural shapes, beginning early in his career with octagons (an American fixture through much of the nineteenth century) and then venturing into circles and spirals. From his point of view, this geometric variation simply demonstrated the flexibility of organic conception. On the other hand, he challenged the organic principle by creating schemes in which the spaces housing the main functions are structurally segregated from those housing secondary functions—a distinction later characterized by Louis Kahn as a separation of "served" and "servant" spaces.

In later years, as Wright perceived that live-in servants could no longer be taken for granted in middle-class households, he refined many of his ideas to correspond to a more informal lifestyle (figs. 9-8, 9-9). These were discussed in several of his books but in none more completely than in *The Natural House,* of 1954. From the 1930s the kitchen became a "workspace" for all sorts of family activities. Although he had formerly shunned the task of fitting it out for use, he devised the unitized kitchen of appliances and cabinets, often with a clerestory at the top of the room, made taller than the rest of the house so as to discharge cooking odors. A hobby room for one or more members of the family might be included, as well as an integral shed—the carport—for the family automobile(s). Built-in furniture was expanded to include cabinets and shelves in hallways and the family dining table, attached at one end to a wall. Basements, banished at the outset, were replaced by platform

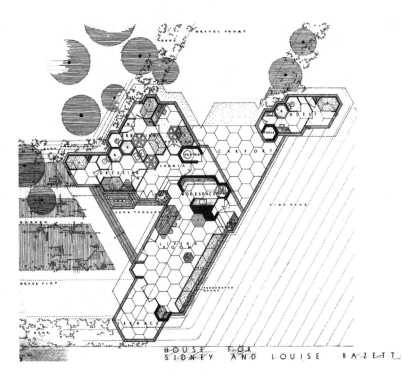

Figure 9-9
Hexagonal grid plan, Sidney Bazett House: Wright (The drawings of Frank Lloyd Wright are Copyright 2002 The Frank Lloyd Wright Foundation, Scottsdale, AZ).

slabs of poured concrete which contained the heating coils. Together, these features denoted a rejection of European formalities and the embrace of an informal, democratic lifestyle. It had been, after all, Wright's deliberate purpose to devise an architecture that is distinctly American. All this added up to what he regarded as a program for organically conceived dwellings suitable for self-confident, democratic individualists. Indeed, each house, he maintained, should be designed to reflect the individuality of the owner.

Le Corbusier proclaimed in *Vers une architecture* that "the plan is the generator." That is, the plan is the idea of the building, from which all the rest is to be developed, including the elevations and the overall mass of the building. The plan, he averred, has the capacity to reshape a lifestyle, which was exactly the social and political result Le Corbusier had hoped for in the formation of a modern architecture. As he put it, formulation of the plan must proceed from within to without, taking shape in the way an organism grows, but functioning in the manner of a machine. Its evolution from initial thought to construction-ready plan is a task in logical problem solving.

Viewing its planning process as one not unlike that for engineering, Le Corbusier characterized a house as a "machine for living in" (figs. 9-10, 9-11, 9-12, 9-13). For him the modern house needed to function like a machine, efficiently and without extraneous parts. That is not to say it should look like a machine, although he was often interpreted as having said so. Rather, he was advocating the suppression of decorative clutter and unnecessary furnishings and possessions. Emulating the efficiency of a machine, the house needs everything necessary for healthful personal maintenance and private cultivation, but nothing materially extraneous. Like Wright, he made bedrooms small, discouraging unproductive indolence. He tried to minimize furniture, encouraging built-ins where possible, especially for storage purposes. At the same time he tried to provide a tall (i.e., two-story) space in part of the living area, a free-flowing scheme for the public spaces, and a private outdoor area, typically on the roof.

Because the plan of a house is so intimately involved with the quality of life, its development is more than a

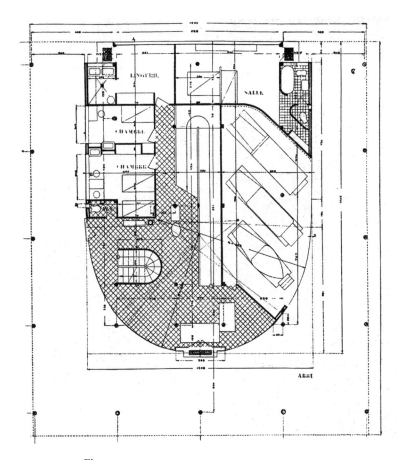

Figure 9-10
"Machine style" plan: ground floor, Villa Savoye, by Le Corbusier
(*Oeuvre complète*) (© 2002 Artists Rights Society (ARS), New
York/ADAGP, Paris/FLC).

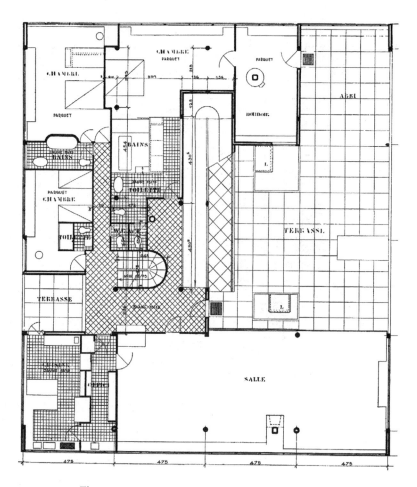

Figure 9-11
"Machine style" plan: first floor, Villa Savoye, by Le Corbusier (*Oeuvre complète*) (© 2002 Artists Rights Society (ARS), New York/ADAGP, Paris/FLC).

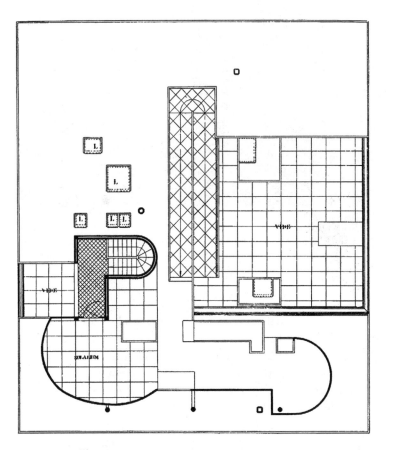

Figure 9-12
"Machine style" plan: roof garden, Villa Savoye, by Le Corbusier
(*Oeuvre complète*) (© 2002 Artists Rights Society (ARS), New
York/ADAGP, Paris FLC).

GENERATIVE PLANNING AS THE BASIS OF DESIGN

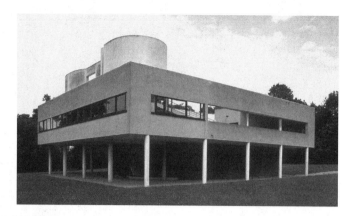

Figure 9-13
"Machine style" exterior: Villa Savoye, by Le Corbusier (*Oeuvre complète*) (© Anthony Scibilia/Art Resource, NY; with permission of © 2002 Artists Rights Society (ARS), New York/ADAGP, Paris/FLC).

material matter; it also raises the moral issues of honesty, authenticity, and integrity. Le Corbusier was aiming at an austere, rational lifestyle that rejected luxuriant excesses imputed to the bourgeoisie of the preceding era. His conception implied a world view that was more socialist than democratic, for the implementation of which he always imagined an unspecified but controlling central authority.

If Le Corbusier conceived of the house in terms of its various functions, the generation of its design required the imposition of formal discipline in the application of proportion. His concern for proportion was manifested in two different theoretical settings. The first was *Vers une architecture,* where it appeared under the rubric of "regulating lines." To demonstrate its application, he imposed various geometric figures, the lines of which cross the center or intersect the corners of prominent features, upon drawings and photographs of famous facades (fig. 9-14). The point was to demonstrate that in an excellent architectural design

Figure 9-14
Le Corbusier's "regulating lines" superimposed on a photograph of the Palazzo Senatorio on the Capitol, Rome (*Vers une architecture*) (© 2002 Artists Rights Society (ARS), New York/ ADAGP, Paris/FLC).

the important incidents follow the discipline of an inherent geometry. Ostensibly the geometric correspondences are meant to indicate that a subtle proportional system was embodied in each of the designs. But he never explained how an architect would or could have arrived at a new design using this method. Nor did he explain the rationale for placing the geometric figures where they happen to fall on the designs: because he imposed them after the fact, he was free to manipulate the figures until he got the desired result. Whether or not such a method could be employed to create designs has, to my knowledge, never been demonstrated either in his work or in that of a follower.

Le Corbusier's second method of employing proportions was gradually developed between the 1920s and the 1940s. It appeared in the guise of a human-figure referent, 1.75 meters tall. This figure, dubbed the Modulor, had one hand raised high above the head to indicate a normal ceiling height. Le Corbusier demonstrated its application in an eponymous treatise (Paris, 1948) and issued another volume of the same name, recording responses by architects who had used it, in 1955. His abstract Modulor figure was subdivided by an obscure set of ratios, based on a mathematical series of increasing quantities (fig. 9-15). These ratios were meant to be transferable to all parts of a building design in order to endow it with a harmony akin to that of classical temples. Whether he employed the ratios while working out a design or applied them only after the fact to refine or justify it, they represented a tool of composition that was somewhat arbitrary in nature. The Modulor was difficult for others to incorporate into their own designs because its ratios did not correspond to standard whole-number measures in either feet or meters. Moreover, it also did not conform to ready-made materials, although Le Corbusier had hoped manufacturers would adopt it as their new standard. Its chief value, then, was less for general applicability than as a reassertion in architectural theory in the modern era of the age-old concern for proportions, particularly for a standard based on the human body. On the part of Le Corbusier it was primarily a gesture of concern for achieving in modern architecture the kind of rationally determined harmony that had distinguished the great architecture of the past.

However well intentioned this effort, the cause of proportions was impeded by the adoption in the late 1940s of standard measurements for mass-produced materials in the United States. In consequence, except for the most privileged of commissions, for which the components could be

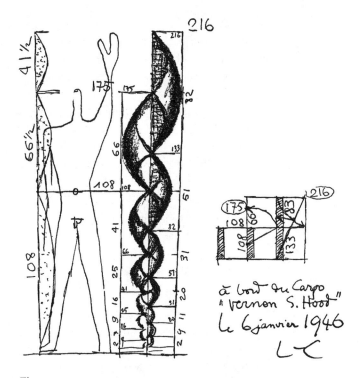

Figure 9-15
Le Corbusier's Modulor figure, representing his system of proportions (*Oeuvre complète*) (© 2002 Artists Rights Society (ARS), New York/ADAGP, Paris/FLC).

custom-made, the use of proportions was reduced to rote application of standard modules. Hence the imposition of subtler ratios on the part of the architect became impractical and the calculation of proportions, for all intents and purposes, passed out of the range of theoretical aspirations, especially for the purposes of generating a plan.

Inherent in all modernist theories of planning is the assumption that a building readily communicates its plan to the user. Even from the exterior the layout of the building should be evident, indicating to a certain extent the nature and variety of activities contained inside. The place of entry outside and the route of circulation inside should be amply manifest. The location of certain kinds of general-access facilities, such as the main auditorium or meeting room of a public building, the reception or information area, and the restrooms, should be apparent without the necessity of inquiry. The distinction between restricted and unrestricted areas should also be clear. And appropriate signage should guide users in locating more specialized facilities. Predictability and clarity are presupposed as qualities of the layout. Simplicity is a virtue. Durand would recognize them all and have been gratified at the durability of his design method.

PLANNING IN TERMS OF SPACE

Modernism in the Netherlands and Germany fostered the notion that architecture is first and foremost about space. Although this concept was already active in Bramante's plan for St. Peter's and was implicitly the subject of Serlio's Book V (fig. 9-16, 9-17), it had not remained an issue in architectural theory. Its reemergence occurred in the writings of Gottfried Semper, who, in *Der Stil* (II, 394), asserted that the Roman exploitation of space in masonry architecture compared to that of the Greeks was like a symphony compared to a solo hymnist accompanied by a lyre. The conception of architecture as space developed, he thought, out of the technique of working in masonry, which fostered first the arch and then, in turn, the vault. The idea was picked up and developed more fully by August Schmarsow, in *Das Wesen der architektonischen Schöpfung* (Leipzig, 1894; see English translation in Mallgrave and Ikonomou 1993, 125–146; also Mallgrave 1996, 289–290). From him it was assimilated and employed by Hendrik

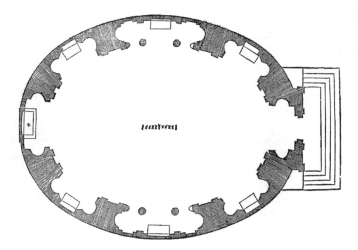

Figure 9-16
Plan of a spatially conceived oval church: Serlio.

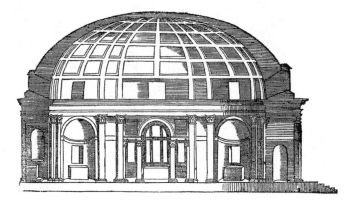

Figure 9-17
Section of a spatially conceived oval church: Serlio.

GENERATIVE PLANNING AS THE BASIS OF DESIGN

Berlage in Amsterdam, who influenced the first generation of modernists in Berlin. Gropius regarded himself as planning in terms of space, and the concept later became associated with the Bauhaus through him. A more particular version of the idea was fostered by Ludwig Mies van der Rohe.

Mies wrote no treatise, but his architectural designs were so widely published in both professional journals and books on the modern movement that virtually anything he said became common currency. Promoting the notion that interior space should be structurally divided only when the needs of stability require it, he advanced the doctrine of unified or "universal" space, in which the occupant is free to erect movable dividers to suit temporary needs. The chief advantage was that such an approach to planning allowed him to pursue the more pressing goal of creating a minimalist architecture. Although he applied the concept mainly to undifferentiated pavilions—an architecture school (fig. 9-18), an art museum, a weekend house—it was readily adaptable to the rented floors of commercial skyscrapers constructed with steel or concrete cage frames.

After World War II, the theoretical principle of spatial planning was rearranged somewhat by the movement known as the new brutalism. Propagandized by critic-historian Reyner Banham in an article announcing the movement in the *Architectural Review* of 1955 and a monograph of 1958, this new wave swelled out of, and in sympathetic response to, the postwar work of Le Corbusier. But as regards plans, the point was to give every function in the program a distinctive space and to flaunt every spatial variation of the interior in the exterior mass (fig. 9-19). As Banham observed, the aesthetic cultivated aformalism, in which topology dominated geometry and explicitness of connectivity was stressed, with no attempt to confer regularity upon the total scheme. It celebrated awkwardness

Figure 9-18
"Universal space": Crown Hall, Illinois Institute of Technology, by Mies (FH).

of composition and embraced what in traditional terms would be deemed ugliness, all in the name of a higher, sterner beauty. Nurtured at the politically radical Architectural Association in London, brutalism meant to reject the traditional standards of beauty associated with the former, elitist establishment. Then, after being patronized by a series of leftist governments, brutalism acquired its own elite status for a time throughout much of the Western world.

In America, the servant/served dichotomy fostered by Louis Kahn belonged to a similar theoretical context. Kahn made a sharp distinction between working spaces and those needed for circulation and technical support. This was famously manifested in his Richards Biological Sciences Laboratory in Philadelphia, in the mid-1960s (fig. 9-20). Another approach to spatial generation of a plan was the neomodern practice of allowing one factor, as the point of

Figure 9-19
"Distinction-of-functions" plan: Leicester University Engineering
Laboratory, by Stirling and Gowan (FH).

Figure 9-20
Distinction of "servant" and "served" spaces: Richards Biological
Sciences Laboratory, University of Pennsylvania, Philadelphia, by
Kahn (Malcolm Smith, for the Louis I. Kahn Collection, Univer-
sity of Pennsylvania and Pennsylvania Historical and Museum
Collection).

Figure 9-21
Plan generated from a single factor: East Wing, National Gallery,
Washington, D.C., by Pei (courtesy Kai Gutschow).

departure, to control the development of the entire scheme.
A notable example was I. M. Pei's process for designing the
East Wing of the National Gallery in Washington, D.C., in
the mid-1970s (fig. 9-21). Pei began by tracing a maximal
footprint for the building, which assumed the same configuration as the site, an irregular trapezoid. Then, in order to
provide accommodation for two distinct institutions on the
site, he subdivided the trapezoid diagonally into two unequal triangles. He then provided for subsidiary functions
by geometrically subdividing the triangles until all the program requirements had been fulfilled. The composition of
the project, then, was primarily determined by an abstract
spatial subdivision of the building site and only secondarily
by a rational arrangement of the functional provisions.

Laugier's call for a return to the structural use of the orders, in the middle of the eighteenth century, came at a time when their decorative application had been so ingrained that his meaning could be made clear only by appealing to the structural schema of Gothic cathedrals as a formal paradigm. By doing this he promoted rational expression in architectural design as an aesthetic concern, not just a better means of construction. So, likewise, did Pugin when he systematically analyzed every feature of Gothic structure, lauded for its aesthetic as well as its pragmatic virtues, as the paragon of rational formulation. It remained for Ruskin, however, to transform structural formulation into a principle of architectural design by obligating it to the expression of honesty.

RUSKIN

Ruskin deemed a building excellent only if it conveyed to the user/viewer a forthright statement of how it was put together. It did not have to display every aspect of structure necessary to assure stability, but it could not appear to be constructed in one way and actually be assembled in another. The essential point was that structure should never dissemble and only conditionally conceal, as in the case of rafters and purlins in a loft, the presence of which can be taken for granted under the sloping planes of a pitched roof. Hence the Gothic cathedral, clearly revealing how it was assembled, was a paradigm of architectural virtue. The impact of this message was to create a sense of moral obligation among architects to make structure explicit and manifest. No particular structural scheme was described and no specific type was recommended. Indeed, from the outset, such theoretical considerations of structure were couched only in terms of principle, so there was never a design imperative regarding structural composition.

VIOLLET-LE-DUC

For Viollet-le-Duc rationality was a more congenial precept than honesty for conceptualizing structure in a design. Moreover, he was willing to go further than Ruskin in staking the excellence of architecture upon the way its structure is handled. He thought that, like a machine, it should have no part that is not necessary for stability and function. He also thought that each element should be joined to the next and to the whole in a manner analogous to the composition of an organic body. Although all structural elements might not be seen, their presence can and should be implicit. In most cases, though, structure ought to be fully evident, both visible and clear in its assembly. It should, moreover, be devised in such a way that it incorporates no more members, and those of no greater size, than are necessary to accomplish the task at hand. (Thereby he introduced the principle of economy of means.) Adhering to those strictures, the rationale of its composition should be amply evident.

Other than the Gothic cathedral, one of Viollet-le-Duc's ideal structural examples was the bamboo domestic architecture of southeast Asia, discussed in *The Habitations of Man in All Ages* (Paris, 1875). It featured numerous short lengths of bamboo fitted together to make a light but strong skeletal structure, which enclosed a broad, tall space and several subsidiary rooms (fig. 10-1). The structure was roofed with a framework of bamboo, thickly covered with matted grass. It took its form

Figure 10-1
Rational design, Asian bamboo house: Viollet-le-Duc (*Habitations of Man*).

HONEST STRUCTURE AS THE FRAMEWORK OF DESIGN

from the properties of the constituent materials, which were obtained from the immediate surroundings. This house, like the Gothic cathedral, met his criteria of economy of means, logic of composition, and explicitness of facture. No rationally conceived structural member—he cited the flying buttress—could be considered unsightly when its appropriateness to the design has been made clearly manifest.

Viollet-le-Duc maintained that while a rationally designed structure may not necessarily be beautiful, no building can be beautiful that does not have a rationally designed structure. Indeed, the pithy dictum "form follows function," which Louis Sullivan later famously employed to express Viollet-le-Duc's theory, signified this sort of structural configuration. The wide currency of this dictum in the twentieth century testifies to the pervasiveness of Viollet-le-Duc's concept in the context of modern architecture.

The hypothetical schemes devised for the *Entretiens* illustrate Viollet-le-Duc's proposals for rational, modern structure. Among them is a scheme for a series of domical vaults covering a great hall, translating a heavy medieval masonry vault into a much lighter modern construction consisting of an iron framework filled in with something like terra-cotta tiles (fig. 10-2). The main point was to create a structural skeleton that could flexibly respond to movements in the building caused by winds or shifting earth. But the most important lesson of this scheme resides in the iron diagonal struts (fig. 10-3), composed of several different pieces—a ball-joint corbel, the strut itself, an "elbow" to effect the shift from diagonal to vertical, and a capital at the top. These pieces differentiate the structural tasks of the strut assembly like the members of an organic body and they are even fitted together in a manner analogous to those of an organism.

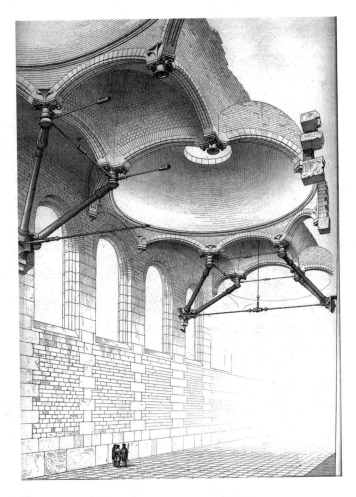

Figure 10-2
Economy of means, iron framework vault, hypothetical great hall:
Viollet-le-Duc (*Discourses*).

HONEST STRUCTURE AS THE FRAMEWORK OF DESIGN

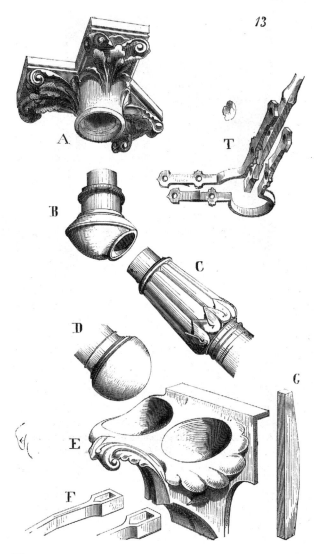

Figure 10-3
Organically conceived structural detail, hypothetical great hall:
Viollet-le-Duc (*Discourses*).

An even more famous example is a scheme for an assembly hall that would hold three thousand people, constructed so as to impose no interior supports that would block sight lines (fig. 10-4). This structure consists of an iron polyhedron, filled in with lightweight masonry webbing and set upon a perimeter of load-bearing masonry walls. In its overall form the domical skeleton reflects the geometry of a crystal and may have been inspired by that metaphor. Like the first hall, this one has diagonal struts to help support the vault, but here the main point is to create a structurally efficient cover over a vast interior. In this instance the efficiency of a metal structural skeleton is a more explicit issue. Perhaps for that reason this example had more important repercussions. Namely, after exposure to this structural concept, Frederick Baumann, a German-born engineer in Chicago, conceived the idea for a multi-story building with a steel frame and non-load-bearing masonry curtain walls on the exterior. He recognized that a framework of this sort could provide the rigidity such a structure would need to withstand Chicago's heavy winds. Published in a pamphlet, *Improvement in the Construction of Tall Buildings* (Chicago, 1884), this idea was taken up by William Le Baron Jenney in his design for the first skyscraper, the Home Insurance Office Building, in Chicago, of the same year (see Turak 1985).

One other hypothetical structure suggested in the *Entretiens* is an iron truss composed of numerous small pieces (fig. 10-5). Viollet-le-Duc proposed it as a substitute for a much heavier box girder, because a truss made in such a fashion is equally strong and is both lighter and better looking. The principle itself was not his and had already been employed in bridges for a century, but he was proposing for use in polite architecture a feature invented in an engineering context and employed earlier mostly in industrial circumstances. His design blatantly allowed the rivets to

Figure 10-4
Iron frame construction, hypothetical assembly hall for three thousand: Viollet-le-Duc (*Discourses*).

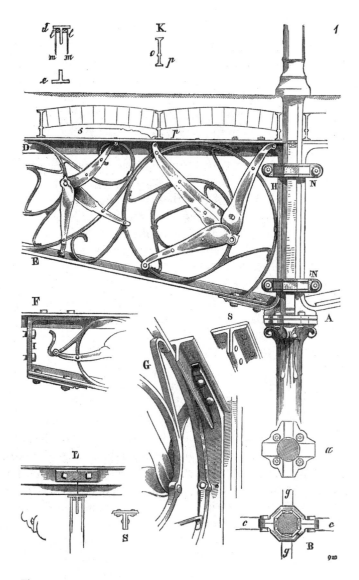

Figure 10-5
Iron truss with decoration incorporated: Viollet-le-Duc (*Discourses*).

HONEST STRUCTURE AS THE FRAMEWORK OF DESIGN

show, asserting the principle that it is acceptable, even desirable, to make the means of structural assembly visible. The implications of using undisguised iron and, indeed, of frankly revealing structural means were absorbed almost at once by the young architects who initiated the Art Nouveau movement.

The theoretical influence of Viollet-le-Duc was at once pervasive and diffuse, inextricably mixed with ideas that had emanated from activities outside the normal scope of architecture, such as engineering and the decorative arts. In the aggregate these ideas did coalesce around his principles, but through generation after generation in the twentieth century they acquired new directions and emphases. A striking example of a nineteenth-century elaboration that became a theoretical line unto itself is the theory of the skyscraper, the one fundamentally new building type of the modern age. The greatest early contributor to that body of theory was the first great master of skyscraper design, Louis Sullivan.

THE SKYSCRAPER: SULLIVAN AND WRIGHT

As Sullivan succinctly put it, the practical realization of the skyscraper depended in the first place on the need for business offices. It also required the mechanical means of getting up and down in the building in an elevator and the development of steel manufacture that made possible the necessary rigid frame. The economic justification presupposed sufficient growth in populations to produce large cities and, with those concentrations of people, a commensurate rise in property valuations. The viability of skyscrapers for high-density occupancy in those circumstances increased the valuations further, and thus the real estate development continued to escalate, in symbiotic fashion.

That left the problem of finding a suitable artistic form for the new type.

The skyscraper frame—a skeletal cage of steel—was necessarily the first component of this new building type to be conceived. The theory of the frame depended primarily upon Viollet-le-Duc's postulation of a structurally efficient skeletal framework, capable of withstanding distortion due to shifting ground and wind loading. Mistakenly perceived in the skeletal structure of the Gothic cathedral, that quality was correctly imputed to skeletal structures of iron (and steel). From that point it was a matter of engineers making the correct calculations. The composition of the exterior elevation, however, posed an aesthetic problem that took longer to solve. It was through a coincidence of talent and circumstance that Louis Sullivan was able to give artistic form to this new type and, moreover, to articulate the theory of the artistic formulation. Published in volume 57 of *Lippincott's Magazine,* 1896, his essay "The Tall Office Building Artistically Considered" became the point of departure for subsequent skyscraper design.

The practical conditions posed by a skyscraper require a basement story to hold the machinery for heating, lighting, and occupant circulation. The ground floor necessarily contains the common entrance, but it is also the natural location for businesses, such as banks, that require large openings and unencumbered spaces. The second floor, easily reached by a broad staircase, will have a similar function with somewhat diminished spatial demands. Above that will be an indefinite number of identical stories devoted to offices. Finally, at the top will be an attic story containing water tanks and other machinery, for which there will be no particular demands either for light source or for spatial division. Such an arrangement automatically creates a three-part composition with a bottom, an intermediate zone, and a top.

Because the typical floors of such a building are unvarying repetitions of the standard office unit, Sullivan indicated, the spatial arrangement of a skyscraper only rarely takes on an aesthetic value. The principal concern in its artistic design, then, is the external elevation. Sullivan started with the individual office as the standard structural unit. Its glazed opening can be almost as wide as the office, excepting only the width of the vertical column at the spatial division. The glazing, of course, requires subdivision with mullions and sashes, the pattern of which can serve as the basic unit for the design, both horizontally and vertically. The ground floor needs a special treatment, with greater height and with bigger windows, and, as the street-level exterior, it also needs richer decoration than the other parts, including a grand portal. The second floor should be of like character although with less lavish decoration. The attic floor has no exterior obligation other than to emphasize the termination of the building. The whole should have a conceptual formulation that expresses emotion.

As Sullivan put it in "The Tall Office Building Artistically Considered":

The chief characteristic of the tall office building . . . [is that] it is lofty. This loftiness is to the artist-nature its thrilling aspect. It is the very open organ-tone in its appeal. It must be in turn the dominant chord of his expression of it, the true excitant of his imagination. It must be tall, every inch of it tall. The force and power of altitude must be in it, the glory and pride of exaltation must be in it. It must be every inch a proud and soaring thing, rising in sheer exultation that from bottom to top it is a unit without a single dissenting line—that it is the new, the unexpected, the eloquent peroration of most bald, most sinister, most forbidding conditions.

It is the pervading law of all things organic, and inorganic, of all things physical and metaphysical, of all things human and all things superhuman, of all true manifestations of the head, of the heart, of the soul, that the life is recognizable in its expression, that form ever follows function. . . . Is it really then, a very marvelous thing, or is it rather so commonplace . . . that we cannot perceive that the shape, form, and outward expression . . . of the tall office building should in the very nature of things follow the functions of the building, and that where the function does not change, the form is not to change?

Sullivan's tripartite composition—analogous, as he acknowledged elsewhere, to the base, shaft, and capital of a classical column—was fundamentally a straightforward arrangement of the various functions to be carried out in the building. But it simultaneously expressed through the vertical office shaft the true nature of the building as a tower. His solution to the problem cut through the difficulties the first designers of skyscrapers had experienced, in which they somehow felt compelled to break up the vertical rise every three or four stories, thereby failing to achieve a coherent format. Instead, he had the vertical columns rise continuously from the base to the cornice, overlapping—and thereby interrupting—the horizontal floor platforms, so as to give distinct dominance to the vertical articulation (fig. 10-6). This composition gives both clarity and simplicity to the building. The alternative, that a tall building can be articulated as a stack of horizontal layers, has also been a successful formulation, but with a much more limited currency. A few designs have managed to combine both of these emphases, usually with stacks of layers at the corners and a vertically articulated shaft in the center of each elevation, but whatever the variations, they begin with or react to Sullivan's formulation.

The most strikingly original alternative to Sullivan's skyscraper scheme was that devised by his most famous and closest protege, Frank Lloyd Wright. Widely published in volumes of Wright's work and tersely explained in his *Autobiography*, this alternative was the rigid-core high-rise

Figure 10-6
Space-cage frame: Guaranty Building, Buffalo, by Adler and Sullivan (courtesy Kai Gutschow).

building with cantilevered floors and suspended curtain walls. Wright justified this format on functional grounds as earthquake-proof. Whether inspired by unimpeachable nature with the example of the tree, as he claimed, or by older architecture in the framework of the Japanese pagoda, as circumstantial evidence indicates, Wright developed this concept in two different versions in the 1920s (see Hearn 1991). The earlier, an unrealized project for the National Life Insurance Company, of 1924, consisted of a tall slab intersected by four subordinate slabs. The later, unrealized project for the St. Mark's-in-the-Bowery apartment towers, of 1929, clustered three slender towers around a church. Two single-tower versions were finally built, the 1949 Johnson's Wax research tower in Racine, Wisconsin (fig. 10-7), and the 1956 Price Tower in Bartlesville, Oklahoma. A more daring rendition, in the unrealized project for a mile-high skyscraper for Chicago, was proposed in 1956.

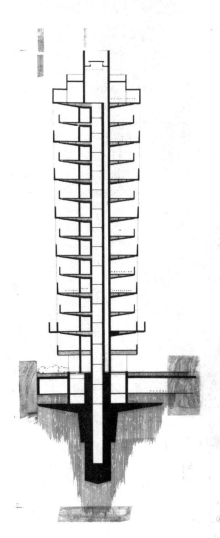

Figure 10-7
Rigid-core frame with cantilevered floors: section, Johnson's Wax Tower, Racine, Wisconsin, by Wright (The drawings of Frank Lloyd Wright are Copyright 2002 the Frank Lloyd Wright Foundation, Scottsdale, AZ).

Beginning in the 1960s, several variations on the steel-cage frame have been developed, primarily for the purpose of making a more efficient structure relative to the quantitative weight of the steel employed. For the John Hancock Center in Chicago, of 1968, the firm of Skidmore, Owings & Merrill designed a rigid external frame with diagonal bracing (fig. 10-8). Then, for the Sears Tower of 1974, also in Chicago, SOM designed a rigid external structure (based on a concept by Fazlur Khan), characterized as a self-reinforcing cluster of nine square tubes, three by three, terminating at different heights (fig. 10-9). And in 1986, for the Bank of China in Hong Kong, I. M. Pei created a rigid frame triangulated in all three dimensions (fig. 10-10). All three of these structural formulations represent conceptual alternatives to the space cage of the first generation of skyscrapers, namely, a more efficient frame to withstand enormous wind loading. These options entered the realm of theory through widely disseminated professional publications.

THE HOUSE (AND BEYOND): WRIGHT, LE CORBUSIER, AND OTHERS

The house has played as central a role in the theoretical conception of structure as in that of the plan in modern architecture, but not to the same degree with the same theorists. Although Downing had defined the house as an important building type in the modern age, he employed only conventional structure. Wright, on the other hand, was as consistent in applying his theoretical principles to the structure of houses as he was to their plans. Having been reared on and near farms, he was particularly attuned to Viollet-le-Duc's injunction to look to nature—particularly to the composition of organisms—for architectural

Figure 10-8
Diagonally braced external frame: John Hancock Center, Chicago, by Skidmore, Owings & Merrill (FH).

Figure 10-9
Tube-cluster external frame: Sears Tower, Chicago, by Skidmore,
Owings & Merrill (FH).

Figure 10-10
Triangulated frame: Bank of China, Hong Kong, by Pei (FH).

HONEST STRUCTURE AS THE FRAMEWORK OF DESIGN

inspiration. Accordingly, Wright based his entire theory of architecture, famously centered on the term "organic," on analogues with nature. As regards structure, Wright unwaveringly served the principle of imitating organic construction, emphasized in his theoretical writings and especially in the essays in *Architectural Record*. Aspiring to a simplicity that transcends fussiness and undue complication, he resisted the structural reductionism embraced by many of his European contemporaries. His notion of organic structure, articulated most memorably in the *Autobiography*, was that each part should be joined to the next in a seamless continuum, not revealing the end of the one and the beginning of the other, as each serves its particular function in the whole.

An examination of any building complex enough to have received his full attention will bear out this intent. Although it is possible to identify the main load-bearing elements of these buildings as distinct from others, the quality of visual continuity always dominates (fig. 10-11). He was particularly prone to applying decorative trim in such a way as to effect this continuity, a practice that would help to explain why he did not see decor as something distinct from structure (fig. 10-12). The realization of the organic principle, which he initially worked out in designs for houses, was then applied to other building types as well. This is fully evident in the mature works of his early period, masterpieces such as the Larkin Building, Unity Temple, and the Robie House. Later, as the organic conception of his structures was more daringly synthesized, for instance in Fallingwater, the Johnson's Wax Administration Building, and the Guggenheim Museum, the application of decorative motifs markedly diminished.

Among modernists, it was Le Corbusier who most radically revised the conception of structure, and that develop-

Figure 10-11
Organic continuity of form: Robie House, Chicago, by Wright (FH).

Figure 10-12
Integration of structure and decor: Unity Temple, Chicago, by Wright (FH).

ment took place in the context of rethinking the house. Having returned to his native Switzerland before the outbreak of World War I—from his peripatetic life of work in Vienna, Paris, and Berlin and travels in central and eastern Europe, Turkey, Greece, and Italy—Le Corbusier set about developing a novel approach to the construction of houses. In the course of doing so he devised a theoretical model that he called the Dom-ino House (fig. 10-13). He had observed that a traditional house is subdivided into a series of boxlike rooms, owing as much to the structural limitations imposed by load-bearing walls as to the spatial conventions imposed by the isolation of discrete functions. So he set out to develop a structural system that would impose minimal restriction and permit maximal freedom.

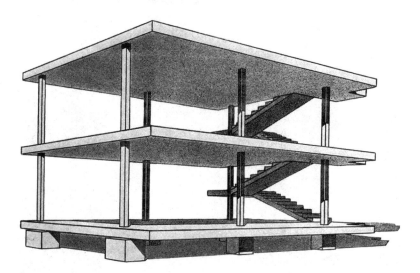

Figure 10-13
Dom-ino structural scheme, by Le Corbusier (© 2002 Artists Rights Society (ARS), New York/ADAGP, Paris/FLC).

The prototype he invented was a system of columns and platforms, which, he assumed, would most likely be fabricated with steel-reinforced concrete. The columns and beams could be engineered to a satisfactory combination of slenderness and breadth of span, both qualities important for the sake of minimizing spatial interruption. Regularly spaced, the columns need not be at the perimeter because they could support a certain amount of cantilevered platform. On any given floor this structure would permit maximal freedom for unifying or dividing space, even facilitating the use of movable partitions. Because no load-bearing walls would be required, the perimeter of the building could be sheathed with a curtain wall, opaque or transparent according to preference or need. Moreover, the structural system would allow the perimeter to assume any shape, either geometric or free form. Assuming a building scaled as a private house, stairs from one floor to the next could be located anywhere they might be desired. The structural system would permit the house to be raised above ground, as if on stilts, to allow free passage underneath. Equally, it would permit functional use of the roof as a garden because the roof, structurally secure as a flat slab, would no longer need to be pitched. Whatever treatment might be desired, the structure could accommodate it and at the same time be minimally intrusive.

In the Villa Savoye of 1929–1931, Le Corbusier let the framework play hide-and-seek with the nonsupporting members (figs. 9-10, 9-11, 9-12). In this house, probably the most famous of the century, the pilotis, the connecting beams, and the supported platform over the ground level are in plain evidence before the glass enclosure of the entry and service rooms (fig. 9-13). By contrast, at the first-floor level the entire perimeter is enclosed by curtain walls, variously treated as opaque areas, as transparent ribbon windows, and as voids open to interior terraces and the sky.

HONEST STRUCTURE AS THE FRAMEWORK OF DESIGN

The second-floor level, partially enclosed by free-form walls to make a roof garden, exercises a formal option not already employed by the other two levels. The completely different designs at the three floor levels, then, exploit to the fullest the structural freedom offered by the minimal framework. In so doing they also make apparent, or implicit, the actual structure. This is a rational, machinelike design, but at the same time one treated in a highly poetic manner.

The value of this structural system for other building types lay in its expandability, both upward and outward. It could, then, be used for skyscrapers or for long ribbon buildings, and for anything between. The most famous early application was made by Mies in two successive projects for a glass skyscraper in Berlin, 1921 and 1922, the latter with a free-form perimeter (fig. 10-14). In 1923, Mies was also the first to envision a multistory commercial building, with curtain walls of glass set back behind cantilevered balustrades on each floor. From these unrealized, but oft-published, schemes most large-scale modernist architecture is descended.

Typical of statements about structure within the modernist movement is the position articulated by Walter Gropius on behalf of the Bauhaus in Germany, which he directed. He combined the rational tenets of Viollet-le-Duc with the moral ones initially enunciated by Ruskin. The latter had been absorbed by William Morris's Arts and Crafts movement and transmitted to Germany by Hermann Muthesius in his Morris-inspired monograph *Das englische Haus,* of 1904–1905. For Gropius, as expressed in *The New Architecture and the Bauhaus* (Cambridge, MA, 1965), a structure should be light (i.e., skeletal), simple (i.e., minimal), and straightforward (i.e., explicit). Bauhaus-inspired buildings, he opined, would have considerable uniformity (e.g., flat roofs) because of the practical objectivity sustained by the adherents of this school of

Figure 10-14
Project for a glass skyscraper, 1922, by Mies (Architecture Photograph collection, courtesy The Art Institute of Chicago. All rights reserved).

thought. Moreover, because they nurtured a predilection for prefabricated elements, Bauhaus architects would foster the dominance in architecture of industrial, machine-made products.

Virtually contemporary with the theoretical development of modernist structure in Europe was the independent generation of a structural theory based on nature and technology by R. Buckminster Fuller in the United States. Educated outside the purview of the architectural profession, Fuller came to the designing of buildings in a roundabout way, his ideas about structure having gradually evolved during a series of work experiences that eventually brought him to the practice of engineering. A combination of concerns— the relationship of human life to the natural world, the maintenance of ecological balance, and the value of technology as the basis for providing for human needs—first led him to propose the Dymaxion House in 1927 (fig. 10-15). It was advanced as a prototype for an architecture composed solely of manufactured components, collected as a kit and shipped to the site ready for assembly, possibly by the occupant. Then another basic prototype, the geodesic dome, was proposed in the years following World War II. It was justified in terms of natural precedents for the use of hexagonal units, in honeycombs, and of polyhedral forms, in crystals. Both prototypes were followed by a succession of models, all published in journals and monographs. Fuller himself explained his intentions and precepts in a collection of essays, *Ideas and Integrities* (New York, 1963).

HIGH TECH AS AN EXTENSION OF MODERNIST
STRUCTURAL THEORY

Fuller's theories had only scattered influence. But they foreshadowed the regeneration of modernist structural

Figure 10-15
Mechanical construction: Dymaxion House model, by Fuller
(courtesy The Estate of R. Buckminster Fuller).

theory, which occurred in England, beginning in the
1960s, as the high tech movement. Spearheaded by Norman Foster and Richard Rogers, this movement was es-
sentially based on a refinement of the modernist principle
of honest expression of structure. In the theory of high tech
architecture, technology was not merely to shape the
means of construction but the form as well. Although heralded by no notable treatise, the theory has become well
known through the publication in professional journals

of individual buildings as they have been designed and erected.

High tech buildings are distinguished by the tendency to hinge the design on a single technological factor related either to structure or mechanical systems. Often unorthodox, usually innovative, and always visually striking, this structural factor is allowed to determine all others. In the Pompidou Center, Renzo Piano and Richard Rogers put all the vertical structure on the exterior in order to create utterly uninterrupted interiors (fig. 10-16). Such a dominance of means over ends has made structural principles the primary consideration, even though the architect may have initially invoked them in the name of serving the intended function of the building. High tech architecture, in its celebration of technology, is also designed with the resolve to make everything involved with the construction and operation of the building blatantly visible (fig. 10-17). Not only must structural members and connections be in plain view, but also the machinery of circulation, ventilation, heating, lighting, and plumbing. Hence the machinelike quality of architecture that was proclaimed by futurism near the beginning of the century, and variously promoted by modernism, was finally realized in high tech architecture.

A typical high tech building may expose both its structural frame and its support services on the exterior. The functional justification would be to leave unencumbered all the interior space. Although such an arrangement entails numerous difficulties in construction and fireproofing of steel, and many more in the operation of the building, it celebrates structure and stands as a monument to uncompromising honesty. Another favorite treatment solves the problem of creating a vast, uninterrupted space by suspending a metal frame over the interior with tension cables secured from stanchions embedded at the sides of the complex, as in Norman Foster's Renault assembly plant,

Figure 10-16
High tech structure: Pompidou Center, Paris, by Piano and Rogers (FH).

Figure 10-17
High tech structural detail: Pompidou Center, Paris, by Piano and Rogers.

Swindon, England, of the latter-1980s, where the space is composed of a series of connected umbrella forms. Paradoxically, as designs that are mostly about structure, high tech buildings hark back to the basic nature of the architecture of the orders as much as they proclaim the wonders of contemporary capability.

Building materials in the modern era assumed a significance in architectural theory that they had not possessed in the past. This change was due to the fact that a multiplicity of materials, newly available due to industrial production, both imposed and invited new ways of building. The choice of materials, then, became much more than a matter of decorum and expense; it became inextricably related to the conception of the design itself. In the theory of architectural conventions, discussion of the use of materials (usually wood, stone, bricks, and rubble and mortar, as well as the secondary stuff of buildings) had been limited mainly to their procurement and proper handling in traditional structural systems. But in the theory of principles, such lore was relegated to the realm of practice. Instead, it became necessary to consider their appropriate use with respect to the site, plan, structural system, and decor—always taking care to honor the physical properties of each substance.

RUSKIN

No theorist writing on the principles governing materials in architecture has had a greater appreciation for the inherent qualities of building matter than John Ruskin. For him the difference between the color and texture of limestone and those of granite or marble was a matter of great import, both for the appearance of a building and for its effectiveness as an element of the built environment. He could equally concern himself with the varieties of brick, for which a number of different colors and textures were available. This sensitivity made him appreciate different techniques of masonry and patterns of bricklaying, and the artistic value of combining types of stone or brick to introduce color patterns. Indeed, his absorption in the *matière* of buildings and in the capacity of materials to establish poetic atmosphere made him the grand romantic on the subject in all the literature of architectural theory.

Ruskin forcefully and memorably inaugurated this perspective on materials when he raised the issue of their honest use. In doing so he set the agenda for their principled employment for the whole modern era. First, no matter which materials are used they should never be other than the highest grade. If the client cannot afford the highest grade of the costliest materials suitable for the purpose, the best quality of a less expensive medium should be chosen. Second, no material should ever be disguised as another, most especially if the substitute is cheaper, although an exception should be allowed if the disguising material patently could not be the actual one through and through. Examples he cited are the gilding of a decorative feature, such as a carved capital, or the covering of a brick wall with plaster and fresco painting. Third, a material should never be used for structural purposes that are contrary to its inherent physical properties. For instance, stone, which has a great capacity for compression but very little for tension, makes an excellent supporting pillar but not a spanning beam. It can, however, be made to cover an appreciable distance in the form of an arch. Fourth, a structural element should not be made in a given material with a technique that has not traditionally been used for that purpose. Thus, a foliate capital that would normally be carved of stone should not be cast in iron, because it will not have the crispness produced by the chisel. Fifth, a material that has not acquired the dignity of traditional use in august architecture should be avoided. Namely, new, industrially produced materials such as cast iron should be avoided in polite circumstances. (Proscription of nontraditional materials is the one tenet of Ruskin's principles for materials that was retrograde.)

The aggregate imperative of all these principles is the doctrine of "truth to the medium." It carries with it the corollary of urging fine workmanship, whether or not the result will be in plain view. On the other hand, exquisite craftsmanship should not be wasted in a location where it cannot be clearly seen and justly appreciated. The main point is that the effectiveness of materials in the appearance of a building depends upon the quality of the workmanship. In this regard, Ruskin generally disapproved of machine production of building elements, favoring instead the minute variations introduced by the human hand. Equally, he preferred a building to be constructed from one basic material, usually traditional stone or brick, rather than mixing them according to the various roles the elements would play in the design as a whole. In this reservation he was, of course, failing to recognize that modern structural needs would soon outstrip the capacity of traditional materials to perform every requisite task.

The implications of his principles were profound, with both conservative and progressive effects. The moral associations with fine workmanship and production by hand inspired William Morris in his founding of the Arts and Crafts movement, originally intended as a progressive antidote to bad quality in industrial production. In time, however, this movement became rather precious and rarefied, even reactionary in character. Yet in the end even this conservative trend paradoxically exerted a progressive influence by encouraging total environment design, first manifested in the Art Nouveau movement and then in the Bauhaus. The motive to make everything well, with good design, had first extended to wallpaper, rugs, and furniture, but by the end of the nineteenth century it also encompassed dishes, flatware, and even the clothing of a building's inhabitants. The vein that was progressive from the outset, the one in which principled use of materials impinged upon the formulation of structure, permanently obligated architects to be on guard against infractions of design integrity. Ruskin's ideas either spread so pervasively that their source soon lost identity or their source was deemed so obvious that attribution seemed unnecessary, but they lived on without acknowledgment in the writings of virtually every theorist of the modern era.

VIOLLET-LE-DUC

Viollet-le-Duc is almost certainly one of the theorists indebted to Ruskin. Although he couched his theory under the blanket of rationalism, his principles regarding materials overlap those that Ruskin subsumed under morality. He held that materials should not appear to have been worked in a manner different from the way they actually were. He cited as an instance the scoring of a single piece of stone, set as lintel, to look instead as if it is made up of the separate voussoirs of a straight arch. He urged that as nearly as possible materials should be made ready for construction at their place of production, to avoid bringing an excess to the building site, costly in the first instance to transport in and costly again to take away as waste. Radically progressive in outlook, he welcomed, even fostered, the availability of new materials that could perform a structural task better than a traditional one. He also advocated the posing of structural problems that would challenge manufacturers to produce new materials or new formats for existing materials.

A very strong reason for accepting new materials to perform various structural tasks was that their inherent virtues could be exploited to make the structure more efficient and the building more commodious. For instance, in a scheme for a hypothetical market hall with masonry load-bearing walls he sought to demonstrate the improvements that would be made possible by substituting nontraditional for traditional materials (fig. 11-1). He proposed substituting diagonal cast-iron struts for stone piers in a vehicular pass-through, iron beams for wooden ones overhead, curved terra-cotta vaulting panels for planks between the beams, and glazed iron framing for heavy masonry in an awning over the sidewalk.

Figure 11-1
Hypothetical market hall: Viollet-le-Duc (*Discourses*).

More generally, Viollet-le-Duc advocated using structural iron rather than masonry alone because it would permit architects to make larger spaces with lighter and stronger construction. In that advocacy resided the principle of economy of means, more readily achievable when the most efficient material to do a given job has been specified. If these materials could be industrially produced by machines, all the better, for that would ensure greater uniformity of quality and reduced labor cost, thus bringing down the expense for construction. In all this there was an implicit assumption that the role of materials in architecture is a means toward an end, whereas for Ruskin—for whom their visual qualities were so palpable—they were also ends in themselves.

SCHEERBART

The prescription of industrially produced materials reached its apogee in Paul Scheerbart's celebration of glass in his manifesto *Glasarchitektur* (Berlin, 1914). Explicitly taking for granted the use of structural frames made either of iron or of reinforced concrete, he advocated their enclosure with glass, mainly sheets of plate glass but of other types as well. To be proof against decay and fire were two of the important justifications, but his principal motive was the creation of a socially and aesthetically revolutionary architecture.

Scheerbart was acutely aware that for human beings to live in virtually transparent buildings would drastically change their sense of relationship both to buildings and to the natural world outside the confines of a room. Not only would placement of furnishings against the wall no longer be appropriate in a room, but the natural environment of the outdoors would also be constantly in proximity. Equally, he was aware that it would alter people's sense of living in the world when they were on view behind transparent walls. In both instances he foresaw an advance in human culture as a result. In order to achieve this he recognized that there were practical problems to be overcome, one of the most pressing of which would be climatic comfort. Toward this end he foresaw the need for double glazing, with provision for heating and cooling in the interval between panes. He also saw in that interval a place where internal lighting could be accommodated.

But he was mainly enchanted with the notion that a built environment of "crystal" buildings would be aesthetically gratifying. He was, in addition, particularly interested in exploiting the opportunities to employ both colored light and colored glass, invoking the precedent of Gothic architecture for its use of stained glass as well as its emphasis on large-scale glazing in principle. He envisioned whole cityscapes of buildings illumined at night with colored light, colored-glass trains moving through the landscape, and airplanes with colored lights flying through the sky. But not all of Scheerbart's glass would be transparent: he advocated the use of translucent glass brick and opaque ceramic tile, brightly colored, as well. Virtually every surface could be made of or covered with some type of glass product.

The value of his prophecy is that, having been generated outside the spheres of the architectural profession, its originality had not been hampered by the confines of recognized practice. His leap of imagination provided the first fundamentally new structural image in the theory of architecture, one that opened a whole new conceptual world. Given his distance from the mainstream of society, by dint of his radical eccentricity, Scheerbart's contribution might well have been lost had he not been a close friend of Bruno

Taut, who took upon himself the task of realizing this vision in his glass pavilion for the 1914 Werkbund Exhibition in Cologne (fig. 11-2). Thereby did this manifesto reach avant-garde architects in Berlin (such as Mies van der Rohe, in his epoch-making, unbuilt projects of 1921 and 1922 for a glass skyscraper, fig. 10-14) and, through them, the rest of the world. Eventually it became the dominant vision for large-scale modernist architecture everywhere.

Figure 11-2
Maximum use of glass: Glass Pavilion, Werkbund Exhibition of 1914, Cologne, by Taut (© Foto Marburg/Art Resource, NY).

Frank Lloyd Wright's theory of materials, which combined and intensified those of Ruskin and Viollet-le-Duc, together with ideas from Japan, was set out in two different contexts and consists of two distinct groups of ideas. The earlier ideas, most strikingly realized in the original construction of Taliesin (1911), were first set out in his series of articles titled "In the Cause of Architecture," in *Architectural Record* in 1908, and colorfully enhanced in accounts of specific buildings in the *Autobiography*, of 1932. The later ideas appeared in two series of articles in *Architectural Record*, one continuing "In the Cause of Architecture," in 1927, and the other titled "The Meaning of Materials," in 1928.

Taliesin represents probably the most radical commitment to the natural expression of materials in Western architecture. Wright constructed it of stone and slate from quarries near the site (fig. 11-3). The stone was neatly cut into rectangular slabs of varying size and thickness, but it was left rough on the outward-facing surface and set in nonuniform courses in which random stones also project beyond the standard surface plane. The effect is of a masonry that belongs to the earth and suggests the natural layering of the stone in its quarry. The house itself is irregularly composed and famously hugs the brow of the hill rather than sitting atop it as if on a pedestal. The roof is covered with thick, roughly cut slates and has no gutters, so that rain can be seen dripping off it and icicles can hang from it all around. The rusticity of the setting has been carefully maintained; the big trees and the lawn and flower beds are kept as informal as possible.

On the interior the materials are left undisguised in their natural state, for the most part repeating the exterior treatments (fig. 11-4). Where there is wood, it is merely

Figure 11-3
Natural materials, exterior: Taliesin, Spring Green, Wisconsin, by Wright (FH).

stained or finished with nothing more than sealant and a coat of wax. Where there is plaster, it is left untreated or given a stain wash. Where there is stone, it remains bare (the same was done elsewhere with brick walls). It is hard to imagine a more starkly honest expression of the character of the materials throughout the building, or a more straight-forward application of them to the structural format. The project as a whole combines a natural exploitation of the site, a natural articulation of the plan and structure, and a natural handling of the materials. Beyond ice igloos and grass huts, it is as organic as architecture can reasonably be.

Wright's later essays take up rather different matters, dis-cussing the use of steel, concrete, stone, wood, glass, and kiln-fired materials such as brick and terra-cotta tile. For the most part they are poetic musings about the materials and the ways, satisfactory or otherwise, in which the traditional ones have been used in the past. But their importance lies in having raised the visionary issue of how materials, through the use of machines to produce or refine them, can be wrought in a fun-

Figure 11-4
Natural materials, interior: Taliesin, Spring Green, Wisconsin, by Wright (photo of Taliesin by Jim Wildeman, courtesy of the Frank Lloyd Wright Archives, Scottsdale, AZ).

damentally new artistic expression. Wright's concern was to work materials with optimum honesty so as to devise inherently artistic structure. He was confident that forms unanticipated by any architecture of the past could be produced. He did not have a specific vision of them in mind, but he counted on young architects to intuit what those forms might be. The final essay, of 1928, was about the creation of poetic form, achieving beauty in architecture by working with principles. (Is it unfair to point out that Le Corbusier had called for a poetry of form in *Vers une architecture,* the English translation of which had appeared in 1927?)

LE CORBUSIER

For Le Corbusier, the theory of materials had nothing to do with the inherent artistic qualities of one building substance as opposed to another. Rather, he concentrated on the handling of materials and their role in the erection of a structure. His pronouncements on the subject were sparse, appearing mainly in discussion of his own hypothetical buildings in the penultimate chapter of *Vers une architecture*. Contrary to Wright, he did not care about the natural qualities of wood and stone and even regarded their color and pattern variations as a defect. Accordingly, he championed the use of manufactured materials, the more artificial and standardized the better. Taking the rationalist position of Viollet-le-Duc to its ultimate conclusion, he proposed the industrial production of all materials in assembly-ready units of standard dimensions. Construction at the site could then be mostly a matter of assembling prefabricated elements. He welcomed the development of new materials in the laboratory, where they could be tested and proved prior to practical adoption, and regretted that all traditional materials and construction methods could not be replaced. The introduction of machines was urged wherever they could be employed, in the creation of artificial substances, in the prefabrication of units, and in work on the site. Such a position was embraced by European modernists in general and did not seem to require detailed restatement by Gropius or others. The modernist outlook marked the apogee of Viollet-le-Duc's rationalist approach.

The romantic, Ruskinian view of materials did have a resurgence of sorts after World War II in the brutalist movement, of which, ironically, Le Corbusier was the primary instigator. It was, however, a theory that Ruskin himself might have deplored, for it fostered a bluntly primitive aesthetic expression, one that embraced ordinary materials and eschewed traditional ideas of beauty in their manipulation. Indeed, it was at heart an anti-art movement. The use of concrete was at the heart of the matter—that is, poured-in-place, metal-reinforced concrete. As Le Corbusier himself wrote apropos his own work in the postwar period, the availability and cheapness of concrete dictated its use in large projects, and technical limitations on the part of the workforce necessitated a tolerance for rough finish. To be sure, lack of maintenance during the war years had exposed the vulnerability of machine-style finishes to the elements and brought their appropriateness into question. But in the construction of his major new buildings, Le Corbusier had discovered the visual expressiveness of the ridges left in the surface of concrete by its oozing into the intervals between planks of the wooden forms. Together with the thick, simplified forms encouraged by the medium of poured concrete, this new approach promised a novel expression of force and vigor. (No one said so, but it aspired to Ruskin's concept of the sublime.) More importantly, it provided for the medium of concrete a visual manifestation of its having been poured into a mold, hence a testament to its most authentic technical handling.

NEW BRUTALISM AND ITS PROGENY

Brutalist architecture was preeminently the architecture of poured-in-place concrete. Indeed, the very name brutalist refers to the French word for concrete, namely *béton brut*. The impulse to define this assertive primitivism theoretically and declare it a new movement came not from Le Corbusier but from young English architects—such as Peter and Alison Smithson, and later James Stirling and Denys Lasdun. As their spokesman, critic-historian Reyner Banham, explained in his eponymous article in the *Architectural Review* of 1955, the movement was largely a radical expression of honesty in both structure and the use of materials, consciously intended as a social and political statement. In general its adherents advocated a much earthier and more boldly articulated architecture than that fostered by the modernist movement. Its novelty lay more in the way plans were developed and materials used than in its structural conception, but those special emphases were sufficient to produce a very different appearance from that of the Villa Savoye or the Bauhaus.

An aspect of the new honesty was to employ materials of ordinary provenance. It became a matter of principle to specify catalog items rather than custom-made ones and to prefer humble materials to those with elite associations. Hence, not only rough concrete but also industrial brick and terra-cotta tile were adopted. Glass was used in smaller, cheaper panes rather than in expensive sheets, and ordinary hardware was preferred to elegant. A typical example was James Stirling and James Gowan's industrial-tile, steel, and glass Leicester University Engineering Laboratory (fig. 9-19), completed in 1962, already discussed in connection with plan and structure. A poured concrete example was Denys Lasdun's National Theater, completed 1975, on London's South Bank. Its boldly blocky forms of exposed concrete, inside as well as out, challenged with their no-nonsense informality all established notions about theater going as an elite social activity. Such an alteration of implicit social expression was the general intention behind brutalist buildings everywhere, as the mode was being adopted for museums, libraries, university buildings, government centers, and apartment complexes. For that very reason the movement did not make much impact on corporate headquarters and shopping malls.

High tech, as a transmogrification of new brutalism, maintains just as rigorously the principle of honesty, but it resubscribes to rationality as well. By way of contrast to its immediate predecessor, it has exchanged the expression of ruggedness for one of sleek sophistication. It accepts only the machine-made and, insofar as possible, the prefabricated, as seen in Renzo Piano and Richard Rogers's Pompidou Center, Paris, of the mid-1970s (fig. 10-17). Materials that are hard, smooth, and shiny are preferred to anything that is otherwise, which means a bias toward metal, glass, and some plastics. Although high tech design favors the use of standardized building elements, the parts almost always have to be specially manufactured for a particular project. Relentlessly urban, even when situated in the countryside, high tech materials denote the cutting edge of modernity. They achieve, even celebrate, the aims of the early modernists in the expression of technology. But, unlike the modernists, high tech practitioners often use unorthodox colors, or unexpected combinations of colors or finishes, in order to be lighthearted or witty.

Decoration and the Integrity of Design

The role of decoration in high-art architecture during the modern era has been so vexed an issue that even to list it as one of the major categories of design principles leaves room for misunderstanding. Debate over the issue has revolved around the question of whether or not decoration is an indispensable aspect of polite architecture or, instead, is something unnecessary that has been merely tacked on for far too many centuries. The nineteenth-century theorists regarded it as being inherent to the nature of architecture, as did their predecessors. Only with twentieth-century modernism did it lose favor to the extent of being shunned.

RUSKIN

John Ruskin never regarded decoration as anything other than the sine qua non of the art of building: for him it was the thing that separates a utilitarian shed from dignified architecture. He was more genuinely philosophical on the subject than any other theorist, having analyzed in *The Seven Lamps of Architecture* what he found satisfactory and unsatisfactory about ornament in numerous buildings and then synthesized his observations into a few coherent principles and a code of application. In *The Stones of Venice* he elaborated his discussion by cataloging every type of ornament he had observed in historical architecture and assessing its relative merits. Overarching all other considerations was the conviction that decoration is an indispensable aspect of architecture. Color as an inherent property of materials should be part and parcel of the fabric of a building, especially in the creation of patterns with colored materials. But beyond that, ornament should be applied to make the general effect richer and more satisfying.

Ornament that is most satisfactory, Ruskin thought, imitates things experienced in the real world. Although the overall design should be first worked out abstractly and its natural motifs simplified, even to the degree of abstraction, purely abstract motifs should be avoided because they are arbitrary and culturally meaningless. The ornament closest to the viewer should be at once more imitative and more finished in detail than what is far away. Indeed, finely worked detail in ornament that is intended to be seen at a distance is not only wasted but less effective than sketchily worked motifs. Equally, color in decoration should be employed in inverse degree of the imitative quality, being applied liberally only to abstracted motifs. Moreover, its application should be independent of form. Namely, separate moldings should not be given separate colors, and a column should not be striped vertically. Instead, color should go against the shape of the form or be used as a background for forms. Decorative motifs should be taken from contemplative aspects of life rather than active, because the former category is evocative and the latter is necessarily limited to banal illustration. Decorations should be located in or on a building where they can be contemplated by viewers at rest, rather than in areas of activity, where they are easily ignored.

Having cultivated his taste with buildings of the late Middle Ages and early Renaissance, Ruskin thought of ornament in terms of mosaics, fresco paintings, and carved capitals, medallions, and friezes. Hence his guidelines for decoration have subsequently been regarded as limited to his own particular time and cultural situation, and even as antithetical to modern aesthetic instincts. Reviewed in the light of postmodernism, however, their continuing value is more evident, warranting their quotation in full (from *The Seven Lamps of Architecture*):

1. Organic form dominant. True, independent sculpture, and alto-relievo; rich capitals, and moldings; to be elaborate in completion of form, not abstract, and either to be left in pure white marble, or most cautiously touched with color in points and borders only, in a system not concurrent with their forms.

2. Organic form sub-dominant. Basso-relievo, or intaglio. To be more abstract in proportion to the reduction of depth; touched with color more boldly and in increased degree, exactly in proportion to the reduced depth and fullness of form, but still in a system non-concurrent with their forms.

3. Organic form abstracted to outline. Monochrome design, still further reduced to simplicity of contour, and therefore admitting for the first time the color to be concurrent with its outlines; that is to say, as its name imports, the entire figure to be detached in one color from a ground of another.

4. Organic forms entirely lost. Geometrical patterns or variable cloudings in the most vivid color.

One of Ruskin's favorite examples illustrating this code was the Doge's Palace in Venice (fig. 12-1), with its richly molded ground-level arcade, embellished with finely detailed figural capitals and large biblical relief sculptures, naturalistically carved, at either corner. The arcade of the next level is somewhat less elaborate and embellished with somewhat abstracted motifs. Above that level, the plain wall is checkered with blocks of pale rose and white

Figure 12-1
Hierarchy of decoration: Doge's Palace, Venice (FH).

PRINCIPLES (THEORY FROM 1800 TO 1965)

marble, the pattern of which takes no account of the placement of the framed windows. With respect to another set of principles, he also appreciated that within this highly coherent overall scheme the windows were not all the same size or evenly spaced. This inconsistency, he thought, has the effect of enlivening the general regularity with the tension of a subordinate irregularity.

SEMPER

Probably no theorist ever ascribed to decoration a more important role in architecture than Gottfried Semper discerned in the buildings of antiquity. He regarded both the ornaments and the color, especially the color, as dressing in meaning the stark scaffold of the structure. They are, then, the aspects of design that transform a mere building into monumental architecture, relating it to reality and making it the bearer of civilization (see Mallgrave 1996, 290–302). In effect, Semper would have been in agreement with Ruskin concerning the role and importance of ornament. Yet his treatise, *Der Stil,* was not posited to advance prescriptions or principles of design for practitioners, even though his analysis of the architecture of the distant past made clear that decoration was always of the essence.

VIOLLET-LE-DUC

Viollet-le-Duc also regarded ornament as a necessary aspect of architecture, but not as something that could be merely applied to a completed structure. Rather, he believed, decoration ought to be integrated with the structure itself, to the extent that it could not be removed without damaging the building in the process. He admired the architectural sculpture of the ancient Egyptians and Greeks to the extent that it was integral with structural components; even more that of the Gothic cathedrals because it made sculpture part of the structure itself. For modern usage, on the other hand, the most important considerations are that embellishment should be subordinate to the design scheme of the building as a whole, that ornament should be concentrated at structurally significant locations, and that its formulation should be appropriate to the material employed. He was, for instance, acutely aware that ornament for new materials such as iron was problematic because there was no earlier tradition to draw upon as a model. Cognizant of color as an aspect of historical decoration, he left unstated any notions he may have entertained concerning its application to modern buildings.

A telling example of how he thought ornament might be used in a modern building is spelled out in *Histoire d'une maison*. He proposed to set the square joists spanning a room on the diagonal, rather than straight, and that they should be held in place by V-shaped cuts in the bearers (fig. 12-2). This disposition, he maintained, would increase their resistance to deflection from the weight of the floor above them and at the same time introduce an interesting pattern and texture into the ceiling. He suggested that these joists might be painted with a stylized design, both to introduce color and to add richness of pattern to these structural members. Still another example was the iron girder made of many small parts, described in the *Entretiens* (fig. 10-5). An abstracted foliate design was introduced into the assemblage of parts composing the girder and another was cast in the capital of the supporting column.

Viollet-le-Duc's position was taken up by the entire generation of Art Nouveau architects of the 1890s. Among them, Louis Sullivan in the United States ideally realized

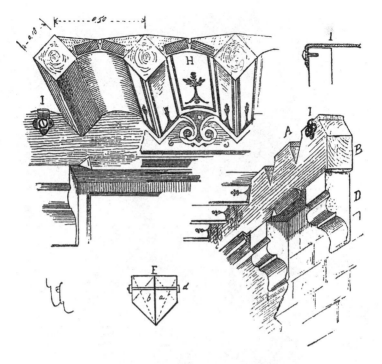

Figure 12-2
Decorative structural detail: dining room ceiling, by Viollet-le-
Duc (*How to Build a House*).

the Frenchman's aspirations, most notably in the terra-
cotta ornaments of his early skyscrapers in St. Louis and
Buffalo (fig. 12-3). Manufactured as small rectangular units,
in which intricately detailed motifs were stamped out by
metal dies before the process of firing, they combined the
qualities of fine workmanship with the virtues of machine
production. The assistant who may have executed some of
the ornamental designs, Frank Lloyd Wright, continued the
tradition and maintained it in his own work, even in the
face of a strongly differing philosophy advanced by European modernists.

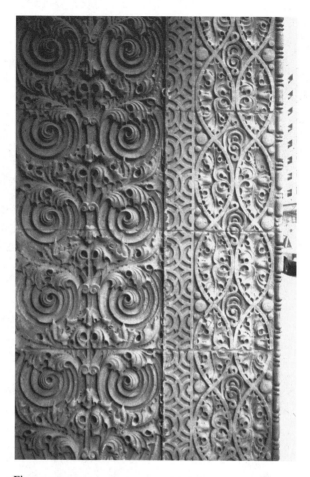

Figure 12-3
Richly decorative terra-cotta detail: Wainwright building, St. Louis, by Adler and Sullivan (FH).

Adolf Loos reacted strongly to the embrace of ornament by the pioneering modern theorists in his essay *Ornament und Verbrechen*, in the early years of the twentieth century. His argument began with an economic concern, namely that the creation of ornament added additional labor and material costs. Moreover, he maintained, the workers who normally produced ornamentation were actually paid less than those who performed straightforward work, in part because they tended to come from a peasant artisan background. A political objection was that ornament is the aspect of the material world that traditionally confers on objects their qualitative distinctiveness, a dispensable carryover from the outmoded elite cultures of the past. Finally, an aesthetic objection was that ornament is a kind of mask, the means of hiding defects of workmanship, materials, or basic design.

Loos's theoretical position was prompted in part by an essay on ornament by Louis Sullivan, which he had read during a sojourn in America in the 1890s. His essay of 1908, originally published in Vienna, was republished in Berlin (1912) and Paris (1913), where it had an impact upon virtually all the leaders of the modern movement, including Le Corbusier. Although all the arguments advanced by Loos against ornament were meaningful to the others, the uncompromising plainness of design that he championed ironically ended by becoming a style (fig. 12-4). Le Corbusier sublimated the arguments against ornament under the rubric of admiration for the machine, but unrelenting austerity in design had, for him, a more direct origin in Loos's essay.

In the years following World War I, Wright continued to uphold the place of ornament in architecture at the same

Figure 12-4
Austerely undecorated exterior: garden elevation, Steiner House, Vienna, by Loos (© Foto Marburg/Art Resource, NY).

time as he smarted under the derisive criticisms of those who regarded it as an outdated practice. The struggle was unequal: he was a lone defender against a generation of opponents, and eventually he virtually gave it up as well in order to maintain his status as a leading modernist. In due course, critics and historians alike have recognized that unadorned structural articulations in themselves take on a decorative value, with the implication that no matter how a building is designed it will inherently possess a decorative character. Accordingly, no influential theorist has taken up the cause of ornament as an essential issue in a subsequent treatise.

Prior to the nineteenth century, the notion of including principles for the restoration of buildings as an aspect of architectural theory would have been meaningless. Vitruvius, Alberti, and even Laugier would have assumed that a damaged building would be repaired or remodeled in the current manner and a largely ruined building would simply be replaced by a new structure. It was cultural romanticism, originator of the concept of the past not just as previous time but as history, that made the preservation of buildings as they were built a serious undertaking of advanced societies. To restore is, of course, a different impulse altogether from that of building in a revived style, an important distinction in view of the nineteenth-century urge to do that as well.

The impulse to restore buildings of the past did not originate simply as a cultural whim. Rather, it was thrust upon the nations that were the first to undertake it, namely England and France, because of the urgent need to compensate for the imprudent alteration and neglect of great buildings of the medieval past. In England the Gothic revival impressed upon responsible agents the value of preserving the real thing in an authentic fashion. This desideratum had lapsed during the eighteenth century, when lack of regard for medieval styles had made tolerable all sorts of incongruous modernizations in the name of greater comfort. In France, the need for restoration was a case of making up for decades of neglect during and after the revolution, not to mention haphazard repairs of earlier times. It was no accident, then, that the first theorists to address the need for principles of restoration were those who had been prompted to write theoretical treatises under the inspiration of Gothic buildings—namely, Ruskin and Viollet-le-Duc. And it should come as no surprise that the former took a conservative view and the latter a liberal one.

Ruskin approached restoration from the standpoint that the quality of the picturesque, highly desirable in architecture, actually depends upon a degree of decay and also that sublimity depends in large measure upon signs of age. He regarded a certain amount of wear and tear as not only tolerable but even a good thing. To him it simply added to the richness of effect. Restoration, on the other hand, is tantamount to destruction of authenticity. Restoring, he averred, is like trying to raise the dead. Hence to recarve a surface removes the surviving expression of the spirit of the time, and any attempt to replicate it in a new stone is doomed to frustration. As he put it in "The Lamp of Memory":

Do not let us talk then of restoration. The thing is a lie from beginning to end. You may make a model of a building as you may of a corpse, and your model may have the shell of the old walls within it as your cast may have the skeleton . . . but the old building is destroyed, and that more totally and mercilessly than if it had sunk into a heap of dust. . . . [If restoration becomes an unavoidable necessity], look the necessity full in the face, and understand it in its own terms. It is a necessity for destruction. Accept it as such, pull the building down, throw its stones into neglected corners; but do it honestly, and do not set up a Lie in their place.

Look that necessity in the face before it comes, and you may prevent it. . . . Take proper care of your monuments, and you will not need to restore them. . . . Watch an old building with anxious care; guard it as best you may and at *any* cost from every influence of dilapidation. . . .

Bind it together with iron where it loosens; stay it with timber where it declines; do not care about the unsightliness of the aid; better a crutch than a lost limb; and do this tenderly, and reverently, and continually and many a generation will still be born and pass away beneath its shadow. Its evil day must come at last; but let it come declaredly and openly, and let no dishonoring and false substitute deprive it of the funeral offices of memory.

Ruskin regarded fine old buildings as nothing less than sacred relics. Their existence in itself constitutes sufficient grounds for preserving them. But they belong to those who made them and not to those who come after, so the society that inherits them has no right to alter them in any way. He discussed this issue only in terms of physical integrity, probably never thinking of circumstances in which reuse for a purpose other than that originally intended might be the sole justification for guaranteeing the survival of the building. Clearly this is an attitude markedly different from our own, and one reason for it may be that he could not imagine that ordinary buildings from the past would become the subject of restoration.

As reactionary as Ruskin's position seems at face value, it was in one sense radically progressive: he was far more willing than we to demolish an old building in order to avoid compromising its form or purpose. He was in favor, then, of preservation not for the sake of maintaining an old building just because it is old, but for the sake of preserving the inspirational spirit of the past. In consequence, his arguments have a boldness not usually attributed to them in their implicit warning against the deleterious effects of meaningless preservation achieved by means of insensitive restoration.

Unlike Ruskin, who viewed buildings only as a lay critic, Viollet-le-Duc was deeply involved in the practice of restoration itself. The decision to save the buildings he worked on had been made far above the level of his discretion, by the national government, and it was his business to carry out this decision rather than to examine its wisdom. Accordingly, he began from the standpoint that the proper approach to restoration is to decide what needs to be done and how, not whether it should be done. The practical issues involved in saving buildings were his province. These were developed at the very beginning of his career, in the cover letter—addressed to the Minister of Justice and Religious Rites—accompanying his proposal soliciting a commission to restore the Cathedral of Notre-Dame in Paris. Later he refined and codified his principles of restoration in the article on that subject in his *Dictionnaire raisonné*.

At the outset, Viollet-le-Duc drew a distinction between the restoration of a scenic ruin and of a historic building that continues to be used for its original purpose. For the ruin, he stated, "it is not necessary to renew; rather, brace, consolidate, and replace . . . the utterly deteriorated stone with new blocks, but refrain from carving new moldings or sculpture." In other words, keep it in as authentic a state as possible, but do not disguise modifications necessary to maintain its preservation. On the other hand, for a building still in use it is necessary to ensure structural stability and to introduce current standards of comfort while making every effort to maintain the historical integrity of the design. In other words, a certain amount of discretion must be exercised, and therein lies the conflict of principle-laden claims that faces every restorer. He was aware that it is seldom possible to address every necessary and desirable concern without compromising one principle or another; indeed, he was to become familiar in time with the vitriolic controversy that such compromises provoke. But he faced the enterprise of restoration as unavoidable if historic buildings are not to be lost altogether.

He pointed out that it is necessary to become as informed about the building as possible before deciding upon alterations or embarking upon the work. Preparation must include familiarity with all documents related to the building, especially old drawings or other records of the former appearance of dilapidated areas. A thorough examination of the building should be made in order to become fully aware of changes made during the live history of the building and to distinguish them from the original state. A careful record must be made of the state of the building before any restoration effort begins. He pointed out that photography was already becoming important in that respect, but he also made careful watercolor renderings of every elevation, both inside and out. It is often in the course of making such a record, he observed, that one becomes aware of vestigial evidence that is not readily noticed in an inspection. A thorough knowledge of the historical style of the building and that of any additions or alterations must be brought to this process, for it is the only way to discipline critical judgment.

Then begins the hard part, involving discretionary decisions on every side. If a portion of the structure must be repaired or replaced, is it necessary to do it exactly as it was originally done, or can it be improved either in material or method? Determining the answer is like moving about in a minefield. If the repair is in an area that does not show, as under a roof, he regarded it as folly not to make changes in method or material that would increase the strength of the structure or make it more durable. If the repair does show, it must be done in an authentic manner. Authenticity is itself sometimes difficult to establish. If, for instance, the original construction was faulty and was altered during the historical life of the building, the new repair should reflect the old improvement. If, on the other hand, a historical alteration was made without actually improving the structure, it is preferable to restore the original configuration. The same applies with replacement materials, meaning that the original type of material should be used unless it is demonstrably inferior to the one later substituted. In no case, however, should modern materials be interposed. The risks of doing so are chemical or structural incompatibility, often resulting in damage to the authentic portions that remain.

Then there are questions about the design. If a portion of the building had been left incomplete, is it appropriate to furnish what was lacking or to invent a likely design for the missing portions? Viollet-le-Duc unequivocally proscribed such "completions," adjuring the restorer to forget his own tastes and instincts in the interest of preserving art rather than making it. However, it is well known that he often gave in to the temptation to do otherwise, particularly at Notre-Dame. If evidence is found indicating that the original design was different from that at the time of restoration, is it appropriate to obliterate the alterations? The answer must be carefully considered, because the patrons and builders may have concluded that that aspect of the design had been faulty and needed correction. In such a case the alteration ought to be regarded as inherent to the historical character of the building. In general, Viollet-le-Duc thought that a restoration ought to respect the evolution of a building throughout the duration of its historical life. On the other hand, changes made during a later, culturally alien era ought to be subject to removal, unless they are of special artistic merit.

In all these considerations, he maintained, one must be practical, respecting the needs of present-day users of the building. If the function of the building has altered since it was constructed, the restoration must accommodate the current use, as in the case of a church, in which liturgical practice has changed since the time of its original design.

Also, although historical patina is important in preserving the character of an old building, it is valid to restore the brightness and richness appropriate to such an edifice. As he famously declared, a carefully wrought restoration must balance all the considerations, so that the final result may not resemble the exact appearance of the building at any specific moment in its historical life. The reasonable pragmatism of this philosophy of restoration reflects his grounding in the real world of work and events, in which the goals of preservation are weighed against those of continuing utility. It is a philosophy that widely separates him from Ruskin's idealized polarity of fastidious preservation or resigned destruction, and its versatility makes him the true founder of the principles still in practice today.

The greatest change between the nineteenth-century outlook toward restoration and that of today is that the concept of what is to be undertaken in the area of renewing old buildings has broadened considerably. Whereas Ruskin and Viollet-le-Duc thought of restoration as applying mainly to major structures, cathedrals and palaces, today's practice extends downward to include quite ordinary buildings. When restoration is carried out for the purpose of preserving historical architecture, it has become painstakingly scientific. But when it is a case of rehabilitation and adaptive reuse, the guiding principles are necessarily less restrictive, shaped more by concerns for economic viability than for artistic integrity. In general, such guidelines have been developed not in a theoretical context but in city-planning and tax offices, where the goals of public policy and practical development are reconciled.

The broadening of the concept of restoration to include adaptive reuse can probably be attributed to the indirect influence of Robert Venturi, whose *Complexity and Contradiction* and *Learning from Las Vegas* were pregnant with cultural implications even he may not have recognized at the time they were written. (Such is the life of books once they are on their own in the world.) One of the implications grew out of the concern for context, namely the need—usually identified by city planners—to retain something of the local ethos of an urban environment by retaining as many older buildings as can be made useful. Hence the tax incentives that make rehabilitation and adaptive reuse attractive to developers. Another emerged from the celebration of both complexity and contradiction, which was projected onto the context and thus helped to create a taste for using buildings for purposes other than those for which they were designed.

Twentieth-century restoration efforts have occasioned refinements of these nineteenth-century principles, but they have not replaced them or even greatly modified them. No subsequent theorist of note has felt called upon to enunciate explicit principles for restoration, so the pioneering modern formulations remain the major statements on the subject. Unlike principles for the design of new buildings, those for restoration cannot be a matter of personal preference, so there can never be a code of principles that is not involved with controversy.

The involvement of architectural theory with the planning of cities has been paradoxical. When theory resided in the realm of conventions, its formulators regarded the design of new cities as the province of architects, even though the activity was limited to practical considerations such as devising defenses and laying out streets. Aesthetic efforts might occasionally be addressed to a square or a city gate, but little more. But when theory came to be couched in terms of principles, and the scope of the profession no longer comprised civil engineering, the aesthetic conception of urban layouts came—to a limited extent, at least—under the purview of architects.

THE AESTHETICS OF URBAN SPLENDOR: LAUGIER AND SITTE

Aesthetic city planning was introduced by Laugier in his call for a fresh approach to the design of everything having to do with architecture. Recognizing in cities the opportunity to create stimulating and awe-inspiring environments that can magnify the pleasure of life, he charged architects with the duty to give cities order, splendor, and rich variety. It is important, he held, for the entries to great cities to be impressive. He recommended, for instance, that the city gate be a large triumphal arch opening onto a grand plaza, from which broad avenues would fan out into both the center and the outlying districts. The plaza and streets should be lined with orderly rows of trees. The street pattern of the city in general should take its cues from great gardens, like those of Le Nôtre's design for the gardens of Versailles (Laugier asserted, nearly half a century before L'Enfant drew upon this design for the layout of Washington, D.C.). The streets should have a pattern that is orderly and easy to negotiate and at the same time made interesting with variety. They should be punctuated with numerous plazas of differing shapes and sizes and ornamented with fountains, monuments, and statues. They should be aligned, but not in a monotonous pattern. The facades lining the thoroughfares should be in proportion with the width of the pathway, tall enough to be impressive but not so tall as to be overbearing. They should be regular in character, but distinctly varied in their ornament and even in their color.

Laugier's conception is an ideal, but it is also one, as he recognized, whose realization could be imposed upon an existing city piece by piece. In making his proposal he was sharing the high aims of Vitruvius and Alberti for the beneficial impact of architecture on the populace, but he was also going beyond them by spelling out how that benefit might actually be achieved. The urban renewal projects carried out by John Nash in London a few decades later may not have been directly instigated by Laugier, but, despite their less formal manner, they were very much in the spirit of Laugier's injunctions.

It was more than a century before another theorist captured the imagination of architects with principles for the design of cities. That writer was Camillo Sitte, whose *Der Städtebau nach seiner künstlerischen Grundsätzen* (Vienna, 1889) is well known in English as *City Planning According to Artistic Principles.* His theory was a more detailed treatment of the kinds of issues Laugier had initiated. He was inspired by Gothic romanticism rather than Laugier's classical rationalism, but their aesthetic goals for urban design were fundamentally similar. They differed in that Laugier set out categorical imperatives while Sitte, like Ruskin, derived his principles from analyses of specific environments. Although his text was expanded in the course of new editions and translations into all the major West European languages, the core concerns were focused on the design of city squares and other punctuating features. His observations of historical examples were expressed in positive terms, but those relating to recent practice were largely negative.

Sitte's design principles consist of a series of correlated injunctions. One should group buildings around plazas, rather than in discrete building blocks, and make plazas of various shapes (especially horseshoe). Monuments, statues, and fountains should be grouped rather than scattered, and they should be situated in relation to buildings. Plazas should be grouped around major buildings and each given a distinctive size, configuration, and character (figs. 14-1, 14-2, 14-3). Streets should open into plazas so that they do not run straight across. One should devise forecourts before major buildings, enclose gardens in the midst of buildings, and avoid placing greenery or rows of trees next to plazas, or even along streets. Irregular terrain should be retained in urban landscapes, along with crooked streets. The visual effects of a building site should be exploited by arranging structures around an open space with a focal monument at the center. Finally, artistic criteria should dominate the design of the principal plazas, while the economic demands of land use should be relegated to secondary areas, such as ordinary streets. It is a daunting list, but these principles helped to foster urban splendor and promote poetic atmospheres. This was the kind of outlook that

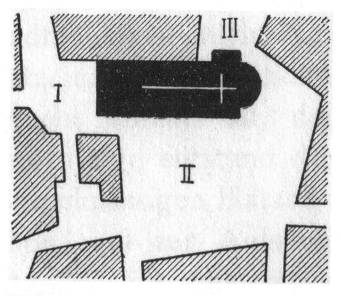

Figure 14-1
Plan of plazas around Modena Cathedral: Sitte.

fostered in Europe the grandiloquent civic buildings of the turn of the century and the City Beautiful movement in the United States.

UTOPIAN VISIONS: HOWARD, WRIGHT, LE CORBUSIER

Contemporary with Sitte's aesthetically instigated vision of the city was the beginning of a series of utopian schemes that were to be as influential upon modernist architecture as Sitte's ideas were upon conservative design. The first was conceived outside the professional realm of architecture by an English stenographer who liked to characterize himself as an inventor. This was Ebenezer Howard's socially inspired formulation for the garden city. Privately published

Figure 14-2
Plaza I, facing the west facade of Modena Cathedral (FH).

Figure 14-3
Plaza II, facing the east end of Modena Cathedral (FH).

in a modest edition in 1898 as *Tomorrow, a Peaceful Path to Real Reform,* its success followed upon commercial re-issue in 1902 as *Garden Cities of To-morrow.* Reacting to the crowded and polluted conditions of British industrial cities, Howard devised a conceptual model for newly founded communities of about 30,000 in which a social fabric based on communal cooperation was assumed. Howard envisioned these garden cities with a circular plan, a series of concentric rings intersected by a radial pattern of streets. At the center was to be a garden, surrounded by the civic and cultural institutions and those, in turn, by a large park. Commerce would be housed in a "crystal palace," sub-divided into shops that would ring the park. Succeeding that would be several residential rings, the middle one of which would be a tree-lined grand boulevard. Beyond the housing would be an industrial ring, then the railroad, and finally a perpetual green belt devoted to agriculture and forests. Growth of the city into this green belt would not be permitted. Instead, more new communities would be founded beyond the green belt and connected by rail.

Howard purposely did not provide formal details and restrained himself from issuing any dicta about design. He assumed that these matters would develop in the cooperative atmosphere he expected to surround the actualization of the project. He was not, after all, an architect but a social visionary. The first such community built, Letchworth, in Hertfordshire, was designed by two architects, Barry Parker and Raymond Unwin, who, as it turned out, were to give Howard's garden city the format that made the concept influential (fig. 14-4). Although Howard led the project, the architects were able to persuade him that the circular scheme ought to be modified. They laid out the street pattern with consideration for the topographical undulations of the site. The civic and cultural buildings remained at the center, but they were surrounded by tree-lined residential streets, which were not strictly regular. The commercial area was off to one side, and the industrial zone was concentrated on one side beyond the railroad. The architecture itself was a modernized version of English vernacular, the sort of thing Ruskin regarded as culturally relevant for all new architecture, envisioned in his "Lamp of Obedience." All the other criteria of Howard's concept were followed, however, and he was always the one credited for the garden city concept. Only one other such community was undertaken in his lifetime, but after World War II the garden city became the model for new communities everywhere.

Whereas Howard did not spell out any aesthetic principles in connection with the garden city, because he was thinking only in social terms, his architects, Parker and Unwin, concentrated on giving visual form to his ideas. Certain aesthetic principles were necessarily invoked, and they were implicitly understood as givens by all those who

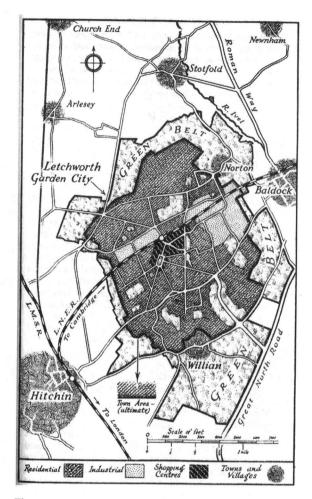

Figure 14-4
A garden city: plan of Letchworth, by Parker and Unwin, inspired by Howard.

were involved in the foundation of garden communities. One is the assumption that no single building or group of buildings stands out as the signature landmark of the city. In such a context, imposing monuments lose their value, all the more so because the dominance accorded to the natural setting would render a formally ambitious effort pompous and ostentatious. Also, Howard's ideal of social cooperation has a visual corollary in both consistency and modesty. For garden cities, then, a modern architecture based on design principles rather than conventions of artifice was the only appropriate aesthetic route. Such an approach ran exactly contrary to that of Laugier and Sitte, and eventually it overwhelmed theirs.

Frank Lloyd Wright's Broadacre City (fig. 14-5), first described in *The Disappearing City* in 1932, set out to be a radically decentralized community, stressing the independence of each family as the basic social unit. His scheme called for the family to own at least an acre of land, on which its members would not only live in privacy but also have room to grow a certain amount of their food in a garden and a small orchard. Such a concept presupposed the centrality of the automobile in modern life, as the basis for getting children to school, adults to work, and everyone to health, recreational, and cultural facilities. Commerce would result from individual initiatives and be housed at roadside markets located at major intersections of roads. Wright was dedicated to maintaining the lowest feasible population density, in a situation in which all the land implicitly would be allocated, leaving no awkward intervals. In the model constructed a few years later by the members of his Taliesin Fellowship, all the buildings were of his own design, meaning that he assumed that only like-minded architects would be involved in realizing the concept. Moreover, the means of bringing this community of individualists into being inevitably had to be a county architect,

Figure 14-5
A low-density city: model plan of Broadacre City, by Wright, executed by the Taliesin Fellowship (FH).

whose complete authority in land allocation and planning Wright assumed would only result in the benevolent benefits of good design.

Scattered loosely through the landscape, the architecture of Broadacre City promised to be individualistic, like the hypothetical inhabitants. Probably only the public buildings would be in plain view from the roads, inviting shows of monumentality, in contrast to the likely incidental nature of the less evident private buildings. Even so, the reliance on cars for transportation meant that parking for public buildings would have to be cleverly (and expensively) concealed if the approach to public buildings was not to be spoiled. As a design principle the greatest opportunity offered by this scheme would be the dramatic exploitation of topographical irregularities—the more rugged the better. In terms of practice, however, Wright's concept presupposed total planning control. Just as Plato's republic was to be governed by a philosopher-king, so Broadacre City would have to be administered by a philosopher-architect.

Le Corbusier also set out his ideas for the design of cities in a book, *Urbanisme,* published in Paris in 1925. Translated into English as *The City of Tomorrow and Its Planning* (London, 1929), it was more successful in inspiring city renovations by others than through schemes of his own design. In contrast to Howard and Wright, Le Corbusier imagined a city more concentrated than even the existing metropolises, but concentrated in a very different way. His city would have a core of concrete and glass skyscrapers flanking the intersecting primary transportation routes and the main station at the center (fig. 14-6). This core would house the elite in luxurious apartments, the major corporations in impressive headquarters, the leading cultural institutions in appropriate pavilions, and would offer glamorous entertainment in the intervals. Each unit could be built individually within vast metal-reinforced concrete frames to ensure both privacy and structural integrity. Between all the towers would be green parks with winding paths, trees, flower gardens, and fountains. Beyond this core would be secondary transportation routes and ribbon buildings of about five stories, set in rectilinear undulations on additional parks. These would house the middle class, professional offices, and shops. Still further beyond would be tertiary routes, garden apartment blocks, and rows of semidetached and detached villas for the most modest portion of the population. Although the whole would be laid out with geometric regularity—roughly a diamond superimposed upon a rectangle—there would be a vast recreational park asymmetrically inserted into one end of the conurbation. By his estimate, only 15 percent of the land area would be covered with buildings, allowing light and air to all and a generous sense of space between them.

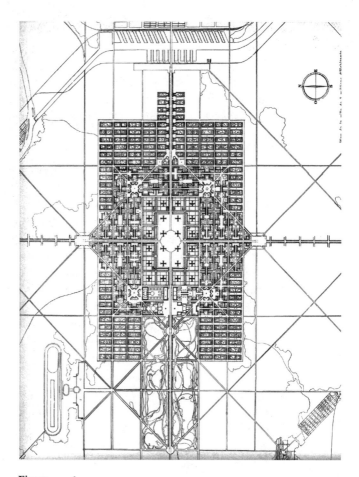

Figure 14-6
A high-density city: plan of the City of Three Million, by Le Corbusier (© 2002 Artists Rights Society (ARS), New York/ ADAGP, Paris/FLC).

To produce and run this city he imagined the imposition of an efficacious central authority, under which the inhabitants would carry on their activities without concerns for governance or maintenance. What began in his mind as the "contemporary city" was gradually glorified to become the "radiant city."

The design principles involved in accommodating millions of people in such a rational scheme necessarily involved geometrical regularity and copious repetition. The buildings would be streamlined to maximal simplicity, made up largely of bulky rectangular forms. Although Le Corbusier probably imagined that the blandness would be redeemed by the beauty of nature in the intervals, the glamour of the glass sheathing of most of the facades, and the smartness of decor in individual units, others leveled charges of sterility and loss of a true urban atmosphere. The juxtaposition of towers housing 12,000–15,000 people with broad expanses of nature was so extreme as to make the interconnection meaningless in terms of urban life. But the promise it held out for the renewal of cities made the scheme attractive enough to city planners in the post–World War II era that it was frequently adopted. Ironically, the central cluster of towers that Le Corbusier assigned to the rich was adopted for large-scale low-income housing in major urban centers and for middle-class accommodation in new capital cities.

The creation of such urban schemes depended heavily upon faith in good design to improve the quality of life, even to effect major improvements in the social conduct of urban populations. In their defense, it should be noted that they had been devised to correct the appalling physical conditions of nineteenth-century cities. These efforts marked the apogee of the notion that architecture has a moral component, and that the architect is the agent of that morality. Its issuance from one particular theoretical strain goes a long way toward explaining why the involvement of architects—and architectural theory—with the design of cities is concentrated in only one generation of practitioner-theorists. In the decades since World War II, there have been major critiques of these ambitious modernist schemes but no additional design guides. Jane Jacobs, in *The Death and Life of Great American Cities* (1961), delivered a powerful argument for the value to cities of organically developed neighborhoods and the interaction of people on streets of moderate scale. And Venturi, Scott Brown, and Izenour, in *Learning from Las Vegas*, defended the messy vitality of urban centers, as they have gradually developed, over schemes that are imposed all at once. If any theoretical formulation of design principles in cities remains in force, it is the value of proceeding incrementally in a contextual manner.

Underpinnings, conventions, and principles as categories of theory are by nature intrinsic: they function in the world in their own right. Convolutions, by contrast, are extrinsic, limited by nature to functioning as modifications of concepts. Hence the adoption of nonparallel categories for the basic schema of this book would seem to be an unwitting rhetorical error. But the switch from one type of term to the other underlines the fact that the new theories of the last third of the twentieth century can function in the world only as variations of previously established norms. Such convolutions could, hypothetically, be applied to underpinnings, conventions, and principles alike, but because they were generated in reaction to the principles of modernism they have functioned thus far only as challenges to that body of theory.

Robert Venturi's *Complexity and Contradiction in Architecture* (1966) made the first big splash in architectural theory that disturbed the waters of modernism. The postmodern movement it helped to provoke did not directly inspire the other reactions, but its defiance of the rational method of modernism as the unquestioned basis for architectural thinking prepared the way for them. Consequently, postmodernism amounted to more than a single ripple in the stylistic stream of late twentieth-century architecture.

Whatever effect Venturi's book was to have was enriched by the publication of *Learning from Las Vegas* (1972, revised 1977), written with Denise Scott Brown and Steven Izenour. These two books entered a social context of rapid change and major cultural ferment. Whatever they were meant to say—which is not entirely clear, even now—they were taken to imply much more than their respective texts actually state. A creative reading opened the way to a radical rethinking of the fundamental principles of modernist theory, although the real sources of inspiration were sometimes quite other.

The aspirations of early twentieth-century modernists to an ahistorical mode of design, eschewing any reference to historical tradition, dovetailed with the rational problem-solving approach of Viollet-le-Duc's design method. Hence modernist architecture tended to be largely an exercise in formalism, ignoring the physical context into which it was inserted and lacking associative cultural references. Indeed, for all his devotion to historical architecture for what it could teach the architect about design, Viollet-le-Duc had been interested neither in the functions for which those buildings were designed nor the aspects of their designs that denoted cultural content. He saw the Gothic cathedral, for instance, as a rational response to certain kinds of functional requirements but not as an expression of the age of faith. Hence his rational design method had ignored the matter of meaning in architecture.

To endow a design with cultural meaning may involve going beyond straightforward rationality. And to understand that is to recognize an important limitation in rational design method, namely the blithe assumption that there is a single right way to go about designing a building, one that, if faithfully followed, will lead inexorably to the right solution to the problems posed by the functional program. By contrast, a postmodern outlook accepts that the logic of a truly satisfactory solution may lead beyond purely rational formulation, tolerating ambiguities that result when competing truths come into conflict. So began a new series of inversions of the accepted verities of architectural theory, creating a mannerism that exists beyond the realm of the classical orders.

VENTURI AND THE POSTMODERN CRITIQUE OF MODERNISM

One of Venturi's great contributions in *Complexity and Contradiction* was to deplore the absence of cultural meaning in modernist architecture and to signal the importance of its presence in the historical styles. Similarly, in *Learning from Las Vegas* he and his coauthors demonstrated that even the lowest common denominator of nonmodernist popular architecture has the value of conveying cultural meaning, which they regarded as indispensable to the built environment. The conclusion to be drawn from those observations is that even the highest quality of formal design does not suffice to replace cultural meaning, nor does the fullest satisfaction of functional requirements compensate for the absence of cultural meaning.

Two blatant examples of the importance to homeowners of cultural content in the domestic environment were noted by the Venturi group in a later study that focused on the repetitious suburban dwellings of Levittown (see Carroll et al. 1972, 1975). They are the prevalence in middle-class homes of one incongruously ceremonial room, usually an elaborately furnished parlor, and also of a customized exterior or landscaping, both contradicting the modernist assumption that functional needs should be the sole determinants of design.

Typically, the calculated decor of the parlor strongly contrasts with the offhand simplicity of the other rooms. A disproportionate share of resources has usually been expended upon its decor, even though it is seldom actually used. At the same time, the utility and comfort of its implements may be markedly less evident than that in the other rooms. The value of such a room to the occupants is considerable, however, because it announces to all who see it the cultural identity assumed by the family as well as their social aspirations. It serves as a locus for social ritual, the setting for the most cherished part of a major holiday celebration and the place to receive the most honored guests.

In suburbs where the occupants buy ready-built houses and where the difference in design from one house to another is minimal, cosmetic features may be added on the exterior in order to make a residence more distinctive. It is all to the better if, as in most modest suburbs, the exteriors are neutral to begin with, because they are easier to modify; indeed, their very plainness invites elaboration. Minor alterations may range from painting the front door a bright color to adding shutters on the windows or wrought iron on the entry, or installing a bay window on the front. Major changes could include modifying the shape of the main elevation or its material to suggest a Tudor half-timbered manor, a Spanish mission, or a Roman temple-front mansion. Equally distinctive effects can be achieved through landscaping. The approach to the front door may be down a winding flagstone path bordered by beds of flowers, or along a straight alley of clipped shrubbery or overarching trees. Accent features might include a birdbath or a reflecting ball on a pedestal, surrounded by a circular planting, sited in the middle of the lawn. Whatever the device, some plant material and an imaginative feature can suggest anything from the quaintly cozy to the gaudily grand or the incongruously exotic.

The value of these examples to illustrate architectural meaning is great because they are recognizable in personal experience by such a high percentage of people in American society. By the same token, the recognizability in a town of various types of shops and public institutions through the use of ordinary emblems of identity is important to making intelligible the built environment of a community. This sense of identity is, in the final analysis, more important to the psychological comfort of the citizenry than aesthetic considerations. Venturi's critique of modernism, then, also addressed by extension the shortcomings of modern design method.

LAYERED MEANING IN ARCHITECTURAL DESIGN

Venturi's initial critique of modernist design implicitly encouraged a revival of mannerist tendencies, in which the rules for form as well as content are broken. His pretext had been the analysis of numerous historical buildings in order to validate his criticisms of twentieth-century structures. His rhetorical purpose was to undermine the boring regularity and unrelenting orderliness of modernist architecture, which, he held, belied the manifold complexities involved in a given planning problem and ignored the opportunities for cultural expression of the patron's motives. But his concern for breaking the rules transcended the unorthodox manipulation of form and extended even into his design method, which was flexible enough to accommodate inconsistent demands.

Venturi's various analytical categories addressed complexity, contradiction, ambiguity, accommodation, and other similar qualities. Though convincingly employed in the assessment of buildings in which he perceived these qualities, his categories are too arbitrary and overlap too much to be adopted by others as a rigorous system of formal classification, applicable to all their own observations. Nevertheless, these categories served to indict as naively bland the universalist outlook of modernist architecture and to encourage an alternative approach to the conception of a design. Although Venturi did not offer an explicit program of recommendations as to how this could be achieved, several inferences were drawn that substantially altered the character of modern architecture.

The very fact that Venturi mainly used historical examples to make his points helped to reinstate in the minds of his readers the value of the past as a legitimate source of inspiration. But possibly because he had made his points by citing specific features, there was a tendency in the work of his followers to employ historicizing quotations, with or without the pragmatic justifications that were inherent in his arguments. An unexpected result was an almost immediate resumption of the premodernist understanding that the architecture of the present best grows out of the architecture of the past. Such a rejection of the modernist premise that the past is both obsolete and irrelevant was a compelling justification for interpreting Venturi's theoretical speculations as initiating a historicizing, postmodern movement.

When his own work confronted him with a difficult situation, Venturi did tend to seek inspiration in the historical examples that had nourished his outlook. His quotations, however, were only occasionally literal and seldom historicizing in purpose. Rather, they were normally used as culturally meaningful devices that also solved a practical problem. Taken out of context, they had the effect of breaking the rules, and their use in incongruous circumstances gave them the kind of layered meaning that is associated with mannerism.

The impact of these references was considerable, expressly because they did convey meaning. They helped to restore the sense of cultural belonging that had been lacking in modernist architecture. Venturi never stated how cultural meaning was to be conveyed or with what means. Under his own hand it was subtly allusive and not programmatically imposed, often breaking the bonds of solemnity, with which almost all previous architecture had been constrained. Indeed, for him meaning seems to have been a matter located behind, or beyond, explicit iconography, addressing instead a preconscious apprehension of the familiar.

An incidental result of Venturi's tendency to draw comparisons to sixteenth-century Italian buildings was that the mannered version of the orders made its way into his architecture, in the form of both direct and indirect references. Both types are effectively illustrated in the most famous example of his work that appears in the treatise, namely the facade of the Vanna Venturi house, of 1962 (fig. 15-1). Direct references include the split pediment treatment of the roof and the segmental arc straddling the lintel of the entrance recess. These features are employed against the foil of classical normalcy, implicit in the pedimented frame of the house, the axial placement of the entry recess, the axial placement of the "chimney," and the molded stringcourse that runs the width of the facade. Indirect references to mannerism occur in the violations of this regularity, manifested in the asymmetrical placement of the windows and their discrepant scale, the location of the front door to one side of the entry recess, and the placement of the flue off-axis on the chimney. The materials are noncommittal, but nontraditional for classicism, and the structure is thin and light, in the tradition of modernism. The combination of these various ways of breaking the rules is at once cultivated, witty, and ironic, denoting a self-assured sophistication. Moreover, the overall composition possesses a dynamic tension that would be lacking in a more regular—and more normally modern—

Figure 15-1
Postmodern design: Vanna Venturi House, by Venturi (Rollin R. LaFrance, courtesy VSBA).

design. Shocking at first, perhaps smacking of an irreverent vulgarity, it appeals to the viewer with a headier aesthetic than that of modernist designs.

Typically, postmodern mannerism has manifested itself through the incongruous appropriation of classical elements or the flouting of decorum in their application. Incongruity might occur with the use of incomplete or schematized—i.e., conceptually deformed—classical elements or their application out of context (fig. 15-2). Violation of decorum might occur through the distortion of traditional proportions of classical elements, as in John Outram's storm water pumping station on the Isle of Dogs, London, mid-1980s, where the elements of the Corinthian capital are reworked in a boldly abstract manner (fig. 15-2). Or it might occur as the juxtaposition of classical elements with popular (low art) elements, such as the Corinthian order with neon lights (as in Charles Moore's famous Piazza d'Italia, New Orleans,

Figure 15-2
Postmodern reconfiguration of classical motifs: storm water pumping station, Isle of Dogs, London, by Outram (courtesy John Outram Associates).

late 1970s) or a comic-strip-like caricature version of classical elements, such as a Doric column cut with exaggerated profile from a flat sheet of building material (as in a well-known house by the Venturi firm). Postmodernism employed incongruity in order to be witty and indecorousness to be charmingly cheeky. Neither quality had previously been deemed admissible to the high art of architecture, but both were undeniably characteristic of the contemporary culture, especially of the pop art movement in painting. Such a tolerance had become the standard of sophistication, a response to the shattering of the traditional cultural codes of Western civilization by the social cataclysms of the twentieth century. This aesthetic layering lies at the heart of postmodernism. Indeed, the use of these references in a piecemeal or mixed manner constituted an analogue to the late twentieth-century perspective on Western culture as damaged and fragmented.

An important contribution came out of the intermingled effect of the implicit historicism unleashed by *Complexity and Contradiction* and the implicit justification of vernacular architecture in *Learning from Las Vegas*. The latter text asserted that "Main Street is almost all right"— namely, that ugly and ordinary architecture has the estimable value of communicating satisfying meaning. This dictum prompted recognition of the reality that in the total fabric of a town each type of building contains signifiers that denote its identity and function, guiding and reassuring the citizens as they go about their daily lives. The linkage of historicism and practical iconography raised the consciousness of architects everywhere to the importance of respecting the context in which any new building takes its place. Quickly acknowledged to be a serious issue, regard for context awakened an awareness that modernist architects had erroneously assumed that their work would eventually take its place as a congenial neighbor to the historical styles, just as each predecessor had done. Such an assumption was inconsistent with the ahistorical aims of modernism, but it was an unconscious holdover from the Gothic revival's romantic attitude toward historical architecture in which modern theory had its origin.

It took several decades of cohabitation to discover that most modernist architecture was never going to form a congenial mix with other styles. For that reason it became an obligation of socially aware architects to study with care all the buildings, indeed the whole district, surrounding a designated building site. In contextual planning, such factors as height, scale, format of building type, and proximity to property lines need to be taken into account, along with color and texture of materials, so that they will all enhance rather than conflict with the setting. The principle of contextualism does not pretend to shape a design but does surround the development with cautionary guidelines.

Venturi's mannerist outlook has also opened the way for acceptance of the wholly new situation in architecture posed by adaptive reuse, namely, the willingness to accommodate a layering of disparate cultural messages. Cultural layering occurs when a format clearly belonging to one building type is employed for a different purpose, or when blatantly incongruous period styles are juxtaposed in a single building or complex. For example, the adaptive reuse of a church as a restaurant or nightclub creates a titillating cultural tension, sending disparate messages about function in the conflict between the obvious original format and the transforming decor. Similar sensations are experienced in the conversion of a multistory commercial building, factory, or school into residential lofts. Aesthetically, an experience of the same sort may be occasioned by the combination of elements of high and popular culture in the same design, or by the juxtaposition of informal modernity with formal tradition. The tensions may denote such qualities as irony or the surreal, but of whatever character, they are imputed, consciously or unconsciously, to the complexity of contemporary culture.

In adaptive reuse, the operative principles are nearly opposite those that apply to historical restoration. Preserving the authenticity of the original design is not a prerequisite, so long as the alterations do not obliterate the original identity—and thereby the disparate associations—of the building vis-à-vis its new function. Indeed, the goals of preservation may not even be desirable in adaptive reuse. In most cases the effectiveness of the makeover depends upon a maximal exploitation of the conflict between the old and new functions, because the attempt to mask the one for the sake of the other would void the effectiveness of the remodeling. For this practice to have attained acceptability implies the accommodation by society of a serious degree of cultural displacement. Although the wrenching events of the last third of the twentieth century may be responsible for that phenomenon, it is the theory of Venturi, in the perspective of the past, that makes it aesthetically palatable.

DECONSTRUCTIVISM AS THE POSTSTRUCTURAL CRITIQUE OF MODERNISM

A markedly different critique of modernism was developed in the 1980s and 1990s, in the movement tentatively labeled as deconstructivism. Instigated by French poststructuralist critical methods of the 1960s and 1970s, this architectural movement represented a conscious effort on the part of architects to incorporate into their work what they regarded as the intellectual ethos of their time. This impulse to make architecture reflect contemporary intellectuality may have been prompted by Erwin Panofsky's *Gothic Architecture and Scholasticism* (1956), which attempted to show that the design of Gothic cathedrals reflected the intellectual methodology of scholastic theology. Powerfully presented, this study launched into the culture of the 1960s the notion that because in the past great architecture has reflected the philosophical bent of its time any new architecture that achieves greatness will necessarily also reflect contemporary intellectual predilections. Hence the adaptation of poststructuralist critical theory to architectural design posed an irresistible challenge.

Stated with schematic simplicity, poststructuralism recognizes that any attempt to explain the causality of a complex situation or to construct a seamless narrative account from a series of events cannot possibly represent the full complexity of what actually happened. Indeed, to the contrary, any such explanation necessarily involves the creation of utile fictions, in which discrete facts are artificially associated in such a manner as to make a narrative or a sequence of causal relationships seem plausible. The reasoned deconstruction of such narrative and causal constructs has occasioned the appropriation of "deconstructionist" as the name for the poststructural intellectual movement in the United States. Hence some architects, keen to have their designs express the most profound level of the culture of their time, have attempted to adopt the concept for their architecture, while a version of the name has been applied by the critics.

Such an architectural movement was promoted in the 1980s as deconstructivism, first by the critic Charles Jencks, then more officially with an exhibition and catalog at the Museum of Modern Art. (The museum, following its triumphs in recognizing and propagating modernism in 1932 and postmodernism in 1966, did not want to miss being the prophet of the next big wave. Its sometime curator of architecture, Philip Johnson, was involved all three times.) In other contexts deconstructivism has been explained largely by Peter Eisenman, in a number of essays no one of which has emerged as the best or most authoritative statement. Most of the architects who were given this label have disavowed it and even Eisenman regards himself as having moved away from it, an appropriate distancing move at a time when the corresponding intellectual movement has lost steam and is now increasingly ignored. Yet, despite all these disclaimers, the concept represents an intriguing theoretical option for structure and one of the most compelling critiques of modernism.

The application of this concept to architecture involves making a viewer unable to apprehend a building as a whole from any single vantage point. Ideally, the user has to make his way in and through it without the aid of conventional signifiers, so that constant discretion must be maintained. Through this means a heightened awareness of the environment—and therefore of one's existence—is promoted. For this purpose normal expectations are thwarted, both as regards spatial arrangement within the building and also its apparent structural composition. Deconstructivist buildings may be made to look as if they are either coming apart or perhaps have been irrationally assembled. To achieve this effect a building may include extraneous structural elements or spaces that cannot be occupied. Barriers may preclude straightforward access, or spatial relationships may be ambiguous. Altogether, deconstructivism aspired to create an architecture that magnifies consciousness.

Eisenman's Wexner Center for the Arts on the campus of Ohio State University, of the mid-1980s, is typical enough to be taken as the signature building of the movement (fig. 15-3). Occupying the interval between and behind two extant performance halls that acutely contrast with its style and format, it creates high drama by looking as if it has collided with the other two and exploded at either end. Each of its entry facades—if such a term can be properly used in this case—is totally unlike the other. One of them inhabits ghostlike reconstructions of burnt-out towers, fake ruins of a building that formerly stood on the site. Another is a white metal frame of open-grid construction that leads down an inclined path into the arterial corridor. The corridor itself is split by a freestanding wall that separates two different paths; one slants upward and the other down. The downward path terminates at the other end of the building, where a broad staircase leads to an upper lobby and the other principal entry (fig. 15-4). The staircase is interrupted by a structural column supporting a beam that does not quite reach the wall, while nearby another ostensible column, suspended from the ceiling,

Figure 15-3
Deconstructivist design: Wexner Center for the Arts, Ohio State University, Columbus, by Eisenman (courtesy David Wilkins).

terminates well above floor level. This adventurous circulation system serves a library, studios, exhibition galleries, performance rooms, offices, and a museum shop. The upper path leads through a series of galleries. Disorienting features continue throughout, so that any visit promises a psychologically stimulating experience.

The basis for the apparent disorganization of this design was the use of two different axial coordinates that meet at an angle and introduce conflicts in the structural grid of the building. The justification for adopting these conflicting axes is that one can be attached to a dominant feature of the campus and the other to the grid of city streets. And the pretext for recognizing both is that the site of the building is near the meeting of campus and city. Yet another consideration was that the ancient indigenous population had built a burial mound on the site, long ago removed. They are memorialized in Eisenman's scheme by the mounds of earth encompassed by the walled garden paths just outside the

Figure 15-4
Deconstructivst structure: Wexner Center interior, Ohio State
University, Columbus, by Eisenman. (D. G. Olshavsky/ARTOG,
courtesy Eisenman Architects).

building. These mounds were even planted with tall wild
grasses to recall the original natural vegetation. Taken together, these references constitute a sensitive and sophisticated appreciation for the physical and historical context of
the site. But there is nothing in the function of the arts cen-

Figure 15-5
Computer-morphed structure: Convention Center interior, Columbus, by Eisenman (Jeff Goldberg/ESTO, courtesy Eisenman Architects).

ter nor in the campus context that predicates such a consideration. In the final analysis, it is all a pretext for making the design take on an irrational appearance.

A variant of this concept of structure is the deliberate malformation of a design scheme, using a computer morphing program. A reasonably straightforward design can be distorted to look as if it has been twisted, bent, or melted. Because only a computer can make this kind of design fea-

Figure 15-6
Computer-morphed design: Convention Center exterior, Columbus, by Eisenman (courtesy David Wilkins).

sible, such malformation becomes the justification for the use of the computer in the design process. The great virtue of this method is that exact measurements reside within the computer record and can be called up or rendered at will. Even better, the measurements can be projected directly to a laser mechanism with which the building materials can be cut to precise shape and size. This method was employed, for instance, in Eisenman's convention center for Columbus, Ohio. Composed of a series of parallel longitudinal structures, the whole was morphed in order to distort the spaces and structural framework. As a result, the interior vistas, which could have been both boring and tiresome, become an adventurous sequence of unexpected episodes (fig. 15-5). On the exterior, the main street facade, facing a row of ordinary shops of moderate scale, is articulated as a series of architectural incidents similar to those across the street, with the exception that they appear to make a rhythmic jumble of distorted units (fig. 15-6).

The postmodern and poststructuralist critiques of modernism exposed gaps or shortcomings in rational design method. In either case the remedy addresses the area of cultural meaning in architecture. Toward this end, postmodernism is likely to gesture in the direction of historical or typological associations. Poststructuralism, on the other hand, is more likely to discover meaning in factors that are lodged in the physical topography of the site or the architectural configuration of the environment.

RECASTING THE INITIAL STAGES OF DESIGN METHOD

Although Venturi diagnosed the absence of cultural meaning in modernist architecture, he did not specify how its absence might be alleviated. His critique implicitly pointed to a lacuna in the rational design method of modernism, which prevailed everywhere in both the curricula of architecture schools and the practice of professional offices. There is nothing seriously wrong with this method except for the vacuity of the assumption that design development is merely a problem-solving process that begins with a list of functions. What it lacks are a few steps that ought to precede the accepted beginning of the method, steps that would prompt the consideration of all sorts of cultural issues.

A good source for this methodological boost is an extant comprehensive theory of creativity, one that has belonged to Western civilization since the early days of Greco-Roman culture, namely the theory of rhetoric. Most fully explicated in an anonymous treatise sometimes ascribed to Cicero, the so-called *Rhetorica ad Herennium*, and Quintilian's *Institutes of Oratory*, the rules of rhetoric—whether employed consciously or unconsciously—underlie many great works of Western art, from the dramas of Shakespeare to the symphonies of Mozart and the novels of Tolstoy. Of the five parts of rhetoric—invention, arrangement, embellishment, memory, and delivery—those that can help supply the missing parts of the theory of architectural design method belong to invention and the initial aspects of arrangement.

Invention involves selecting and defining the theme and identifying the purpose behind it. The relevant aspects of arrangement involve projecting the theme into the process of composition. When these stages of creative development are applied to architecture, at least as much responsibility lies with the patron as with architect, although in the best of circumstances collaboration will have been entered into from the outset. It is in the nature of things that the choice of theme, that is, the type of building to be designed, and perhaps the site as well, have been decided upon by the patron before the design process has begun. The patron also necessarily has a purpose—whether consciously articulated or not—and probably some notion of the manner in which it is to be carried out. Indeed, the extent to which those issues have already been defined will undoubtedly have influenced the selection of the architect. Consequently, the patron needs to know something about the former work of the architect and be confident that that person has the capacity to realize the purpose in an appropriate manner. But for optimum results neither patron nor architect should embark upon the project with a fixed image in mind. If the user(s) of the proposed building will be other than the client, either they or responsible representatives of their interests may (indeed, ought to) be involved in the process also.

The important issue at this point is not to start with the functional program. That should be drawn up only following a thorough discussion of the nature of the project and its purpose. The cultural role of the project must be defined after examining several different options. In that process the social and political implications of each role option must be carefully considered. In most cases it will be necessary to determine these matters with reference to an already existing context. Whatever is to be built will either complement or confront the context. Hence the purpose of the project is much more than just the housing of certain functions. The new building will necessarily make a statement about the nature of those functions and their place in the communal context. In doing so it will embody certain values and will project them upon the neighboring environment and the community. Architectural forms have a way of working this way even when the designer has proceeded without conscious intentions, never mind programmatic objectives, just as a photographer inevitably interprets a subject whether intending to do so or not. For that reason it is better to consider beforehand what values ought to be communicated rather than to discover too late that the message sent was not the most constructive that could have been devised. No matter how conveniently the various practical functions may be housed, the building will never be satisfactory unless it has first properly addressed its cultural purpose.

The theory of rhetoric defines four steps to accomplish these aims. The first is the *charge,* the decision to build a building of a certain type. Next follows the *division into issues:* What is to be accomplished by constructing this building? Who is to be served, in what manner, and at what location? What will the building express in the course of carrying out its function? To answer these questions it is necessary to lay out the *alternatives,* which will represent the various ways in which the purpose could be accomplished and specify the good each of them should be able to do. When these have been articulated a *choice with justification* needs to be made.

Ancient rhetoricians explained their theory by citing examples, and that is probably the best way to show how this enhancement of the theory of design method might be employed. Toward this end I shall take three different building types through this initial stage of planning. The first is a public library, to represent institutions that are open to virtually all comers. The second is a commercial office building, with moderate access limited to working occupants and certified clients. The third is a freestanding, private house, with access restricted to occupants and guests.

From a postmodern point of view, the alternatives for the library are degrees of impressing and welcoming while defining the nature and function of a library. If the library is defined as a collection of cultural treasures, meant to enhance the spirits of the clientele, it could be formulated as a temple of learning, which would impress and uplift, or as a palace of learning, which would impress and delight. On the other hand, if it is defined as simply a storage and circulation facility for information and entertainment, a more informal public image may be sought. In that case the library might be formulated as a factory of learning, a laboratory of knowledge, a high tech information retrieval center, a community cultural club, or even an information circus. Each definition will call for a strikingly different design, which will announce the intended institutional purpose and, in turn, affect the communal use of the library and also the formation of the communal self-image. Once the purpose has been defined, it is appropriate to make some basic functional stipulations, such as whether to have open or closed stacks, complete or partial circulation of the collection, structured or informal reading areas, and maintenance of nonprint resources.

For the commercial building, the alternatives depend upon how the occupants are to be attracted to lease or rent spaces and how their clientele are to be accommodated. For instance, it could be a building with a self-selected and self-assured clientele of limited numbers, who get an ego boost from the building. In this case the design could be forbiddingly stylish, dauntingly sophisticated, challengingly hip, exclusively clubby, or unabashedly ethnic. If it is for a clientele with narrowly specialized activities, the design could be illustrative of the relevant product or service or expressive of expertness in that specialty. If, on the other hand, it is to have broad popular appeal, attracting a large and heterogeneous clientele, it should be openly accessible, friendly, and unchallenging in character. It could be formulated as technically forward, culturally evocative of the region, or self-referentially witty.

For the house, the alternatives range among different types of formality and informality. Formal houses are meant to separate the occupants from the surrounding community by distinguishing them in a particular way. Such a house can be a cultural symbol, for instance a temple-like design formulated in one of the classical orders, evoking cultivation and refinement. Or it might be a class status symbol, such as an additive Tudor manor house evoking the prosperity of inherited land ownership. Such a symbol could also be a strikingly sumptuous urban palazzo, bespeaking liquid wealth. Informal houses, on the other hand, are meant to connect the occupants with the surrounding community or at least with the natural environment. They usually denote a relaxed lifestyle and hospitality, as in a rustic ranch house, or a cozy domesticity, as in a cottage, or oneness with nature, as in a berm house. Or such a residence can denote participation in urban modernity, as in a high tech villa. The functional program, whether for an austere or hedonistic lifestyle or something between, will be determined in part by cultural and social definitions.

In each case the thematic choice needs to be justified by the commissioning client, whether that entity is an individual, a board of directors or trustees, or a focus group representing the community. The choice ought to be justified in terms of both the architectural (or natural) context and the values of the community. In some instances this choice may govern the choice of site as well. Be that as it may, when these four steps are taken prior to embarking upon the method prescribed by Viollet-le-Duc, it is much more likely that the resulting scheme will be culturally satisfying than if the design process begins with nothing more than a list of functions.

A poststructuralist approach to all three building types is more likely to address the history and geography of the community, drawing upon factors not immediately relevant to each building type, or not inherent in the cultural definition of the project. When creatively discerned, these factors help to define or localize the design schemes just as aptly as do traditional signifiers. As with thematic content, the focus on these factors needs to precede articulation of the functional program.

COMPUTERS AND DESIGN METHOD

In the last two decades of the twentieth century the computer has assumed an increasingly important role in architectural planning. Initially it was chiefly a tool useful in the process of laying out a design. Then it became a medium for devising the design. Now it is being recognized as a force that will significantly reshape the architectural environment itself.

As tools, computers can be used to generate and store detailed design schemes. Although the initial entry of a scheme may be more time-consuming than for a traditional board drawing, the value of doing so is that the computer image can be easily altered without the necessity of drawing the scheme all over again. It also permits the conversion of two-dimensional schematic drawings into three-dimensional images, which can be examined from all sorts of angles, both inside and out. For complex projects the computer permits linkage of several different programs that are employed to help realize various aspects of the design—such as one for functional space allocation, another for the structural systems, and still another for technical systems and quantitative code requirements. The value of this linkage is that it permits the designer to combine data systems that are usually difficult to reconcile in manual drawings. Moreover, the linkage can detect inconsistencies between plan and section, thereby avoiding practical problems and undue expense after construction has begun. But beyond the reconciliation of technical discrepancies and their other functions as tools, computer programs also leave room for creative improvisation in the leeway between the restraints imposed and the "affordances" permitted. In this way they serve the play of imagination as well as performing mechanical tasks (see Mitchell 1995; also McCullough 1996).

As a medium of design, computers permit a degree of targeted differentiation of details within the system of a large complex that is simply not feasible in a manually composed scheme. The necessary variances of materials and dimensions can be easily noted and stored, after which the relevant data can be extracted to draw up the specifications. Although computers readily serve the rational design method of modern architecture, they are equally capable of storing visual component data for the assemblage of conventional features employed in a traditional design. To wit, the various components of the classical orders, their normal window and door treatments, and even conventional combinations of formal elements can be stored as predetermined components and then assembled at will in varying compositions and at any scale. This ready access permits the designer to experiment with combinations of components and different proportional arrangements (Mitchell 1995, McCullough 1996).

As a medium of stylistic innovation, the computer has thus far mainly encouraged the adoption of design complexity, achieved in conceptually opposite ways. The first way is, having made a normal configuration, to distort it to make it look bent, folded, twisted, or melted. The other is to devise free-form shapes and then translate them into computer images that can be fully charted and measured. With either method the measurements can be projected directly to a laser mechanism with which the building materials can be cut to precise shape and size. Because reconciling the complexities of these kinds of design is feasible only with the aid of a computer, the ability to make such designs has become the artistic justification for using computers in the design process.

Frank Gehry has employed both methods. Morphing was adopted in his Netherlands National Building in Prague, of the mid-1990s (fig. 16-1). Nicknamed "Fred and Ginger," it sports a distorted circulation tower that suggests the swaying movement of an elegantly waltzing couple. The windows of the office stories undulate in the facade as if responding to music. Created as a straightforward structural design and then morphed into distortion, its effect is

Figure 16-1
Computer-determined design and construction: Netherlands National Building, Prague, by Gehry (FH).

whimsical but manifests a redemptive seriousness of creative purpose. The Guggenheim Museum in Bilbao (fig. 16-2), on the other hand, was artistically composed and then rendered technically possible by entering the design into a computer. Created in the spirit of sculptural play and then reconciled to the functional program of displaying art, its relationship to the computer was one of technical facilitation rather than artistic formulation. Both designs beg the question: if such capability were not residing in the computer, would anyone think to make buildings that look like this? They bespeak cutting-edge modernity, but only because they derive from the technical frontier. One cannot reasonably expect to build whole cities in this manner; such

Figure 16-2
Computer-facilitated design: Guggenheim Museum, Bilbao, by Gehry (courtesy David Wilkins).

fantastical schemes can be no more than accents to the built environment, never the norm. The real design direction for architecture made with computers, then, remains unclear.

The environmental impact of computers begins with the architectural office itself. Thanks to data storage, most of the furniture of a traditional office, and consequently much of the square footage of the office that is normally occupied by such furniture, has been rendered unnecessary. Drawing tables and spacious design studios, together with cabinets for storing drawings and the blueprint machines for reproducing them, are, in such circumstances, nearly obsolete. It is no longer necessary even to convene under one roof all the professionals needed to coordinate a complex project. William J. Mitchell, in *City of Bits: Space, Place, and the Infobahn* (Cambridge, MA, 1995), notes that as telecommunications become more complex and are more seamlessly integrated with computers, the cyber-machinery becomes part of the fabric of buildings, and buildings themselves become computers. Hence the implications for the design of buildings are profound, but how they will take form is still unclear.

To perceive the scope of this transformation one needs only to reflect that prior to the industrial revolution a building was basically just a structural shell, into which activities and their supports were installed. But afterward buildings came in gradual progression to have plumbing and lighting systems, elevators, heating and cooling systems, communications systems and, more recently, surveillance and security systems. In a phrase, buildings came to be machines as well as structures. As a machine, however, a building was still the locus for a specific population carrying out specific activities in a limited venue. Now the computer makes possible the conduct of many activities without their taking place in a single, fixed location. Not only is a reversal of the separation of home and workplace (begun in the seventeenth century) occurring, but also a general decentralization, the implications of which for cities are only just becoming apparent. In this respect the computer is much more than a tool or a medium of architectural design; it is also the basis for the likely transformation of the built environment, as it has been known for millennia (Mitchell 1995). How that is to happen has yet to be imagined, much less designed and constructed.

Conclusion

The preceding chapters have distinguished the fundamental topics of architectural theory as universal underpinnings, conventions, principles, and convolutions, the last three characteristic respectively of the eras before 1800, from 1800 to 1965, and after 1965. This categorization associates the types of theory with the chronological circumstances of their development, but it does not foreclose the validity of employing the earlier theories in the present. Old theories have a way of reasserting their value, either in combination with new theories or as options alongside the others. The distinctive characteristic of the most recent theories, those designated as convolutions, is their capacity to enrich and enlarge the scope of design potentialities without voiding the ability of the older theories to nurture culturally relevant designs. In other words, it is still possible to create worthwhile buildings using the theory of classical conventions—even with a computer—just as it is also possible to do so with the theory of modernist principles. Indeed, to embrace the convolutions as the only theories relevant to the present is to risk falling into a morass of self-indulgence. The architect who would be maximally free to produce optimal designs for particular situations is one who recognizes the importance of being conversant with the entire range of architectural theory, free to pick and choose theories according to their appropriateness to a given situation.

Time Line of Treatises
by John Hearn

Date	Author	Title	Location
30 B.C.E.	Marcus Vitruvius Pollio	*De architectura* presented to Caesar Augustus	Rome
1414	Marcus Vitruvius Pollio	complete version of *De architectura* rediscovered	Saint-Gall
1450	Leon Battista Alberti	*De re aedificatoria* presented to Pope Nicholas V	Rome
1485	Leon Battista Alberti	*De re aedificatoria* printed	Florence
1511	Fra Giovanni Giocondo	Translation of Vitruvius into Italian	Venice
1537	Sebastiano Serlio	*Architettura,* Book IV	Venice
1540	Sebastiano Serlio	*Architettura,* Book III	Venice
1545	Sebastiano Serlio	*Architettura,* Books I, II, and V	Paris
1551	Sebastiano Serlio	*Extraordinario libro di archi-tettura*	Venice
1556	Daniele Barbaro	Translation of Vitruvius into Italian	Venice

Date	Author	Title	Location
1562	Giacomo Barozzi da Vignola	*Regola delli cinque ordini d'architettura*	Rome
1567	Philibert de l'Orme	*L'architecture*	Paris
1570	Andrea Palladio	*Quattro libri d'architettura*	Venice
1584	Sebastiano Serlio	*Tutte l'opere d'architettura*	Venice
1615	Vincenzo Scamozzi	*L'idea della architettura universale*	Venice
1650	Roland Fréart de Chambray	*Parallèle de l'architecture antique et de la moderne*	Paris
1675	François Blondel	*Cours d'architecture,* vols. 1 and 2	Paris
1683	François Blondel	*Cours d'architecture,* vol. 3	Paris
1683	Claude Perrault	*Ordonnance des cinq espèces de colonnes*	Paris
1706	Jean-Louis Cordemoy	*Essai sur l'architecture*	Paris
1753	Marc-Antoine Laugier	*Essai sur l'architecture* (rev. ed. 1755)	Paris
1788–1823	A.-C. Quatremère de Quincy	*Encyclopédie méthodique*	Paris
1800	Jean-Nicolas-Louis Durand	*Recueil et parallèle des édifices de tout genre*	Paris
1802–1819	Jean-Nicolas-Louis Durand	*Précis des leçons d'architecture*	Paris
1803	A.-C. Quatremère de Quincy	*De l'architecture égyptienne*	Paris
1836	Augustus Welby Northmore Pugin	*Contrasts*	London

Date	Author	Title	Location
1841	Augustus Welby Northmore Pugin	*Principles of Pointed or Christian Architecture*	London
1849	John Ruskin	*The Seven Lamps of Architecture*	London
1850	Andrew Jackson Downing	*The Architecture of Country Houses*	New York
1851–1853	John Ruskin	*The Stones of Venice*	London
1860–1863	Gottfried Semper	*Der Stil in den technischen und tektonischen Künsten*	Frankfurt
1863	Eugène-Emmanuel Viollet-le-Duc	*Entretiens sur l'architecture, vol. 1*	Paris
1872	Eugène-Emmanuel Viollet-le-Duc	*Entretiens sur l'architecture, vol. 2*	Paris
1873	Eugène-Emmanuel Viollet-le-Duc	*Histoire d'une maison*	Paris
1875	Eugène-Emmanuel Viollet-le-Duc	*Histoire de l'habitation humaine*	Paris
1879	Eugène-Emmanuel Viollet-le-Duc	*Histoire d'un dessinateur, comment on apprend à dessiner*	Paris
1889	Camillo Sitte	*Der Städtebau nach seiner künstlerischen Grundsätzen*	Vienna
1896	Otto Wagner	*Moderne Architektur*	Vienna
1896	Louis Sullivan	"The Tall Building Artistically Considered"	New York
1898	Ebenezer Howard	*Tomorrow, a Peaceful Path to Real Reform*	London

Date	Author	Title	Location
1902	Ebenezer Howard	*Garden Cities of To-morrow*	London
1904–1905	Hermann Muthesius	*Das englische Haus*	Berlin
1908	Adolf Loos	*Ornament und Verbrechen*	Vienna
1908	Frank Lloyd Wright	"In the Cause of Architecture," *Architectural Record*	New York
1912–1914	Antonio Sant'Elia	*La città nuova*	Milan
1914	Antonio Sant'Elia	*Manifesto dell'architettura futurista*	Milan
1914	Paul Scheerbart	*Glasarchitektur*	Berlin
1917	Tony Garnier	*Une cité industrielle*	Paris
1923	Walter Gropius	*Idee und Aufbau des staatlichen Bauhauses Weimar*	Dessau
1923	Le Corbusier	*Vers une architecture*	Paris
1925	Le Corbusier	*Urbanisme*	Paris
1927–1928	Frank Lloyd Wright	"The Nature of Materials," *Architectual Record*	New York
1932	Philip Johnson and Henry-Russell Hitchcock	*The International Style*	New York
1932	Frank Lloyd Wright	*An Autobiography*	New York
1932	Frank Lloyd Wright	*The Disappearing City*	New York
1941	Sigfried Giedion	*Space, Time and Architecture*	Cambridge, MA
1948	Le Corbusier	*Le Modulor*	Paris

Date	Author	Title	Location
1952	Frank Lloyd Wright	"The Nature of Materials," *Architectural Record*	New York
1954	Frank Lloyd Wright	*The Natural House*	New York
1955	Le Corbusier	*Modulor 2*	Paris
1966	Robert Venturi	*Complexity and Contradiction in Architecture*	New York
1972	Robert Venturi, Denise Scott Brown, and Steven Izenour	*Learning from Las Vegas* (rev. ed. 1977)	Cambridge, MA
1988	Philip Johnson and Mark Wigley	*Deconstructivist Architecture*	New York
1991	William J. Mitchell and Malcolm McCollough	*Digital Design Media*	New York
1995	William J. Mitchell	*City of Bits: Space, Place, and the Infobahn*	Cambridge, MA
1996	Malcolm McCullough	*Abstracting Craft: The Practiced Digital Hand*	Cambridge, MA

Bibliography

This bibliography consists of works cited, consulted, or deemed relevant to the discussions of the theories in the text. It does not purport to be comprehensive either for architectural theory in general or even for the treatises discussed in the foregoing pages.

Alberti, Leon Battista. c. 1450. *De re aedificatoria*. Trans. Joseph Rykwert, Neal Leach, and Robert Tavernor as *On the Art of Building in Ten Books*. Cambridge, MA, 1988.

Banham, Reyner. 1955. "New Brutalism." *Architectural Review* 118: 355–358.

Banham, Reyner. 1966. *The New Brutalism: Ethic or Aesthetic?* London.

Banham, Reyner. 1967. *Theory and Design in the First Machine Age*. New York.

Banham, Reyner. 1969. *The Architecture of the Well-Tempered Environment*. London.

Benevolo, Leonardo. 1967. *The Origins of Modern Town Planning*. Trans. H. J. Landry. Cambridge, MA.

Benevolo, Leonardo. 1971. *History of Modern Architecture*. 2 vols. Trans. H. J. Landry. Cambridge, MA.

Blondel, François. 1675 (vols. 1, 2), 1683 (vol. 3). *Cours d'architecture*. 3 vols. Paris.

Carroll, Virginia. 1975. "These Houses Are All Exactly the Same. They Just Look Different." *Lotus*.

Carroll, Virginia, Denise Scott Brown, and Robert Venturi. 1972. "Levittown et Après." *Architecture d'aujourd'hui* 163: 38–42.

Chambers, William. 1791. *A Treatise on the Decorative Part of Civil Architecture*. London. Reprint, New York, 1968.

[Cicero?]. 1954. *Rhetorica ad Herennium*. Trans. Harry Caplan. Cambridge, MA.

Conrads, Ulrich, ed. 1970. *Programs and Manifestoes on 20th-Century Architecture*. Trans. Michael Bullock. Cambridge, MA.

Dacos, Nicole. 1969. *La découverte de la Domus Aurea et la formation de la grotesque à la Renaissance*. London.

de l'Orme, Philibert. 1567. *L'architecture*. Paris.

Downing, A[ndrew] J[ackson]. 1850. *The Architecture of Country Houses*. New York.

Durand, Jean-Nicolas-Louis. 1800. *Recueil et parallèle des édifices de tout genre*. Paris, 1800.

Durand, Jean-Nicolas-Louis. 1802–1819. *Précis des leçons d'architecture*. Paris.

Eisenman, Peter, Rosalind Krauss, and Manfredo Tafuri. 1987. *Houses of Cards*. New York.

Fishman, Robert. 1977. *Urban Utopias in the Twentieth Century: Ebenezer Howard, Frank Lloyd Wright, and Le Corbusier*. Cambridge, MA.

Fréart de Chambray, Roland. 1650. *Parallèle de l'architecture antique et de la moderne*. Paris.

Fuller, R. Buckminster. 1963. *Ideas and Integrities*. New York.

Garnier, Tony. 1917. *Une cité industrielle*. Paris.

Ghirardo, Diane. 1996. *Architecture after Modernism*. London.

Giedion, Sigfried. 1941. *Space, Time and Architecture: The Growth of a New Tradition*. Cambridge, MA.

Gropius, Walter. 1923. *Idee und Aufbau des staatlichen Bauhauses Weimar*. Berlin. Trans. P. Morton Shand as *The New Architecture and the Bauhaus*. 1935; reprint, Cambridge, MA, 1965.

Hart, Vaughn, with Peter Hicks, eds. 1998. *Paper Palaces: The Rise of the Renaissance Architectural Treatise*. New Haven.

Hays, K. Michael, ed. 1998. *Architecture Theory since 1968*. Cambridge, MA.

Hearn, M. F. 1981. *Romanesque Sculpture: The Revival of Monumental Stone Sculpture in the Eleventh and Twelfth Century*. Ithaca.

Hearn, M. F. 1991. "A Japanese Origin for Frank Lloyd Wright's Rigid-Core High-Rise Buildings." *Journal of the Society of Architectural Historians* 50: 68–71.

Herrmann, Wolfgang. 1984. *Gottfried Semper: In Search of Architecture*. Cambridge, MA.

Hitchcock, Henry-Russell, and Philip Johnson. 1932. *The International Style: Architecture since 1922*. New York.

Howard, Ebenezer. 1902. *Garden Cities of To-morrow*. London.

Hubbard, William. 1980. *Complicity and Conviction: Steps toward an Architecture of Convention*. Cambridge, MA.

Jacobs, Jane. 1961. *The Death and Life of Great American Cities*. New York.

Johnson, Philip, and Mark Wigley. 1988. *Deconstructivist Architecture*. New York.

Kroll, Lucien. 1983. *Composants—faut-il industrialiser l'architecture?* Brussels. Trans. Peter Blundell Jones as *An Architecture of Complexity*. Cambridge, MA, 1983.

Kruft, Hanno-Walter. 1994. *A History of Architectural Theory: From Vitruvius to the Present*. Trans. R. Taylor, E. Callander, and A. Wood. London and New York.

Laugier, Marc-Antoine. 1753. *Essai sur l'architecture*. Paris. Rev. ed., 1755. Trans. Wolfgang and Anni Herrmann as *An Essay on Architecture*. Los Angeles, 1977.

Lavin, Sylvia. 1992. *Quatremère de Quincy and the Invention of a Modern Language of Architecture*. Cambridge, MA.

Le Corbusier. 1923. *Vers une architecture*. Paris. Trans. Frederick Etchells as *Towards a New Architecture*. London, 1927.

Le Corbusier. 1925. *Urbanisme*. Paris. Trans. Frederick Etchells as *The City of To-morrow and Its Planning*. 1929; reprint, New York, 1987.

Ligo, Larry. 1984. *The Concept of Function in Twentieth-Century Architectural Criticism*. Ann Arbor.

Long, Pamela Olivia. 1979. "The Vitruvian Commentary Tradition and Rational Architecture of the Sixteenth Century." Ph.D. diss., University of Maryland.

Loos, Adolf. 1908. *Ornament und Verbrechen*. Vienna.

Lynch, Kevin. 1960. *The Image of the City*. Cambridge, MA.

Lyttelton, Margaret. 1974. *Baroque Architecture in Ancient Rome*. Ithaca.

Mallgrave, Harry Francis. 1996. *Gottfried Semper: Architect of the Nineteenth Century*. New Haven.

Mallgrave, Harry Francis, and Eleftherios Ikonomou, trans. 1993. *Empathy, Form, and Space: Problems in German Aesthetics, 1873–1893*. Santa Monica.

McCullough, Malcolm. 1996. *Abstracting Craft: The Practiced Digital Hand*. Cambridge, MA.

Meyer, Esther da Costa. 1995. *The Work of Antonio Sant'Elia: Retreat into the Future*. New Haven.

Mitchell, William J. 1995. *City of Bits: Space, Place, and the Infobahn*. Cambridge, MA.

Mitchell, William J., and Malcolm McCullough. 1991. *Digital Design Media: A Handbook for Architects and Design Professionals*. New York.

Mitrović, Branko. 1990. "Palladio's Theory of Proportions and the Second Book of the *Quattro libri dell'archittetura*." *Journal of the Society of Architectural Historians* 49: 279–292.

Muthesius, Hermann. 1904–1905. *Das englische Haus*. 3 vols. Berlin. Trans. Janet Seligman as *The English House*. New York, 1979.

Palladio, Andrea. 1570. *I quattro libri dell'architettura*. Venice. Trans. Isaac Ware as *The Four Books of Architecture*. 1738; reprint, New York, 1965. New trans. Robert Tavernor and Richard Schofield as *The Four Books on Architecture*. Cambridge, MA, 1997.

Panofsky, Erwin. 1956. *Gothic Architecture and Scholasticism*. Latrobe, PA.

Payne, Alina A. 1999. *The Architectural Treatise in the Italian Renaissance: Architectural Invention, Ornament, and Literary Culture*. Cambridge.

Pérez-Gómez, Alberto. 1983. *Architecture and the Crisis of Modern Science*. Cambridge, MA.

Perrault, Claude. 1683. *Ordonnance des cinq espèces de colonnes selon la méthode des anciens*. Paris.

Pugin, Augustus Welby Northmore. 1836. *Contrasts*. London.

Pugin, Augustus Welby Northmore. 1841. *True Principles of Pointed or Christian Architecture*. London.

Quatremère de Quincy, Antoine-Chrysostome. 1788–1823. *Encyclopédie méthodique*. Paris.

Quatremère de Quincy, Antoine-Chrysostome. 1803. *De l'architecture égyptienne*. Paris.

Quintilian. 1921. *Institutio oratoria*. Trans. H. E. Butler. 4 vols. Cambridge, MA.

Ruskin, John. 1849. *The Seven Lamps of Architecture*. London.

Ruskin, John. 1851–1853. *The Stones of Venice*. London.

Rykwert, Joseph. 1972. *On Adam's House in Paradise: The Idea of the Primitive Hut in Architectural History*. New York.

Saarinen, Eliel. 1948. *Search for Form: A Fundamental Approach to Art*. New York. Reprint as *The Search for Form in Architecture*. New York, 1985.

Sant'Elia, Antonio. 1914. *Manifesto dell'architettura futurista*. Milan.

Scamozzi, Vincenzo. 1615. *L'idea della architettura universale*. Venice. Reprint, Ridgewood, NJ, 1964.

Scheerbart, Paul. 1914. *Glasarchitektur*. Berlin. Trans. James Palmes as *Glass Architecture*. New York, 1972.

Schmarsow, August. 1894. *Das Wesen der architektonischen Schöpfung*. Leipzig.

Scott, Geoffrey. 1914. *The Architecture of Humanism: A Study in the History of Taste*. London.

Semper, Gottfried. 1860, 1863. *Der Stil in den technischen und tektonischen Künsten oder praktische Aesthetic: Ein Handbuch für Techniker, Künstler, und Kunstfreunde*. Frankfurt. Reprint, Mittenwald, 1977.

Semper, Gottfried. 1989. *The Four Elements of Architecture and Other Writings*. Trans. Harry Francis Mallgrave and Wolfgang Herrmann. New York.

Sergeant, John. 1976. *Frank Lloyd Wright's Usonian Houses: The Case for Organic Architecture*. New York.

Serlio, Sebastiano. 1551. *Extraordinario libro di architettura*. Venice.

Serlio, Sebastiano. 1584. *Tutte l'opere d'architettura et prospettiva*. Venice. Trans. for Robert Peake as *The Five Books of Architecture*. London, 1611; reprint, New York, 1982. New trans. Vaughn Hart and Peter Hicks as *Sebastiano Serlio on Architecture*. New Haven, 1996.

Shepheard, Paul. 1994. *What Is Architecture?* Cambridge, MA.

Sitte, Camillo. 1889. *Der Städtebau nach seiner künstlerischen Grundsätzen*. Vienna. Trans. George R. Collins and Christiane

Crasemann Collins as *City Planning According to Artistic Principles*. New York, 1965.

Soleri, Paolo. 1969. *Arcology: The City in the Image of Man*. Cambridge, MA.

Stuart, James, and Nicholas Revett. 1858. *Antiquities of Athens and Other Monuments of Greece*. 3rd ed. London.

Sullivan, Louis. 1988. *The Public Papers*. Ed. Robert C. Twombley. Chicago.

Summers, David. 1972. "Michelangelo on Architecture." *Art Bulletin* 54: 146–157.

Summers, David. 1981. *Michelangelo and the Language of Art*. Princeton.

Summerson, John. 1966. *The Classical Language of Architecture*. Cambridge, MA.

Szambien, Werner. 1986. *Symétrie, goût, caractère: théorie et terminologie de l'architecture à l'âge classique, 1550–1800*. Paris.

Tafuri, Manfredo. 1967. *The Origins of Modern Town Planning*. Cambridge, MA.

Tafuri, Manfredo. 1976. *Architecture and Utopia: Design and Capitalist Development*. Trans. Barbara Luigia La Penta. Cambridge, MA.

Tafuri, Manfredo. 1979. *History of Modern Architecture*. New York.

Tschumi, Bernard, et al. 1988. "Deconstruction in Architecture." *A. D.: Architectural Design* 58.

Turak, Theodore. 1985. "Remembrances of the Home Insurance Building." *Journal of the Society of Architectural Historians* 44: 60–65.

Venturi, Robert. 1966. *Complexity and Contradiction in Architecture*. New York.

Venturi, Robert, Denise Scott Brown, and Steven Izenour. 1972. *Learning from Las Vegas*. Cambridge, MA. Rev. ed., 1977.

Vidler, Anthony. 1992. *The Architectural Uncanny: Essays in the Modern Unhomely*. Cambridge, MA.

Vignola, Giacomo Barozzi da. 1562. *Regola delli cinque ordini d'architettura*. Rome.

Villari, Sergio. 1990. *J. N. L. Durand (1760–1834): Art and Science of Architecture*. Trans. Eli Gottlieb. New York.

Viollet-le-Duc, Eugène-Emmanuel. 1843. "Rapport addressé à M. le Ministre de la Justice et des Cultes." [The cover letter for his proposal to restore the cathedral of Notre-Dame in Paris.]

Viollet-le-Duc, Eugène-Emmanuel. 1854–1868. *Dictionnaire raisonné de l'architecture française du XIe au XVIe siècle*. 10 vols. Paris.

Viollet-le-Duc, Eugène-Emmanuel. 1863, 1872. *Entretiens sur l'architecture*. 2 vols. Paris. Trans. Henry Van Brunt as *Discourses on Architecture*. Boston, 1875, 1881. Trans. Benjamin Bucknall as *Lectures on Architecture*. London, 1877, 1882; reissued as *Discourses on Architecture,* London, 1889.

Viollet-le-Duc, Eugène-Emmanuel. 1873. *Histoire d'une maison*. Paris. Trans. George M. Towle as *The Story of a House*. Boston, 1874. Trans. Benjamin Bucknall as *How to Build a House, an Architectural Novelette*. London, 1874.

Viollet-le-Duc, Eugène-Emmanuel. 1875. *Histoire de l'habitation humaine depuis les temps préhistoriques*. Paris. Trans. Benjamin Bucknall as *The Habitations of Man in All Ages*. London, 1876.

Viollet-le-Duc, Eugène-Emmanuel. 1879. *Histoire d'un dessinateur, comment on apprend à dessiner*. Paris. Trans. Virginia Champlin as *Learning to Draw, or the Story of a Young Designer*. New York, 1881.

Viollet-le-Duc, Eugène-Emmanuel. 1990. *The Architectural Theory of Viollet-le-Duc: Readings and Commentary*. Ed. M. F. Hearn. Cambridge, MA.

Viollet-le-Duc, Eugène-Emmanuel. 1990. *The Foundations of Architecture: Selections from the Dictionnaire Raisonné*. Intro. Barry Bergdoll. Trans. Kenneth D. Whitehead. New York.

Vitruvius. c. 30 B. C. E.. *De architectura*. Rome. Trans. Morris Hickey Morgan as *The Ten Books of Architecture*. Cambridge, MA, 1914; reprint, New York, 1960.

Wagner, Otto. 1896, 1898, 1902, 1914. *Moderne Architektur*. Vienna. Trans. (1902 ed.) Harry Francis Mallgrave as *Modern Architecture*. Santa Monica, 1988.

Wiebenson, Dora, ed. 1982–1983. *Architectural Theory and Practice from Alberti to Ledoux*. Chicago.

Wittkower, Rudolf. 1962. *Architectural Principles in the Age of Humanism*. London.

Woods, Mary N. 1999. *From Craft to Profession: The Practice of Architecture in Nineteenth-Century America*. Berkeley.

Wright, Frank Lloyd. 1932, 1943, 1970. *An Autobiography*. New York.

Wright, Frank Lloyd. 1932. *The Disappearing City*. New York.

Wright, Frank Lloyd. 1954. *The Natural House*. New York.

Wright, Frank Lloyd. 1958. *The Living City*. New York.

Wright, Frank Lloyd. 1975. *In the Cause of Architecture*. Ed. Hugh S. Donlon and Martin Filler. New York. [This volume collects the essays published under the same title in *Architectural Record* in 1908 and 1927, and as "The Meaning of Materials" in the same journal in 1928 and 1952.]

Credits

The quotation in chapter 7 from *Ars poetica* is reprinted by permission of the publishers and the Trustees of the Loeb Classical Library from *Horace: Satires, Epistles, The Art of Poetry,* translated by H. R. Fairclough, Loeb Classical Library, volume 50 (Cambridge, Mass.: Harvard University Press, 1926), p. 194. The Loeb Classical Library is a registered trademark of the President and Fellows of Harvard College.

Quotations from Alberti in chapter 4, from Vitruvius in chapter 6, from Louis Sullivan in chapter 10, and from John Ruskin in chapter 12 are deemed to be in the public domain.

Sources for illustrations deemed to be in the public domain are as follows: Sir William Chambers, *A Treatise on the Decorative Part of Civil Architecture* (London, 1791; reprint, 1968): fig. 5-1; Philibert de l'Orme, *L'architecture* (Paris, 1567; reprint): fig. 5-19; A. J. Downing, *The Architecture of Country Houses* (New York, 1850): figs. 9-2, 9-3, 9-4, 9-5, 9-6; J.-N.-L. Durand, *Précis des leçons d'architecture* (Paris, 1802–1819): figs. 8-1, 9-1; Ebenezer Howard, *Garden Cities of To-morrow* (London, 1902): fig. 14-4; Marc-Antoine Laugier, *Essai sur l'architecture* (Paris,

1755; reprint): fig. 2-1; Andrea Palladio, *The Four Books of Architecture* (New York: Dover Reprints, 1965): figs. 4-6, 4-7, 5-8, 5-20, 5-21, 7-1, 7-2, 7-3, 7-4, 7-5; Sebastiano Serlio, *The Five Books of Architecture* (New York: Dover Reprints, 1982): figs. 3-1, 3-2, 3-3, 3-4, 5-7, 5-17, 5-18, 6-7, 6-8, 9-15, 9-16; Camillo Sitte, *Der Städtebau nach seiner künstlerischen Grundsätzen* (Vienna, 1889): fig. 14-1; James Stuart and Nicholas Revett, *Antiquities of Athens and Other Monuments of Greece* (London, 1858): figs. 5-3, 5-9, 5-12; Eugène-Emmanuel Viollet-le-Duc, *Dictionnaire raisonné de l'architecture française du XIe au XVIe siècle* (Paris, 1854–1868; reprint): figs. 3-8, 3-9; idem, *Discourses on Architecture* (Boston, 1875, 1881): figs. 3-6, 3-7, 9-7, 9-8, 10-2, 10-3, 10-4, 10-5, 11-1; idem, *The Habitations of Man in All Ages* (London, 1876): fig. 10-1; idem, *How to Build a House* (London, 1874): figs. 8-2, 8-3, 8-4, 8-5, 12-2.

The following illustrations were furnished by the author or were kindly lent without restrictions on use: figs. 3-11, 4-1, 4-3, 5-2, 5-4, 5-5, 5-6, 5-11, 5-15, 5-22, 6-4, 6-9, 9-17, 9-18, 10-8, 10-9, 10-10, 10-11, 10-12, 10-17, 10-18, 11-3, 12-1, 12-3, 14-2, 14-3, 14-5, 16-1 (author); Kai Gutschow: figs. 9-20, 10-6; Jana Hearn: fig. 6-3; Anne Thomas Wilkins: fig. 5-10; David Wilkins: figs. 3-5, 15-3, 15-6, 16-2.

The following illustrations are under copyright and are used with permission: Architecture Photograph Collection, courtesy the Art Institute of Chicago, all rights reserved: fig. 10-14; Art Resource: figs. 3-12, 4-2, 4-4, 4-5, 5-14, 6-1, 6-5, 6-6, 11-2, 12-4; © 2002 Artists Rights Society (ARS), New York/ADAGP, Paris/FLC: figs. 9-11, 9-12, 9-13, 9-14, 10-13, 14-6; D. G. Olshavsky/ARTOG, courtesy Eisenman Architects: fig. 15-4; Jeff Goldberg/ESTO, courtesy Eisenman Architects: fig. 15-5; courtesy The Estate of R. Buckminster Fuller: fig. 10-15; Malcolm Smith, for The Louis I.

Index

Alberti, Leon Battista, 3–4, 5, 8, 13, 25–26, 32, 35, 37, 41–42, 48, 54, 83–88, 92–93, 124–127, 130, 133, 152, 169–175, 281, 290

Banham, Reyner, 219–267
Barbaro, Daniele, 4
Blondel, François, 7, 159

Cordemoy, Jean-Louis, 9

de l'Orme, Philibert, 6–7, 129–130
Downing, Andrew Jackson, 14, 194–199, 202, 238
Durand, Jean-Nicolas-Louis, 9–10, 13, 179–181, 216

Eisenman, Peter, 21, 316–321

Fréart de Chambray, Roland, 7

Garnier, Tony, 15, 36
Giedion, Sigfried, 18
Giocondo, Fra Giovanni, 4
Gropius, Walter, 17, 18, 28, 34, 36, 218, 246, 266

Hitchcock, Henry-Russell, 17

Horace (Quintus Horatius Flaccus), 139–141
Howard, Ebenezer, 15, 292, 294–297, 299

Izenour, Steven, 20, 302, 304, 306–308, 313, 315

Johnson, Philip, 17, 316

Laugier, Marc-Antoine, 9, 15, 48–49, 57, 135, 159, 223, 281, 289–291, 297
Le Corbusier (Charles-Édouard Jeanneret), 15, 17–18, 28–30, 36, 51, 72–73, 202, 208–216, 218, 242, 244, 265–268, 279, 299–301
Loos, Adolf, 16, 279

McCullough, Malcolm, 329–330
Michelangelo Buonarroti, 133, 148–150
Muthesius, Hermann, 14, 36, 246

Palladio, Andrea, 6, 54, 56, 88–92, 108–109, 129–133, 157, 174
Perrault, Claude, 7, 159, 176

Pugin, Augustus Welby Northmore, 12, 13, 26, 59, 223

Quatremère de Quincy, Antoine-Chrysostome, 10, 26, 50–51

Ruskin, John, 12, 14, 16, 17, 18, 26–27, 36, 37–38, 42–45, 59–61, 70, 93, 223–224, 246, 255–258, 260, 263, 266, 267, 271–275, 282–283, 287, 291, 295

Sant'Elia, Antonio, 16, 36, 71, 191
Scamozzi, Vincenzo, 7, 35, 157, 159
Scheerbart, Paul, 16, 27–28, 36, 191, 260–262
Scott Brown, Denise, 20, 302, 304, 306–308, 313–315
Semper, Gottfried, 10–11, 50, 216, 275
Serlio, Sebastiano, 5–6, 54–56, 88, 106, 121, 127–129, 146–148, 150, 152–156, 175, 216
Sitte, Camillo, 15, 69–70, 290–294, 297
Sullivan, Louis, 188, 226, 232–235, 276–278, 279

Venturi, Robert, 19, 76–78, 287–288, 302, 303–304, 306–315, 323
Vignola, Giacomo, 6, 16
Viollet-le-Duc, Eugène-Emmanuel, 12, 13, 15–16, 17, 18, 19, 26, 32–33, 35, 45–46, 51, 59, 61–69, 93, 97, 151–152, 181–191, 193, 199–202, 224–232, 238, 246, 258–260, 263, 266, 275–276, 282, 283–287, 290, 305, 328
Vitruvius (Marcus Vitruvius Pollio), 1–2, 3, 8, 13, 25, 30–32, 33, 34–35, 36–37, 39–41, 45–47, 53, 81–82, 88, 93–95, 104–109, 110, 114, 115–116, 119–122, 123–124, 126, 137–146, 161–170, 173, 175, 281

Wagner, Otto, 16
Wright, Frank Lloyd, 15, 17, 28–29, 36, 51–52, 73–75, 188, 198, 202–207, 235–237, 238, 242, 263–265, 277, 279–280, 297–299